Springer Series on
Comparative Treatments for Psychol

*Series Editor: Arthur Freeman, EdD*

**1999** **Comparative Treatments for Substance Abuse,**
edited by *E. Thom*  *PhD, and Loreen Rugle, PhD*

**E. Thomas Dowd** is Professor of Psychology at Kent State University and previously taught at Florida State University and the University of Nebraska. He is a Fellow of the American Psychological Association in two divisions and holds Diplomates from the American Board of Professional Psychology in Behavioral Psychology and Counseling Psychology. He is President of the American Board of Behavioral Psychology, was President of the International Association for Cognitive Psychotherapy, and has served on numerous other professional boards and committees. His interests are in Cognitive Behavior Therapy, hypnotherapy, paradoxical interventions, and psychological reactance.

**Loreen G. Rugle** received her Ph.D. in Clinical Psychology from Kent State University. She was Deputy Director of the Veterans Addiction Recovery Center (VARC) for several years at the Brecksville Unit of the Cleveland Department of Veterans Administration Medical Center. Her areas of expertise are in addiction treatments of all kinds.

# SUBSTANCE ABUSE

### — A PRACTITIONER'S GUIDE TO —
## COMPARATIVE TREATMENTS

**E. THOMAS DOWD, PhD**
**LOREEN RUGLE, PhD, Editors**

SPRINGER PUBLISHING COMPANY

**New York**

Springer Publishing Company, LLC
11 West 42nd Street
New York, NY 10036

Acquisitions Editor: Bill Tucker
Production Editor: Jeanne Libby
Cover design by Mimi Flow

06  07  08  09  /  5  4  3  2  1

New ISBN-13: 978-0-8261-2095-3 © 2006 by Springer Publishing Company, LLC

---

**Library of Congress Cataloging-in-Publication Data**

Comparative treatments of substance abuse  /  E. Thomas Dowd,
   Loreen Rugle, editors.
         p.  cm. — (Springer series on comparative treatments for
psychological disorders;1)
   Includes bibliographical references and index.
   ISBN 0-8261-1276-5
   1.  Substance abuse — Treatment.  2.  Psychodynamic psychotherapy.
I.  Dowd, E. Thomas.  II.  Rugle, Loreen.  III.  Series.
RC564.C6515  1999
616.86'06—dc21
                                                           99-14661
                                                              CIP

---

Printed in the United States of America by Berryville Graphics

# Contents

# Contributors

**Jane Baron, R.N., M.Sc.**
4016 McBean St.
Richmond, Ontario K0A 2Z0
Canada

**Kimberly Barrett, Ed.D.**
Department of Psychology
University of Washington
Seattle, WA

**Raymond DiGiuseppe, Ph.D.**
Department of Psychology
St. John's University
Grand Central & Utopia Pkwys.
Jamaica, NY

**E. Thomas Dowd, Ph.D.**
Department of Psychology
Kent State University
Kent, OH

**Michael Foster, Ph.D.**
Department of Psychology
Kent State University
Kent, OH

**Kathryn Graham, Ph.D.**
Addiction Research Foundation
100 Collip Circle, Suite 200
London, Ont. N6G 4X8
Canada

**Richard Hirschman, Ph.D.**
Department of Psychology
Kent State University
Kent, OH

**G. Alan Marlatt, Ph.D.**
Department of Psychology
University of Washington
Seattle, WA

**Jennifer Mascolo, M.A.**
Department of Psychology
St. John's University
Grand Central & Utopia Pkwys.
Jamaica, NY

**William J. Matthews, Ph.D.**
School Psychology Program
College of Education
University of Massachusetts
Amherst, MA

**Pamela J. Millas, M.A.**
23208 E. Baintree Road
Beachwood, OH

**Robert J. Meyers, Ph.D.**
Center on Alcoholism
Substance Abuse, and Addictions
2350 Alamo Street SE
University of New Mexico
Albuquerque, NM

**Cory Newman, Ph.D.**
Center for Cognitive Therapy
The Science Center (8th Floor)
3600 Market Street
Philadelphia, PA

**Carol Putt, Ph.D.**
415 Longbeach Pkwy.
Bay Village, OH

**Christine L. Ratto, Ph.D.**
Center for Cognitive Therapy
The Science Center (8th Floor)
3600 Market Street
Philadelphia, PA

**Helen S. Raytek, Ph.D.**
Center of Alcohol Studies
Smithers Hall, Busch Campus
P.O. Box 969
Piscataway, NJ

**Frederick Rotgers, Psy.D.**
Program for Addictions
   Consultation and Treatment
254 Easton Ave.
New Brunswick, NJ

**Loreen G. Rugle, Ph.D.**
8344 Villa Marina
Mentor, OH

**Douglas H. Ruben, Ph.D.**
4211 Okemos Road, Suite 22
Okemos, MI

**Jane Ellen Smith, Ph.D.**
Department of Psychology
University of New Mexico
Logan Hall
Albuquerque, NM

**V. Ann Waldorf, Ph.D.**
Veterans Administration
   Medical Center
2100 Ridgecrest Drive, SE
Albuquerque, NM

# Series Editor's Note

*Comparisons are odious . . .*
—Cervantes, *Don Quixote*

The general view of comparisons is that they represent measurements against some standard or that they entail evaluating one experience or object against another. If one has had a sibling, one has likely come up against the parental statement, "Why can't you be like . . .?" Teachers also invariably compare students one with the other when they post grades or grade papers for all to see.

This view of comparisons is that they are somehow adversarial-one person, group, or effort "wins" and one "loses." In psychology we often use the construct of comparison as synonymous with the term "versus" (e.g., "The treatment of depression: Psychotherapy versus pharmacotherapy" or "A comparison of two treatments for Obsessive Compulsive disorder"). This implies that whenever there are two or more systems or objects available, one will be better than another. Yet not all comparisons are clear-cut. One choice may be appropriate for a certain sub-group, while another choice may work better in a different setting or with a different population. (This adversarial view seems to be very popular among mental health professionals. After all, we are a group that over the years when under attack have been known to circle our wagons and shoot at each other!)

Our goal in this series is to examine not who is better than whom, or what model works better than other models, but rather to examine and to compare, as cleanly as we can, the similarities and differences between different psychotherapeutic approaches. To do this most efficiently, we have used a standard patient. All contributors were asked to respond to the sample case prepared by the volume editors. In this way the reader can compare the thinking, conceptualization, interventions, and questions that would be asked by the contributing authors. We have invited authors who are exemplars of a particular school, understanding that other therapists of the same school, might see or do things differently. By aligning apparently diverse therapies side-by-side, we can look at what models share specific conceptual frameworks, philosophical biases, strategic foci, or technical interventions, as well as help us to make clearer distinctions between therapeutic models.

We have set as our goal the examination of those problems most frequently seen in clinical practice. We have not seen this need for cross-model comparison as an issue of professional discipline inasmuch as these clinical syndromes are seen by psychologists, psychiatrists, nurse practitioners, social workers, pastoral counselors, and counselors.

This series sprang from four roots. First the powerful influence of the classic "Gloria" series produced by Dr. Everett Shostrum, when he arranged for Carl Rogers (Client-Centered Therapy), Albert Ellis (Rational Emotive Therapy), and Fritz Perls (Gestalt Therapy) to demonstrate their representative model of therapy with a standard patient, Gloria. He gave viewers the opportunity to compare and contrast the three models as practiced by the founders of the particular school of therapy.

The second influence on this series was the present state of affairs in psychotherapy. Between the models that are promoted for their purported science and efficacy and those models that are promoted for their purported humanism and eschewal of science, there are many treatment models. Without attempting to judge the value, efficacy, and importance of a model, we believe that it is important to offer mental health professionals the opportunity to make their own decisions about diverse treatment models.

The third impetus for this series was the availability of so many experts in the treatment of the broad range of psychological disorders. Both as editors and as contributing authors, it is their work that is being highlighted in this series.

Finally, this series was the result of encouragement and support from Bill Tucker, Acquisitions Editor of Springer Publishing Company, and Dr. Ursula Springer, the President of Springer Publishing Company. When I first approached Springer with the idea for the series, they were enthusiastic and eagerly agreed not to just produce one volume, but committed their resources to a series of several volumes. Given the publishing history of Springer, the breadth and quality of their book list, and the many professional groups that they reach, I can think of no better place for this series on comparative psychotherapy.

ARTHUR FREEMAN, EdD, ABPP
Department of Psychology
Philadelphia College of Osteopathic Medicine

# 1

# Substance Abuse in American Society

## *E. Thomas Dowd and Loreen G. Rugle*

Substance abuse is one of humanity's oldest afflictions. As far back as Homer, there are references to what would today be called hallucinogenic and mind-altering substances. The "lotus eaters" in ancient Greece apparently used them and of course there was Bacchus, the god of wine and the vineyard. Throughout the ages hallucinogenic substances have been used in religious ceremonies, which reflect an awareness of their symbolic properties and their ability to alter consciousness and enable believers to commune with the gods. The first miracle of Jesus was changing water into wine at a Jewish wedding and there are indications that the guests became quite drunk. Native Americans have long used peyote in their religious ceremonies, which became a point of some controversy recently. Most forms of Christianity use wine in their ceremonies as a form of communion with the Deity.

Mind-altering substances have also been recognized as providing medicinal benefits, including relief of tension and pain, as well as for their ability to increase energy. For example, Sigmund Freud, in his essay "On Coca," described the benefits of cocaine as warding "off hunger, sleep, and fatigue and steels one to intellectual effort" (Freud, 1885/ 1974). He further reported, based on his personal use, that the euphoria was not followed by depression and that repeated doses produced no compulsive desire for further use. He had become interested in coca based on reports from American physicians that it reduced the cravings of opiate addicts and alcoholics. However, the friend that Freud had hoped to

*1*

cure of other addictions through the use of cocaine disintegrated into a state of cocaine delirium and Freud withdrew his support for the drug in 1907.

Along with the ingestion of these substances, however, it became apparent that not all individuals could handle them equally well. The excessive use of alcohol eventually became a social problem. For years, it was assumed that drunkenness was an individual moral failing that could be overcome only by a staunch exercise of the "will" aided by religion. "Drunks" were commonly thought to be weak-willed people, lacking in common moral, civic, and religious virtues. Much effort in Christianity was and still is devoted to rescuing "fallen" people from sin; which in modern times was generally alcohol- or sex-related. Other religions, such as Islam and the Church of Jesus Christ of Latter-Day Saints (Mormons), solved the problem by prohibiting mind-altering substances entirely, as did certain denominations within mainstream Christianity at times as well. Mormons even prohibit coffee because of the caffeine.

Perhaps because of alcohol's association with "debauchery" (i.e., casual sexual behavior), drunkenness was more often condemned in women than in men. Although women often suffered sexually from substance abuse problems, men suffered occupationally. Habitually drunken men were often unable to hold steady jobs, crucial in an age in which the welfare of the entire family depended on the income of the husband. The greatest catastrophe for a wife was to have a drunkard for a husband.

With the rise of the Alcoholics Anonymous (AA) movement in the early 20th century, the moral failing, or sin, of drunkenness began to be replaced by the disease of alcoholism. Thus, the problem of overindulgence in alcohol moved from the realm of religion to that of medicine. Rather than being seen as sinful moral failures in need of spiritual renewal, alcoholics began to be seen as sick and in need of treatment. Like insanity before it, the hope was that the change from a moral model to a disease model would remove the social stigma associated with alcoholism, a change that has not necessarily occurred with mental illness (Mehta & Farina, 1997). Alcoholics Anonymous is still perhaps the most common and widespread treatment for alcoholism and has spawned a collection of related approaches to the treatment of other addictive disorders, such as Al-Anon (for family members), Al-Ateen (for children), Narcotics Anonymous, Cocaine Anonymous, Overeaters Anonymous, and Gamblers Anonymous. Some wags have even suggested an Anonymous Anonymous program for those who are addicted to addiction treatment programs.

The culture of the United States has always had an ambivalent attitude toward alcohol. Although its use was nationally illegal only for a brief period, the sale (if not the use) of alcohol has been and still is prohibited or heavily regulated in many jurisdictions. Many of the most influential denominations in the early history of the country condemned its use, though with mixed success. The Temperance (really abstinence) Movement of the late 19th century was religiously based, much as the Abolition Movement had been earlier and the Civil Rights Movement was almost a century later. This movement reached its high water-mark in the early 20th century with Prohibition ("The Great Experiment"). Its failure demonstrated the public's ambivalent attitude; although the regulation and occasionally the limited prohibition of the *sale* of alcohol was tolerated, people would not tolerate an absolute and national prohibition of its *use.*

The use of drugs other than alcohol has shown a somewhat different pattern. There appear to have been three phases to America's first cocaine epidemic (1885–1920s). It was initially introduced in the 1880s and caught on more readily than it had in Europe where there were laws restricting its use. Cocaine use then spread rapidly. When Freud first published his paper, pure cocaine along with the milder coca was available to Americans in drug and grocery stores, saloons, and from mail-order vendors. By 1885, Park, Davis & Co. was selling cocaine and coca in 15 forms, including coca-leaf cigarettes, cocaine inhalant, a coca cordial, cocaine crystals, and cocaine in a solution of hypodermic injection (Kosten & Kleber, 1992). Cocaine was also offered as an asthma remedy and a cure for toothache pain. At that time, Coca-Cola contained a minute amount of cocaine (from whence its name). There was a repressive stage after the turn of the century. By 1892, medical journals were beginning to report hundreds of cases of habitual use and limited statistics from import and manufacturing data suggest that cocaine use peaked around 1900. At that time, Coca-Cola eliminated both alcohol and cocaine from "coke," thus allowing it to be marketed as a soft drink. Laws restricting its use began to be passed (Kosten & Kleber, 1992). In 1907, New York State passed legislation restricting cocaine availability to physician prescription and required record keeping. The Harrison Narcotics Act of 1914 required records to be kept of all opiates and cocaine from the importer or manufacturer down to the patient's prescription. It also limited the amount of opiates and prohibited any cocaine in nonprescription remedies. As a result, cocaine use gradually faded in the United States.

The current resurgence in cocaine use began about 1970. At that time, there were calls for legalization based on the view of many medical professionals that it was relatively harmless and did not lead to dependency (Kosten & Kleber, 1992). The increased use of cocaine and other illegal drugs has resulted in more polysubstance use than formerly. By 1990, the abuse of alcohol and drugs together was the most common pattern with 43% of clients abusing both substances. The remaining clients were equally divided between alcohol-only (28%) and drug-only (29%). Between

1991 and 1995 the proportion of drug-only clients declined from 29% to 23% while the proportion of clients with both problems increased from 26% to 46%. The proportion of alcohol-only clients decreased from 45% to 28% (Uniform Facility Data Set (UFDS): Data for 1996 and 1980–1996; 1997).

Probably due to changes in broad cultural acceptability, the use of alcohol and illegal drugs has waxed and waned over the years in the United States. There is no question that at present their use is widespread and constitutes a major social problem in terms of crime, lost occupational productivity, increased family problems, and personal misery. Perhaps as a result of the loosening of many cultural prohibitions and standards in the 1960s and the increasing use of legal medications, illegal drug use increased steadily from that time, reaching a peak in 1979 and declining about 50% since then (National Drug Control Strategy, 1997). In the early 1960s, only about 2% of the population had experimented with illegal drugs. By 1982, almost one-third of the population over 13 had and by 1985 almost half had (Drake, McLaughlin, Pepper, & Minkoff, 1991).

In spite of the recent drop, more than a third of all Americans over 12 years of age have tried an illicit drug at some time in their lives. An estimated 12.8 million Americans, about 6% of the population over 12 years of age, have used illegal drugs within the past 30 days. Ninety percent of these have used marijuana or hashish and one-third of these have used cocaine or taken a prescription-type drug for nonmedical reasons. Approximately 45% of Americans know someone with a substance abuse problem (National Drug Control Strategy, 1997). Other statistics indicate that approximately 18 million people abuse or are addicted to alcohol, up to 1 million use heroin, at least 2 million are addicted to cocaine or crack, 4.4 million get high on marijuana more than once a week, and 11 million abuse tranquilizers or other psychotropic drugs (Crow & Reeves, 1994). In 1988, an estimated 15.3 million people in the United States over 18 years of age met criteria for treatment of alcohol abuse, dependence, or both (Grant et al., 1991).

There is some indication that the use of some illegal drugs is declining (National Drug Control Strategy, 1997). In 1995, about 1.5 million Americans were current cocaine users, a 74% decline since 1985. There were an estimated 533,000 first-time users in 1994, a 60% decline from 1980–1984. However, the number of *frequent* users has not changed significantly since 1985—estimated at 582,000 in 1995. In addition, while the number of total cocaine users has dropped, the amount of cocaine used has not. These figures are similar for marijuana. In 1995, an estimated 9.8 million Americans smoked marijuana (77% of all illicit drug users) and 5 million smoked it frequently—significantly lower that the estimated 8.4 million in 1985. However, the numbers may be rising again; the annual number of marijuana initiates has risen from less than 1.5 million in 1991 to 2.3 million in 1994.

In addition, although total usage may be down, this may be deceptive. Children appear to be using at younger ages and prison populations include increasing numbers of inmates whose only crime is the use of the illegal drug.

Whereas earlier substance abusers were primarily alcoholics only, the recent trend has been towards polysubstance use (McCormick, Dowd, Quirk, & Zegarra, 1998). The greater number of polysubstance abusers is likely due to the increasing acceptability and use of illegal drugs. In addition, increasing numbers of individuals with psychiatric disorders have also been diagnosed with substance abuse problems, known as dual diagnosis (Putt, 1996). The reasons for the increase in the number of dual diagnoses are unclear but are probably related to deinstitutionalization and the increasing use of addicting substances among the entire population, as previously noted. Also, behavioral problems such as anger, aggression, and hostility are closely associated with both substance abuse and many types of mental illness and likely both cause and are caused by substance abuse. Putt (1996), for example, found that changes in levels of hostility and aggression were predictive of improvement in substance abuse symptoms for alcoholics and polysubstance abusers at 12 month follow-up.

Substance abuse is costly, both to society and the individual. Drug-related illness, death, and crime cost the nation approximately $66.9 billion. Every man, woman, and child in the U.S. pays nearly $1,000 annually to cover the cost of unnecessary health care, extra law enforcement, auto accidents, crime, and lost occupational productivity resulting from substance abuse (National Drug Control Strategy, 1997). Alcohol was a contributing factor in half of all fatal auto accidents in 1990 (Crowe & Reeves, 1994). Many instances of domestic violence and broken marriages are due, at least in part, to substance abuse—and these problems are often passed down through the generations. In 1994, there were 1.14 million arrests for drug law violations; 75.1% of these were for possession. Likewise, 59.5% of federal prisoners were drug offenders as were 22.3% of state prisoners. The increase in numbers of incarcerated drug offenders accounts for nearly three-fourths of the total growth in number of federal inmates since 1980 (National Drug Control Strategy, 1997). The result is that the United States has the highest percentage of its population in prison compared to any major industrial nation, and the increased prison costs have siphoned off significant funding from other important societal needs such as education.

There is evidence that substance abuse treatment is cost-effective. A 1992 California Department of Alcohol and Drug Programs (CALDATA) survey (National Drug Control Strategy, 1997) concluded that treatment can generate a 7:1 return on investment. Illegal drug use dropped by 40%

among participants, hospitalization rates dropped by a third, and overall criminal activity dropped by two-thirds after treatment completion. When one considers the number of inmates in prison for illegal drug use *alone*, it is apparent that additional savings could be realized from a lower prison population as well. The United States already has a larger percentage of its population incarcerated than any other major industrial nation; any reduction would be for the better.

Thus, it is possible to conclude that substance abuse in all of its manifestations is one of the major public health problems the nation currently faces. Punishment and incarceration have had limited effectiveness; many experts across the political spectrum feel that, despite the recent substance use decrease, we are losing the "War on Drugs." The failure of Prohibition has shown us that a free society will not tolerate outright proscription of chemically addicting substances, even if problematic, but will tolerate and even welcome regulation and treatment of such addictions. The movement from the moral failure model of addiction to the illness model implies that treatment and recovery are more likely to succeed than judgment and condemnation.

However, in a recent and ironic turn, it appears that the moral failure model may once again be gaining ascendency. For example, the state of South Carolina has reportedly imprisoned a number of mothers whose only crime is using crack cocaine while pregnant (this has been interpreted as child abuse). Likewise, a sizeable percentage of incarcerated felons are guilty only of using and trafficking in marijuana. Imprisoning large numbers of people for the sole crime of using illegal drugs implies that they are "bad" rather than "sick." It is therefore important that effective and lasting treatments be developed and fostered in order to counteract this movement. Religion, despite its unfortunate historical association with the moral failure model, potentially has an important role to play in treatment. It is to the further development of the treatment model of substance abuse that this book is devoted.

## REFERENCES

Crowe, A. H., & Reeves, R. (1994). *Treatment for alcohol and other drug abuse: Opportunities for coordination*. Rockville, MD: U.S. Department of Health and Human Services, Public Health Service Substance Abuse and Mental Health Services Administration Center for Substance Abuse Treatment.

Drake, R. E., McLaughlin, P., Pepper, B., & Minkoff, K. (1991). Dual diagnosis of major mental illness and substance disorder: An overview. *New Directions for Mental Health Services, 50*, 3–12.

Freud, S. (1885/1974). In R. Byak (Ed.), *Cocaine papers by Sigmund Freud*. New York: Stonehill.

Grant, B. F., Harford, T. C., Chou, P., Pickering, R., Dawson, D. A., Stinson, F. S., & Noble, J. (1991). Epidemiological Bulletin No. 27: Prevalence of DSM-III-R alcohol abuse and dependence: United States, 1988. *Alcohol Health Research World, 5*, 91–96.

Kosten, T. R., & Kleber, H. D. (Eds.). (1992). *Clinician's guide to cocaine addiction: Theory, research, and treatment.* New York: Guilford.

McCormick, R. A., Dowd, E. T., Quirk, S., & Zegarra, J. H. (1998). The relationship of NEO-PI performance to coping styles, patterns of use, and triggers for use among substance abusers. *Addictive Behaviors, 23*, 497–507.

Mehta, S., & Farina, A. (1997). Is being "sick" really better? Effect of the disease view of mental disorder on stigma. *Journal of Social and Clinical Psychology, 16*, 405–419.

*National Drug Control Strategy.* (February, 1997). Office of National Drug Control Policy. Washington D.C.: U.S. Government Printing Office.

Putt, C. A. (1996). *Relationship of pre-existing levels of hostility and aggression to substance abuse and psychiatric symptom severity.* Unpublished doctoral dissertation, Kent State University.

Uniform Facility Data Set (UFDS): Data for 1996 and 1980–1996. (1997). Department of Health and Human Services, Substance Abuse and Mental Health Services Administration. Rockville, MD: Office of Applied Studies.

# 2

# Outcome Research in Substance Abuse Treatment

*Carole A. Putt*

## GENERAL EFFECTIVENESS OF SUBSTANCE ABUSE TREATMENT

There are an estimated 5.5 million people currently in need of drug abuse treatment in the United States; the detrimental effects of drug abuse are widely recognized. It is a significant factor in accidents, illness and disease, crimes and violence, disability, suicide and homicide, and lost productivity. Costs to society associated with drug abuse are estimated to be approximately $72 billion annually and reduction of this abuse and its related problems are among primary national health objectives. Because of escalating costs, reduced appropriations, increased health ramifications and treatment demands, the development and provision of effective drug abuse treatment is critical (Mejta, Naylor, & Maslar, 1994). The following review examines current outcome research in substance abuse treatment and addresses issues such as the general effectiveness of treatment, outcome predictors, correlates, comparative treatment effectiveness and outcomes with special populations.

A preliminary review of the rich database gathered on the evaluation and outcome of substance abuse treatment points clearly to a singular conclusion: Treatment is effective. Upon closer scrutiny however, the question of exactly what treatment, for whom, and how measured poses a myriad of problems that makes comparison very difficult indeed. The following discussion will address effectiveness outcomes of several national multi-program studies as well as state and private studies. Issues, concerns and problems inherent in the research will receive consideration.

According to Hubbard (1997) the emergence of the community-based alcohol treatment system in the late 1960s saw a proliferation of inpatient, short-term programs. As use and abuse of drugs mounted in succeeding years, these programs incorporated drug treatment as well. A national system of drug abuse treatment programs was developed to treat the growing heroin addiction problem as well as to deal with the high rate of substance abuse of returning Vietnam Veterans. This led to three major types of publicly funded treatment programs in the United States: The outpatient methadone clinics (OMC); therapeutic communities (TC); and outpatient drug-free programs (ODF). The OMCs treated opioid abusers, primarily IV heroin users; TCs involved long-term, 24-hour stays in communities that basically provided peer group counseling for all types of drug abuse; and ODFs provided counseling treatment generally in community mental-health-center settings. Fletcher, Tims, and Brown (1997) added a fourth program—Short-term detoxification. Programs within these categories are by no means homogeneous. Hubbard stated "Among these modalities, there are great variations in program size, setting, organization, philosophy, structure, therapeutic approach, services, and funding" (p. 499).

Several nationally funded drug abuse treatment studies have emerged from data generated from these programs. Studies of individual programs and clinical trial designs have also been conducted. They have all indicated that existing treatment, whether behavioral, psychosocial, and/or pharmacological is effective, can reduce drug use, and can help manage drug dependence and addiction, thereby producing benefits that far outweigh the costs of treatment (Hubbard, 1997; Simpson et al., 1997).

The first national program to study drug abuse treatment evaluation research was called the Drug Abuse Reporting Program (DARP) which began collecting data in 1969 on 44,000 clients being treated in 52 federally funded treatment programs between 1969 and 1973. Program modalities were the four listed above and intake only. Research results indicated that community-based drug abuse treatment was effective in reducing drug use and criminal behavior. Using the criteria of no drug use or criminality in the 12 months after treatment, there was no difference between treatment modalities and intake only for those in treatment less than 90 days. There was also no long-term effect for 21-day detox. Favorable outcomes for the other 3 modalities (OMC, TC, and ODF) were found for patients remaining in treatment longer than 90 days. There was a linear relationship between length of treatment and outcome for OMC patients. DARP remained in operation for 20 years and was one of the longest and most productive outcome studies ever conducted, generating six books and over 150 articles (Fletcher et al., 1997).

Fletcher et al. (1997) and Hubbard (1997) described the next national study. The Treatment Outcome Prospective Study (TOPS) was designed to expand on DARP and provide longitudinal data on long- and short-term treatment outcomes. It gathered data from 11,000 patients in 41 treatment programs in 10 cities between 1979 and 1981. Modalities were methadone maintenance, outpatient drug-free, and long-term residential, selected to represent optimal types of stable, established programs. Follow-up was conducted at 1, 2, and 3–5 years posttreatment. Results showed that treatment was effective in reducing heroin and other drug use and reducing crime rates both during and after treatment. Posttreatment rate of daily heroin, cocaine, and psychotherapeutic drug use was half the rate of pretreatment use for patients remaining in treatment for at least 3 months. Posttreatment rates for weekly or more-frequent-use patients remaining in treatment for at least 3 months were 10%–15% lower than for patients who left treatment earlier. Time spent in treatment was one of the most important predictors of favorable outcomes.

Even with the major reduction of usage, however, patients in each modality reported continued posttreatment use of at least one drug other than alcohol or marijuana. Daily or weekly use was reported by 40% of methadone, 30% of residential, and 20% of outpatient drug-free treatment method clients who had remained in treatment at least 30 days. Pretreatment levels of marijuana and alcohol use also continued posttreatment. Hubbard (1997) stated that these data indicate that even though treatment may be successful, much work is still needed to maximize treatment effectiveness.

Changing patterns of drug use were noted, with less daily use of opiates and more polysubstance abuse. However, over three-fourths of TOPS clients stated opiates were their primary drug of abuse. TOPS clients experienced a substantial decrease in depression in the years following treatment. Another interesting finding was that patients with legal involvement, including those mandated to treatment, fared well in the programs. This may be due to the fact that they remained in treatment longer than those without legal involvement, but the end result was that compulsory drug treatment could be effective in interrupting early criminal and drug abuse careers. According to Hubbard (1997), reduction of criminal activities due to treatment of drug abuse resulted in an overall return of $7 for each dollar invested in treatment and an overall savings of $1.5 billion.

In 1989, the National Institute of Drug Abuse (NIDA) initiated the Drug Abuse Treatment Outcome Study (DATOS), which was to become the next, and most current, major outcome research study. The goal of this project was to study drug abuse treatment in typical, stable programs to ascertain effectiveness for current populations and drug abuse patterns. Several of these programs included a high percentage of criminal justice and dual diagnosis patients. Of the 75 programs chosen to participate in the project, 10 were long-term residential (LTR), 9 were short-term inpatient (STI), 24 were outpatient methadone (OMT), and 22 were outpatient drug free (ODF). Program structure, operations, treatment, and services were studied.

DATOS is a cooperative study between NIDA and 4 collaborating research sites. Data were collected on both adult and adolescent populations to determine long-term outcomes posttreatment, to investigate factors related to relapse, and to identify patterns of drug abuse health service use over time (Etheridge, Hubbard, Anderson, Craddock, & Flynn, 1997)

Hubbard, Craddock, Flynn, Anderson, and Etheridge (1997) presented an overview of the one-year follow-up outcomes in DATOS. This study of 2,966 patients in the four modalities from 1991–1993 indicated that there was a 50% reduction in prevalence of weekly or more frequent cocaine use from preadmission by LTR and ODF patients. Reductions were even greater for patients treated for 3 months or more. Patients remaining in OMT for at least 6 months reported less weekly or daily heroin use than those who left the program. Illegal activity decreased 50% and full-time employment increased 10% for LTR patients who stayed in treatment 6 months or longer. Drug use of most types was lower for all modalities at follow-up, especially for patients who remained in treatment for 3 months or more. The association of reduced use and treatment duration remained after other potential explanatory variables were statistically removed. Hubbard et al. stated: "Most important, evidence of the effectiveness of treatment for cocaine use in LTR and ODF is demonstrated. A treatment duration of more than 6 months is associated with statistically significant and clinically important decreases in odds of weekly or more frequent cocaine use in the follow-up year" (p. 176). This was also true for alcohol and marijuana use when treatment duration was at least 6 months. The authors concluded that these findings further confirm the fact that treatment of sufficient duration improves the odds of change in drug use. This is reiterated by Simpson et al. (1997) who analyzed DATOS' program diversity and retention rates. The authors stated that regardless of recent shifts in client characteristics and services delivered in nationally funded programs, "length of stay in treatment still serves as one of the most consistent predictors of follow-up outcome" (p. 289).

Further evidence of treatment effectiveness for substance abuse is found in outcome studies that are not funded by national organizations. A sampling of these follows.

Hartmann, Wolk, and Sullivan (1995) presented an analysis of treatment effectiveness in state-supported programs in Missouri. Based on self-reports of clients at 1-year follow-up, they found that a significant percentage had remained abstinent after discharge. In a study that examined outcome data from private programs, McLellan et al. (1993) conducted a 6-month follow-up of 198 alcohol and/or cocaine abusing male patients referred by their EAP to 4 private treatment programs. They found that 59% were completely abstinent, 82% were working, and only 8% required additional treatment.

International outcome research also indicated treatment effectiveness. In a 2.5-year follow-up study conducted in London, Oppenheimer, Sheehan, and Taylor (1990) found high rates of abstinence among opioid and other drug users: Overall, 37% were totally drug free; of the 71% still living in the community, 73% were opiate free and 35% were totally drug free; 18% had injected drugs in the prior 4 weeks; 13% were in prison; and 12% were in therapeutic communities. A Swedish study describing a 6-year follow-up of 50 alcohol-dependent persons who completed a 2-year treatment program was conducted by Ojehagen, Berglund, and Moberg (1994). They found that a favorable outcome at 1–2 year follow-up correlated with a favorable outcome 6 years later, and the same held true for unfavorable outcomes. Favorable outcome was defined as no >7 abuse days for each half-year and no >14 abuse days during each year of the 2-year follow-up period.

In determining what constitutes an effective program, Waltman (1995) listed key ingredients as easy accessibility of care, treatment flexibility, involvement of collaterals, good therapists, motivated clients, matching treatment to client variables, client accountability for their sobriety, focused treatment approaches, and follow-up of drop-outs and graduates. He stated that a program based on these elements had a 64% abstinence rate among clients in the Action stage of recovery and a 56% rate with clients in the Contemplation stage.

Miller (1992) explored treatment effectiveness and found several reasons for pessimism (e.g., the propensity for relapse over time and the ineffectiveness of some treatments). He continued with reasons for optimism, however, stating that in over 200 carefully controlled studies that can infer causality, more than 40% have reported statistically significant differences. He focused on several promising specific approaches such as social skill training, behavioral marital therapy, behavioral self-control training, and stress management. He also looked at mechanisms for change such as the impact of conditioning in addictive behaviors, client compliance, and therapist style.

The literature also focused on issues, concerns, and problems inherent in substance abuse treatment outcome research. The heterogeneous nature of various treatment programs, even within the same domain, makes comparison very difficult. The variability of patient characteristics further complicates the picture. These include but are not limited to number and types of substances used, severity and duration of use, socioeconomic status and educational level, social supports available, previous treatments, and comorbidity of psychiatric diagnoses. Nathan and Skinstad (1987) stated that where people are treated is usually related to the adequacy of their personal resources, and these resources often play a very important role in the outcome of their treatment. They stated that ". . . interventions are not always implemented as effectively or consistently as planned and that environmental factors external to treatment can strongly affect treatment outcome" (p. 334).

Drop-out rates and noncompliance with treatment were issues cited by Hubbard et al. (1997), Nathan and Skinstad (1987), and Rohrer, Vaughan, Cadoret, and Carswell (1996). Clients may not remain in treatment long enough to benefit from its effects and repeatedly cycle through addiction centers at high cost to treatment resources. Drop-outs are generally regarded, correctly or incorrectly, as treatment failures who have likely returned to their addiction, thus impacting negatively on treatment success outcome figures.

Other issues of concern were differences in the definition of treatment effectiveness, determination of an adequate follow-up interval leading to reliable conclusions regarding treatment success, and the validity of self-reports (Sobell, Sobell, & Gavin, 1995).

Wolk, Hartmann, and Sullivan (1994) maintained that adherence to an abstinence-only model of success may be counterproductive. Nathan and Skinstad (1987) talked about the controversy between abstinence and controlled drinking as an outcome measure. Sobell and Sobell (1989) addressed the issue of defining successful outcomes and stated that reported treatment success rates were highly dependent on small changes in the criteria used to define success.

Vaillant (1983) was most widely cited in the literature regarding the natural history of the addiction career, which is marked by periods of abstinence, non-problem drinking, and abusive drinking. For this reason, it was felt that follow-up information must be gathered for longer than the usual 1–2 year period used in most outcome research in order to provide a more valid perspective. Nathan and Skinstad (1987) concurred with this view, stating that alcoholism is a remitting disorder and 3- to 6-month follow-ups are not likely to provide evidence of long-term effects of treatment. Desmond, Maddux, Johnson, and Confer (1995) described several procedures to enhance effective follow-up.

The validity of using self-report for outcome data was considered by Emrick and Hansen (1983) who emphasized the importance of using multiple sources to gather data and advocated the use of multiple follow-up measures beyond the self-report to increase outcome validity. These included treatment completion, recidivism, mortality, health, drinking behavior, other substance use, and legal problems, among others.

Floyd, Monahan, Finney, and Morley (1996) reviewed 229 alcoholism treatment outcome studies between 1980 and 1992 and compared investigator, study and patient characteristics, treatment modalities, follow-up points, and outcome variables. They concluded that ". . . there are important differences in single and multiple-group studies, that the field has remained male dominated in terms of both investigators and patients studied, that the reporting of patient characteristics is inconsistent across studies, that minimal or no treatment control conditions are examined in fewer than one-third of multiple group studies, and that outcome domains other than drinking behavior are examined infrequently" (p. 427).

To summarize, the literature overwhelmingly supported the fact that substance abuse treatment is effective if it is of sufficient duration. However, several issues must be considered before valid and reliable conclusions can be drawn. These include defining appropriate criteria for measurement of outcome, controlling the heterogeneity of programs and subjects, and determining an adequate length of time for follow-up so that treatment effectiveness can be determined with more certainty.

## PREDICTORS OF TREATMENT OUTCOME

The one treatment outcome predictor that stands out in the literature as the most important is retention in both active treatment and aftercare (Booth, Dale, Slade, & Dewey, 1992: Condelli & Hubbard, 1994; Leshner, 1997; Miller & Hoffmann, 1995; Montgomery, Miller, & Tonigan, 1995; Moos & Moos, 1995; Ojehagen, Skjaerris, & Berglund, 1988; Ojehagen et al., 1994; Wright & Devine, 1995). Miller and Hoffman (1995) for example, found that the continuum of care should be extended for at least one year posttreatment including participation in self-help groups; and Montgomery et al. affirmed the value of becoming actively involved in AA after treatment. Moos and Moos stressed the need for long-term supportive care for patients with more severe and chronic disorders, while Wright and Devine recommended retention in treatment for at least 3 months. In a study of outcome after an extensive (2-year) treatment program for alcoholics, Ojehagen et al. (1988; 1994) observed that early success in treatment (0–6 months) was not predictive of long-term successful outcome, but that a successful adjustment between 6 and 24 months during treatment was.

Concomitant psychiatric disorders were addressed in several studies predicting outcome. Ravndal and Vaglum (1994) explored the relationship between self-reported depression and treatment outcomes in 144 clients in an 18-month therapeutic community program and found that although depression did not predict dropout during the treatment phase, it did significantly predict dropout after 1 year. In fact, being depressed increased the dropout risk 5 times when compared with not being depressed. McLellan, Luborsky, O'Brien, Barr, and Evans (1986) also found that the nature and severity of pretreatment psychiatric problems were the best predictors of treatment response.

In a study that examined psychopathology in alcoholics as a predictor of treatment outcome, Rounsaville, Dolinsky, Babor, and Meyer (1987) found that 77% of the 321 alcoholics they studied had a co-occurring Axis I or Axis II disorder. The most common diagnosis for females in the study was major depression and the most common diagnosis for the males was antisocial personality disorder. In measuring outcome one year after treatment the authors found 3 types of predictors: psychiatric diagnosis, a global rating of psychopathology, and the degree of alcohol dependence. This replicated earlier findings that male alcoholics with primary drug abuse or primary antisocial personality disorder had poorer prognoses than primary alcoholics. The Rounsaville et al. study yielded more prognostic power when the primary/secondary distinction was disregarded.

Gregson and Taylor (1977) and Miller (1991) examined the role of cognitive impairment in predicting relapse and recovery in alcoholics. Gregson and Taylor used the Patterned Cognitive Impairment Test (PCIT) to determine the extent of cognitive deterioration in 90 male alcoholics during a 12-week inpatient treatment program in New Zealand. They found PCIT scores were significantly related to abstinence 1 month after release from the hospital and to holding a job for 5 months after. The relative cognitive efficiency of the subjects served as a predictor of relative relapse rates. They found that the number of previous hospitalizations was not predictive of subsequent relapse, implying that duration of full-time therapy (at least in New Zealand) was of little value. While age per se was not a predictor of relapse in this sample, PCIT scores in alcoholics tended to get worse with age, indicating on-going cognitive deterioration. The authors stated that better PCIT scores were associated with longer abstinence, but cautioned that causal mechanisms might be indirect and involve intermediary variables. They also found a relationship between having active religious beliefs and joining AA, and between joining AA and staying abstinent. However, the patients who stayed abstinent without joining AA were less cognitively impaired on the average. The authors found that the worst prognosis for abstinence was for patients with low PCIT scores who had no religion and did not join AA.

Miller (1991) stated that "The majority of chronic, dysfunctional alcoholics and addicts seem to be characterized by a nonreflective, impulsive cognitive style that relates to an inability to use inner speech and other verbal self-regulatory mechanisms to evaluate, plan, and guide behavior" (pp. 277–278). He cited Gregson and Taylor's 1977 study as concluding that the best predictor of relative relapse rates was the measure of relative cognitive efficiency and discussed other studies that supported these findings. According to Miller, people with greater cognitive abilities participate more effectively in therapy, are more likely to get off drugs, have better jobs, go back to school, and are more likely to remain abstinent. Those with poorer outcomes have an impulsive, nonreflective cognitive style and may be more likely to use psychoactive substances to help modulate thought processes and feelings. Substance abusers with good planning and language skills have better outcomes. Miller indicated that neuropsychological tests that measure these cognitive skills may be measuring a "cognitive competency" factor that appears to be predictive of outcome for a variety of symptoms and circumstances. He discussed other studies that cited the negative relationship of comorbid disorders to successful treatment outcome, including major depression, antisocial personality disorder and other substance abuse, as well as psychiatric symptom severity and changes in perception of self-efficacy.

Weinstein and Shaffer (1993) also stressed the importance of neuropsychological dysfunction as an essential marker in predicting substance abuse treatment outcome. They stated that the prefrontal/frontal brain region is often impaired among substance abusers, resulting in reduced attention, impulsivity, and disinhibition. If brain dysfunction was not recognized and left untreated, many substance abusers would not be able to benefit from traditional treatment. The authors included a neurocognitive functions guide for clinicians to use during assessment and treatment.

Several studies described outcome predictors for specific substances, i.e., opiates, cocaine, and marijuana. Jacobsen and Kosten (1989) found that opiate addicts who had high levels of addiction at intake had poorer program retention and elevated symptoms of depression at 3-month follow-up. This also was predictive of higher frequencies of positive urine tests for illicit substances during treatment.

Kosten, Rounsaville, and Kleber (1987) examined pretreatment sources of income as predictors of outcome in opiate addicts at 2.5-year follow-up. Sources of income were employment, welfare, and criminal activities. At follow-up, all 3 groups had significantly improved in substance abuse, family, legal, and psychological problems. Welfare subjects improved most in medical status, social adjustment, and depression, and least on employment and legal problems. Employed and criminal subjects on methadone maintenance had less illegal income and more employment than those with detoxification only.

In a 2.5-year follow-up study of 361 opiate addicts, Addiction Severity Index Psychiatric Severity ratings were the best predictors of poorer outcome functioning, according to Rounsaville, Kosten, Weissman, and Kleber (1986), and when these scores were controlled for, the only diagnosis that remained significantly related to treatment outcome was major depression. Later studies of alcoholics replicated these findings.

The problem of polysubstance use was addressed by Brower, Blow, Hill, and Mudd (1994) who compared groups consisting of alcoholics, cocaine users, and combined alcohol and cocaine users. Although all 3 groups significantly decreased substance use at around 1-year follow-up, the alcohol-only group had higher rates of abstinence than the dual-use group. Gainey, Wells, Hawkins, and Catalano (1993) found predictors of treatment retention among 110 cocaine users were living alone, use of multiple substances prior to treatment, length of cocaine use, and external motivation.

Carroll, Power, Bryant, and Rounsaville (1993) stated that one-third of the 94 cocaine abusers in their study who were followed up at one year reported complete abstinence during that 12 month period. Predictors replicating other studies were severity of drug use, poorer psychiatric functioning, and presence of concurrent alcoholism. Subjects who continued to use alcohol were unlikely to renounce cocaine. Their most striking finding was the consistency of baseline severity of drug use as a predictor of outcome. The authors considered why this finding was so consistent with alcoholics and cocaine abusers, but did not seem to hold true for opiate users. They addressed the issue of a unidimensional (regarding abstinence as the sole determinant of treatment effectiveness) versus a multidimensional (using criteria besides abstinence) model of outcome and supported the unidimensional model for cocaine abuse. They found, however, that abstinence was not necessarily associated with improvement in other areas such as medical, legal, and employment.

Stephens, Wertz, and Roffman (1993) examined the role of self-efficacy, among other variables, as a predictor of treatment outcome for marijuana abusers. They found that pretreatment marijuana use, psychological distress, and perceived self-efficacy for avoiding use made a significant contribution to the regression equation at 3- and 6-month follow-up, but only the marijuana use and abuse variables were predictive at 12-months.

Matching of patient-staff beliefs as well as patient-treatment (McLellan, Woody, Luborsky, O'Brien, & Druley, 1983) as successful predictors of outcome were considered. Looking at matching of patient-staff beliefs, Colon and Massey (1988) found that outcome was better for patients who endorsed more fully the disease model of alcoholism that the staff subscribed to. A more successful outcome was also apparent when patients' symptom severity was matched with intensity of treatment in McLellan et al.'s 1983 study.

In summary then, predictors for successful outcome were length of time in treatment and aftercare, comorbidity, symptom severity, cognitive impairment, self-efficacy perceptions, and matching. Length of time in treatment should be at least 3 months, but extensions from 6 months to 2 years have been cited as important to successful outcome. Equally important was retention in aftercare programs posttreatment, and involvement in support groups such as AA.

The comorbid disorders most related to poor outcome were depression, antisocial personality disorder, and drug use other than the drug of choice. Levels of use at admission had a negative relationship to outcome, as did severity of symptoms of co-occurring psychiatric disorders.

## CORRELATES OF SUBSTANCE ABUSE

The issues that will be addressed in this section include comorbidity, incidence of polysubstance abuse, incidence of substance abuse and Axis I and II disorders, and the effect of these issues on treatment outcome.

The rate of co-occurring substance use and mental illness reaches or exceeds 50%, as substantiated in the literature (e.g., Blow, Cook, Booth, & Falcon, 1992; Jones & Katz, 1992; Miller, Belkin, & Gibbons, 1994; and Sheehan, 1993). An examination of data from the Epidemiologic Catchment Area studies revealed that 21%–39% of persons studied met criteria for both a substance abuse disorder and psychiatric diagnosis within the past 6 months (Kofoed, Kania, Walsh, & Atkinson, 1986). Also reporting on data from this study, Helzer and Pryzbeck (1988) found that 34% of the 20,000 respondents from the Epidemiologic Catchment Area had a core diagnosis of substance abuse and/or a psychiatric diagnosis and alcoholics were much more likely than the rest of the sample to have a dual diagnosis; co-addiction (alcohol and other drugs) was common, with alcoholism being highest in cocaine users (84%), followed by barbiturate users (71%) and opioid users (67%). Every one of the psychiatric diagnoses examined was more likely to occur in alcoholics than in nonalcoholics (Putt, 1996).

Robertson (1992) differentiated the population, stating that approximately 19% of people with mental disorders were also chemically dependent, while 50% of those who were drug dependent and 37% of alcohol-dependent persons had coexisting mental disorders. Some studies found significantly more men than women met criteria for co-occurring addictive and mental disorders while others did not find this, according to Alexander (1996).

The changing pattern of drug use among the mentally ill was noted. A longitudinal study by Rosenheck, Massari, Astrachan, and Suchinsky (1990) indicated that between the years of 1976 and 1988, the percentage of Mentally Ill Chemical Abusers (MICAs) doubled from 22.6% to 43.6%; Stockfisch, Galanter, and Lifshutz (1995) looked at trends in the dually diagnosed between the years 1988 and 1994 and found that the 1994 group of inpatients was older and had a higher incidence of marijuana, opiate, and cocaine abuse during the 24 hours pre-intake. An increasing number had used self-help groups, outpatient drug treatment clinics, and private therapists for substance abuse treatment.

Polysubstance use was associated with higher dropout rates (Kofoed et al., 1986); and a higher incidence of a comorbid diagnosis—90% according to Tomasson and Vaglum (1995), and 46% in the Miller et al. (1994) study. Women were more likely to be single vs. polydrug users in a study of sex differences among the dually diagnosed conducted by Comtois and Ries (1995). Polysubstance abuse did not appear to predict time to readmission in a study that examined readmission rates for 225 alcoholic patients discharged from a treatment program, but a history of heavy drinking, high daily alcohol consumption, and previous treatment did (Booth, Yates, Petty, & Brown, 1991).

Comorbid disorders of substance abuse and Axis I diagnoses were addressed by several authors. Roth and Fonagy (1996) cited a review of 17 studies of patients who presented for alcohol abuse treatment. The authors estimated lifetime prevalence of major depressive disorder among alcoholics was within the range of 30% to 40%, and lifetime rates of panic and phobic disorders in this population were between 2% and 60%. Most studies cited rates under 15% for panic and generalized anxiety, with a median of about 20% for phobic disorders. Miller et al. (1994) concurred with the fact that the most common co-occurring Axis I diagnosis among alcohol/drug users was major depression (31%), followed by bipolar disorder (16%), and schizophrenia (14%). Co-occurrence of substance abuse and dissociative disorders was 15% in a study of 100 subjects completing a VA treatment program (Dunn, Ryan, Paolo, & Van Fleet, 1995).

Attention-deficit hyperactivity disorder (ADHD) commonly occurred with substance use disorders, according to Wilens, Prince, Biederman, Spencer, and Frances (1995), and the authors recommended that patients with ADHD who were active substance abusers should be treated to stabilize the substance use before starting pharmacologic interventions for ADHD. Patients at a VA hospital who had coexisting substance abuse problems and Posttraumatic Stress Disorder (PTSD) reported more substance abuse related problems, more psychological distress, and less social support than substance use only or other dually diagnosed patients at follow-up (Ouimette, Ahrens, Moos, & Finney, 1997).

Co-occurrence of substance abuse and Axis II disorders was relatively common, the most frequent being antisocial, borderline, narcissistic, and mixed (Putt, 1996). Roth and Fonagy (1996) cited the incidence of antisocial personality disorder and substance abuse to be 41% to 44%. Poldrugo and Forti (1988) examined the relationship between personality disorders and alcoholism treatment outcome at 1-year follow-up and found that 25% of the 717 subjects studied had personality disorders, basically antisocial, dependent, and borderline, and that alcohol abuse was specifically related to antisocial personalities. Of the group, those with antisocial personality disorders had the worst outcome; they did not benefit from group therapy, but those with dependent personality disorders did.

In two other studies that examined the effects of personality disorders, Clopton, Weddige, Contreras, Fliszar, and Arredondo (1993) found personality disordered patients were as likely as other patients to complete a 4-month aftercare program while maintaining abstinence; and Nace and Davis (1993) found significantly greater decreases in the use of marijuana, amphetamine, and LSD among patients with personality disorder upon 12-month follow-up. The non-personality disordered (non-PD) group had significantly greater decreases in the use of beer and hard liquor, and were more satisfied with life, emotional health, and social relationships than the PD group. There was no difference in the use of drugs between the groups at follow-up, but the PD group was using significantly more alcohol.

Hirschel and Keny (1990) examined the issue of drug use and criminal activity, emphasizing the enormous drain on the nation's economy and on the resources of social, welfare, treatment, and criminal justice agencies. They cited a $59 billion annual toll brought about by drug use and related crime; this figure did not include costs resulting from alcohol abuse. The authors quoted a 1987 NIDA report that stated that by their mid 20s, nearly 80% of young adults had tried an illicit drug, including approximately 60% who had used illicit drugs other than and usually in addition to marijuana; over 90% of high school seniors had used alcohol, and two-thirds of these had used alcohol within the past month. Because there is little effective treatment of substance abuse in penal settings, a cycle of "addiction—arrest—release—readdiction—rearrest" is fostered.

The effects of these issues on treatment outcome were varied. Osher (1996) stated that although treating persons with co-occurring addictive and mental disorders (COAMD) was costly, "not treating them will ultimately break the health-care bank" (p. 74). Dickey and Azeni (1996) concurred, stating that in their study, "psychiatrically disabled substance abusers had psychiatric costs that were almost 60% higher than those of nonabusers" (p. 973) and that most of the cost differential was due to more acute psychiatric inpatient treatment. They found that even moderate drinking by persons with major mental illness carried the risk of their eventually becoming substance abusers. The authors described an offset effect (treatment in one area reducing costs in another) that treatment reduced mean monthly medical costs more than 20% in the 4-year follow-up. Other studies corroborated this effect. Miller et al. (1994) referenced several studies that indicated treatment of psychiatric disorders without concurrent treatment of substance abuse disorders did little to alter the course of either illness, stating, ". . . treatment of a psychiatric disorder is neither specific nor adequate for treatment of the addictive use of alcohol and drugs" (p. 390).

In problematic patient groups, those with a dual diagnosis are overly represented according to Kofoed et al. (1986); the dually diagnosed demand irregular discharges from psychiatric hospitals, show up more frequently in emergency rooms, comprising half of psychiatric emergencies, and become treatment failures in substance abuse treatment programs. Women with COAMD experienced more childhood physical and sexual abuse than women without substance use problems according to Alexander (1996) and were more likely to be victimized and initiate conflict as well. Alcoholic women were four times more susceptible to major depression than male alcoholics.

Drake, Mueser, Clark, and Wallach (1996) described several effects of substance abuse correlates. They stated that the dually diagnosed had poorer psycho-social adjustment, as measured by homelessness and institutionalization. For patients discharged from psychiatric hospitals, use of alcohol and drugs strongly predicted homelessness. Comorbid homeless men who were moved from homeless shelters to stable housing were more likely to be rehospitalized and to return to homelessness. The dually diagnosed had higher rates of rehospitalization; this was also true for those with schizophrenia who drank even moderately. Persons with schizophrenia who abused marijuana had more psychotic relapses.

Traditional treatment programs for those with severe mental illness had little effect on substance abuse disorders and this tended to persist over time. The authors discussed the problem of the "poor fit between dually diagnosed patients and the existing treatment system" (p. 45) and strongly supported an approach which integrated mental health and substance abuse treatment at the level of clinical delivery. Some advantages of the integrated approach were: the avoidance of a substance abuse system that was typically unresponsive to persons with severe mental illness; avoidance of breakdowns between separate agencies and systems that address each issue separately; ability to take advantage of ready access to patients already within the mental health system; and the requirement that clinicians and programs, rather than clients, make the treatment compatible.

Findings from current research on integrated programs were summarized, listing the following results: All programs were successful in engaging clients in outpatient services and retention rates were 75% to 85%; engagement in these services reduced inpatient and institutional services utilization; there was minimal or no reduction in substance abuse during a one-year period; treatment was complicated by measurement difficulties, short follow-up periods, and lack of patient motivation to become clean and sober. The authors recommended motivational interventions be utilized to help prepare dually diagnosed clients for traditional, abstinence-oriented interventions and examined studies that showed a percentage (from 25% to 61%) of severely mentally ill, substance-abusing patients were able to become abstinent with such treatment within a 4 to 7 year period. They concluded that "Initial evidence indicates that integrated treatments, if consistently applied over several years, are quite effective" (p. 49).

To summarize, the rate of co-occurring substance use and mental illness is approximately 50%; i.e., about half of persons who have substance abuse problems also have a comorbid psychiatric diagnosis. Drug use among the mentally ill is increasing, having doubled between 1976 and 1988. Co-addiction of alcohol and other drugs is common, and polysubstance use is associated with higher dropout rates.

The most common comorbid disorder on Axis I is major depression, followed by anxiety disorders, bipolar disorder, and schizophrenia. Attention-deficit hyperactivity disorder and posttraumatic stress disorder also commonly occur with substance use disorders. Axis II disorders that most commonly occur in substance abusers are antisocial and borderline personality disorders. Less commonly occurring comorbid personality disorders include dependent, narcissistic, and mixed. Persons with comorbid disorders are difficult and costly to treat, requiring lengthy and specialized programs.

## COMPARATIVE TREATMENT EFFECTIVENESS

### Introduction

Before comparative treatment effects can be determined, there must be agreement as to the desired outcome goals. Definition of goals to be accomplished remains a recurring problem in outcome measurement. One commonly agreed upon goal is eliminating or reducing drug use. Secondary goals often include: decreasing criminal activity; increasing educational level and improving vocational skills; attaining steady employment; establishing stable social and family relationships; developing coping, social, and communication skills; improving physical and psychological health;

and eliminating or lessening health risks associated with drug use, such as those associated with HIV transmission and infection (Mejta, Naylor, & Maslar, 1994).

While total abstinence remains the goal for most treatment centers, studies continue to indicate that abstinence is an unlikely outcome of treatment even in the short term. Outcome studies on inpatient treatment during the decade 1980 to 1990 indicated that only 31% to 43% of individuals treated for alcoholism had maintained abstinence at 1-year follow-up. The 6-month follow-up rates ranged between 44% and 51%. Recovery is a multifaceted process and abstinence does not automatically result in improved physical, psychological, or social functioning, according to Schneider, Kviz, Isola, and Filstead (1995). The authors stated "Examining only whether or not abstinence was achieved fails to provide comprehensive information about the impact of treatment. Moreover, this perspective ignores the course of alcoholism as a life-long chronic condition, and recovery as a process where coping skills are learned and periods of normal functioning or remission may be followed by periods of relapse" (p. 2).

Most treatment research involves basic comparative designs, which are appropriate means for estimating average effects of treatment that addresses the fundamental question of whether or not the treatment works. Finney (1995) discussed the importance of additionally examining mediators and moderators of treatment effects to determine which treatments work for whom and which variables within the treatment lead to differential effects. He described the process of explanatory analyses and listed advantages such as indicating ways in which programs might be improved, offering greater precision in estimating how well treatment-effect findings generalized to new situations, and providing new information that could result in changes in how treatment effects are thought to be exerted.

Literature reviewed in this section will describe which treatments work best, with whom, and under what conditions. Due to the quantity of variables affecting treatment outcome, the section will be divided into the specific focus areas of particular substances of abuse, treatment models, and specific populations.

## Treatment Effectiveness Based on Substance of Abuse

The substances addressed most often in the current literature were alcohol, cocaine, and methadone. The following describes this research.

### Alcohol
Roth and Fonagy (1996) reviewed various treatments for alcohol dependency. They stated that treatment has shifted from intensive residential

and rehabilitation treatment toward more brief interventions. The authors reviewed controlled studies and compared 200 treatment outcomes. Effectiveness included not only reduction in drinking, but improvement in physical and emotional well-being. They listed the following as treatments with good evidence of effectiveness: social skills training; self-control training; brief motivational interviewing; behavioral marital therapy; community reinforcement approach; and stress-management training. Among treatments that were promising but not proven were: covert sensitization; behavioral contracting; disulfiram; antidepressant medication; nonbehavioral marital therapy; cognitive therapy; hypnosis; and lithium. Treatments with no evidence of effectiveness were: chemical or electrical aversion therapy; educational lectures/films; anxiolytic medication; general counseling; and residential milieu therapy. The authors stated that treatments focusing on improving social skills and relationships seemed to have good cost/benefit ratios, and by contrast, treatments such as residential milieu therapy, psychodynamic therapy, and some drug treatments appeared to have high costs with little evidence of efficacy.

Retention in treatment was associated with positive outcome. In a study of alcoholics comparing Hazelton-type treatment to traditional-type treatment, Keso and Salaspuro (1990) found that the Hazelton-type treatment was significantly more involving, supportive, encouraging of spontaneity, and personal-problem focused than the traditional type of treatment. This resulted in a much lower dropout rate (7.9% compared to 25.9%)

## Cocaine

Many studies addressed the issue of cocaine abuse, reflecting the recent upsurge in its use. Most of these studies compared various treatment approaches.

In an outpatient treatment program for cocaine abusers that compared relapse prevention with 12-Step approaches, Wells, Peterson, Gainey, Hawkins, and Catalano (1994) gathered self-report data at baseline, at the end of the 12-week treatment program and at 6 months. They found that subjects in both treatment conditions had reduced their use of cocaine, marijuana, and alcohol posttreatment. Those in the 12-Step program showed less use of alcohol from pretreatment to follow-up than the relapse prevention group, and treatment attendance was negatively related to cocaine use at posttreatment and to cocaine and marijuana use 6 months later.

Carroll, Nich, and Rounsaville (1995) looked at symptom reduction in depressed cocaine abusers who were treated either with psychotherapy or pharmacotherapy. They compared depressed and nondepressed patients, and found that the depressed subjects remained in treatment longer and had better cocaine outcomes than the nondepressed subjects.

While desipramine had an effect in reducing depression, it did not reduce cocaine use more than a placebo did. Cognitive-behavioral relapse prevention treatment was associated with longer abstinence periods among the depressed as compared to supportive clinical management. This was also true for retention in treatment.

A comparison of six psychosocial treatment approaches and client characteristics for 303 cocaine abusing subjects indicated that retention was significantly enhanced by more frequent and intensive group therapy or by adding more treatment services to traditional group therapy. The authors concluded that a successful approach for treatment of cocaine abusers was increasing the frequency, intensity, and types of services offered (Hoffman et al., 1994).

In a 1996 study, Hoffman, Caudill, Koman, and Luckey looked at 12-month outcomes for psychosocial treatment of cocaine abusers. They reported that overall, there were substantial pre-post treatment gains, including reduced cocaine and other drug use and less involvement in illegal activities. Variables associated with regular cocaine use during the year after treatment were attending fewer sessions during treatment, being female, being less educated, and regular use of cocaine prior to treatment. The authors concluded that treatment positively impacted posttreatment gains and suggested that selective tailoring of additional services may result in additional gains. These included services particularly tailored for women, and adjusting the cognitive and behavioral skills level for those with less education.

A description of the Matrix Model for treatment of cocaine abuse was presented, along with results of various studies comparing this model with other treatment options (Rawson et al., 1995). The Matrix Model was developed during the early 1980s as cocaine use escalated and the first wave of cocaine abusers began to seek help. It was developed in response to previous research that had indicated an optimal treatment dose for cocaine abusers seeking outpatient treatment, after finding that weekly outpatient therapy was ineffective both in retaining subjects in treatment and in initiating or sustaining abstinence from cocaine use. The Matrix Model is a structured, 2-phase treatment program lasting 12 months. The goal of the model is to "provide a framework within which cocaine abusers can achieve the following: (a) cease drug use, (b) remain in a treatment process for 12 months, (c) learn about issues critical to addiction and relapse, (d) receive direction and support from a trained therapist, (e) receive education for family members affected by the addiction, (f) become familiar with the self-help programs, and (g) receive monitoring by urine testing" (p. 119). The studies concerning this model demonstrated that patients with fewer resources were more difficult to engage and retain in treatment; that there was a clear positive relationship between duration and amount of treatment involvement and positive outcome at 1 year; and patients treated within the model demonstrated significant reductions in drug and alcohol use and improvements in psychological indicators.

In a study by Richard, Montoya, Nelson, and Spence (1995), the Matrix Model (here called the neurobehavioral model) was adapted for use with an indigent urban population of mainly African-American cocaine abusers. The authors looked at the effectiveness of this model, used either alone or in combination with one of three adjunct therapies in the treatment of cocaine addiction. Adjunct therapies included acupuncture; medications such as desipramine and bromocriptine, a fast acting nonaddictive anti-craving medication; and biofeedback. Follow-up, conducted at 9 months after intake, found that adjunct therapy significantly improved retention in treatment independent of motivation at intake; retention in intensive outpatient treatment significantly improved drug use outcomes at 9 months as measured by urinalysis; and adjunct therapies did not directly improve drug use outcomes beyond improvement attributable to retention in the treatment program.

Other studies involving cocaine abuse indicated that a community reinforcement approach that improves social behavior and vocational functioning was effective (Higgins & Bickel, 1993); that length of abstinence prior to admission to treatment was positively correlated with retention; and that subjects in functional relationships did better in treatment compared to those living alone or in dysfunctional relationships (Means et al., 1989). Piotrowski, Clark, and Hall (1994) studied the efficacy of different recruitment strategies and found that active recruitment efforts by personnel on an inpatient substance abuse unit of the VA resulted in a large number of potential subjects, but that they tended to be primarily white polysubstance abusers who used crack cocaine secondarily. Media-based strategies for recruitment, e.g., fliers and outreach approaches resulted in obtaining more primary crack cocaine users, and these strategies were more effective with African-Americans.

## Methadone

Three studies examined outcome utilizing methadone treatment. Desmond and Maddux (1996) looked at the difference between treatment outcomes of subjects admitted to methadone maintenance while on probation or parole as compared to those admitted to the program without compulsory supervision and found that the compulsory supervision group had worse outcomes regarding retention, productive activity, and incarceration. However, a higher number of noncompulsory subjects were discharged from the program for noncompliance. The authors concluded that the findings of this study do not support a policy of exclusion of opioid users from methadone maintenance just because they are on parole or probation.

A comparison of relative efficacies of 50 mg and 20 mg of methadone with methadone-free treatment was made by Strain, Stitzer, Liebson, and Bigelow (1993). All patients improved on measures of psychosocial functioning and psychological symptoms over time, indicating that methadone-free treatment is effective on those measures. Subjects on 50 mg of methadone had lower frequency of heroin use than the other two groups. In comparing outcome of abstinence-oriented with indefinite methadone maintenance treatment, Caplehorn (1994) indicated that subjects assigned to the abstinence-oriented program were significantly more likely to use heroin (one-third more) and amphetamines (3 times more) than those in the methadone program during the first 2 years of treatment, but less likely to use benzodiazepines. Abstinence-oriented subjects were more likely to relapse and return to maintenance treatment; and the abstinence-oriented program was less able to attract heroin addicts into treatment.

A 24-year follow-up study examined long-term patterns and consequences of use among narcotics addicts (Hser, Anglin, & Powers, 1993) . The authors found that substance use and criminal activity remained high in the 581 subjects into their late 40s. Only around 5% entered treatment voluntarily with the primary objective of becoming totally abstinent. Few (<10%) participated in community-based programs such as methadone maintenance; and disability, long periods of heavy alcohol and tobacco use, and heavy criminal involvement were strongly correlated with mortality. Consistent with other studies, they found a cyclical pattern of treatment, abstinence, and relapse in the addiction history. The authors concluded that the "eventual cessation of narcotics use is a very slow process, unlikely to occur for some addicts, especially if they have not ceased use by their late 30s" (p. 577).

## Effectiveness of Treatment Models

A study by Timko, Moos, Finney, and Moos (1994) compared 1-year outcomes for 515 problem drinkers who had self selected into four treatment modalities: No treatment; AA only, outpatient treatment; and residential or inpatient treatment. All four groups improved on drinking and functioning outcomes, but subjects who entered the two treatment conditions and the AA groups improved more than those who received no treatment, especially on drinking-related outcomes. Inpatient subjects were more likely than outpatient or AA subjects to be abstinent. More AA attendance was associated with the three treatment groups; among outpatients and inpatients, more formal treatment was associated with abstinence, and other drinking-related outcomes showed improvement. Burnam et al. (1995) found that at 3-month follow-up, residential treatment, as compared to nonresidential treatment, seemed to provide more positive effects on outcomes but by 6 months these effects had eroded.

Stockwell et al. (1991) compared home detoxification with inpatient care, and found that both rates of completion and complication were identical in the two groups. They concluded that home detoxification was equivalent in both safety and efficacy to more expensive inpatient treatment. A comparison of residential vs. nonresidential treatment for homeless mothers with young children was conducted by Smith, North, and Fox (1995). Dropout rates were high for both groups, but residential subjects had a lower dropout rate than those in nonresidential treatment. Both groups improved in alcohol and drug problems and housing stability regardless of time spent in the program.

Patients with alcohol and cocaine addictions whose appropriate level of care evaluation suggested inpatient treatment were placed in an intensive day treatment program and compared with those who were properly matched to day treatment (McKay, McLellan, & Alterman, 1992). Mismatched patients were no more likely to drop out of day hospital treatment than matched patients and there was no evidence during follow-up that they were drinking or using cocaine more frequently. They did not do worse on any other outcome measure except psychological status.

In a comparison of 12-step and cognitive-behavioral models of treatment, Ouimette, Finney, and Moos (1997) showed both programs to be equally effective in reducing substance use and improving most other areas of functioning. Patients with substance-abuse-only diagnoses, with concomitant psychiatric diagnoses, and those mandated to treatment all showed similar improvement at 1-year follow-up regardless of the type of treatment received. Twelve-step involvement was also studied by Hoffmann and Miller (1992) who found that AA attendance after treatment resulted in greater likelihood of sobriety than nonattendance. Around 70% who attended AA but not aftercare remained sober; the same proportion remained true for those who attended aftercare but not AA. The best results were obtained (90% remained abstinent) by those who attended both aftercare for one year and weekly AA meetings. The authors concluded that addictions need to be addressed as chronic, not acute, conditions.

Comparing several private treatment programs, McLellan et al. (1993) found that the "quantity and range of the treatment services actually delivered during rehabilitation can be one of the major factors accounting for differential effectiveness of treatment programs" (p. 254). Behavioral couples therapy was superior to individual therapy in terms of relationship and drug-related outcomes, according to Fals-Stewart, Birchler, and O'Farrell (1996).

Cognitive-behavioral relapse prevention treatment was effective, especially for reducing severity of relapses and for patients with higher levels of impairment, either psychopathology or dependence severity (Carroll, 1996). Cognitive-behavioral group therapy was more effective than two other group approaches for dually diagnosed subjects in an outpatient setting in reducing alcohol use, improving social and family relations, and enhancing psychological functioning, according to Fisher and Bentley (1996).

## Treatment Effectiveness With Specific Groups

Several studies examined treatment outcomes with adolescents and the elderly, the homeless population, the severely mentally disabled (SMD) population, and those persons who were mandated to treatment.

### Adolescents
Studies regarding adolescents stressed the importance of family relationships as factors influencing severity and treatment issues. Blood and Cornwall (1996) examined the impact of childhood sexual abuse on treatment of substance-abusing adolescents and found that those reporting sexual abuse had more serious involvement with substances, suffered more physical abuse, had substance-abusing parents, and that males showed increased suicidal ideation and school failure. Compared to subjects who were not exposed to sexual abuse, there were no differences on rate of treatment completion, change scores pre- and post-treatment, nor on ratings of treatment effectiveness. Therapists, however, felt that subjects who reported sexual abuse were more in touch with their feelings and more likely to be involved in aftercare.

In a study that examined family and client characteristics as predictors of outcome for outpatient treatment of adolescent drug abusers, Friedman, Terras, and Kreisher (1995) found that the more positively the subjects described family functioning and relationships at pretreatment, the more improvement they reported at 15-month follow-up. Those who were self referred had reduced levels of substance abuse.

Doyle, Delaney, and Tobin (1994) found that adolescents who participated in treatment and reported no abstinence or reduced alcohol use at 4-year follow-up had early personality difficulties and unsatisfactory school experiences. They also indicated illicit drug use in addition to continued problem drinking. Both the good and poor outcome groups initially had similar forensic histories, but the poor outcome group continued to have marked legal problems, and also continued to make heavy demands on medical services during the follow-up period.

In an evaluation of treatment programs for adolescents, Hird, Khuri, Dusenbury, and Millman (1996) reiterated what has already been pointed out above, i.e., "It is difficult to draw conclusions based on the literature, due in part to variations between studies in operational definitions and terminology, as well as in measures of outcome effectiveness. However, reviews in the field conclude that any treatment is better than no treatment and the best predictor of treatment outcome is the amount of time spent in treatment. Success also appears more likely when skills training is part of the treatment and when families participate, and attending aftercare, including self-help and support groups, favorably influence outcome" (p. 690). The authors stated that adolescents who had the best prognosis were those who attended school or other educational programs, were older when substance use began, were not involved in opiate use, polysubstance use, or criminal behavior, and who had fewer problems to start with. Of those who relapsed, one-third did so in the first month posttreatment, and two-thirds within the first 6 months. Adolescents most often relapsed as a result of peer pressure, and those who believed substance use would help in social interaction had a more difficult time remaining abstinent.

## Elderly

A study involving older alcoholic VA patients compared two types of treatments: One was operated by a tolerant staff that specialized in treatment of elderly alcoholics and used reminiscence therapy with goals of developing self-esteem and peer relationships (OAR); the other was traditional therapy that emphasized confrontation, focusing on past failures and present conflicts. The OAR patients were two times more likely to report abstinence at 1-year follow-up; response was best for patients over 60 years of age (Kashner, Rodell, Ogden, & Gugenheim, 1992)

Stoddard and Thompson (1996) addressed issues for professionals who treat the alcohol-abusing elderly. They stated that alcoholism in this population is a growing social concern and estimated that it occurred in 5%–6% of the elderly who live independently. The majority of elderly alcoholics said that feelings of loneliness and depression preceded their first drink. The authors suggested that treatment for this group be age-specific, address both substance abuse and aging problems, and involve aggressive recruitment of family involvement and education.

Gambert (1996) discussed physiological changes that lead to altered tolerance and increased morbidity with substance abuse in the elderly, diseases that coexist or interact with substance abuse, and effects of chronic alcohol ingestion. He stated that many elderly alcoholics were unaware of the effects of aging on the dynamics of alcohol use or how greatly alcohol affected their cognition. While discussing this may lead to limiting the use of alcohol among older persons, the goal of treatment must be total and complete abstinence. Dietary and vitamin deficiencies must be addressed, as well as medical support for alcohol-related illnesses. Many elderly benefitted from AA involvement, while programs specially tailored to the elderly appeared to be most successful.

## Homeless
Treatments that were effective for the homeless population included an integrated cognitive-behavioral therapeutic community approach in a residential rehabilitation program (Burling, Seidner, Salvio, & Marshall, 1994), and placement in a halfway house posttreatment vs. placement in community-based housing (Hitchcock, Stainback, & Roque, 1995). Braucht et al. (1995) found that homeless persons who received intensive case management posttreatment initially improved more than those who received less service, but the rate of improvement decreased during follow-up.

Joseph and Paone (1996) in a comprehensive article on issues affecting the homeless, looked at several national demonstration projects geared toward treatment of this population. Problems encountered included the fact that homeless clients were difficult to track and treat and often did not complete follow-up. Service needs were many and varied and included housing, unemployment, education, drug and alcohol problems, and health and mental care issues. Resources were unavailable to coordinate community facilities and services needed for effective treatment and currently funded programs did not have the research capacity to evaluate their efforts. There was also the problem of community resistance and hostility toward the homeless. The authors listed five conclusions from evaluations of the demonstration projects dealing with this population:

"1. Addiction programs must also focus on housing needs, means of support and gainful employment.

2. Dropout rates in all programs were high. Programs must develop more user friendly programs that clients and patients can respond to and commit themselves to upon admission. More intensive therapeutic measures can be gradually introduced.

3. Of those who remained in treatment, both subjects and controls improved significantly by the end of the treatment episode. Controls received minimal services as compared to the subjects. In some programs, controls received as many services but of a different type including 12-step programs.

4. Positive posttreatment outcomes diminish over time suggesting the need for posttreatment interventions and after care programs.

5. Patients or clients with higher levels of education, lower levels of severe substance abuse, less criminal activity, and greater social integration

have more positive outcomes than others who participated in the program" (pp. 741–742).

## Severely Mentally Disabled

The SMD population with concomitant substance abuse problems presents especially difficult treatment issues, as was previously pointed out. Treatment that appears effective with this population was addressed in several studies. Woody, McLellan, Lubursky, and O'Brien (1986) stated that substance abusers with high levels of psychopathology showed greater improvement when they received therapy in addition to drug counseling rather than receiving drug counseling only.

Continuous, intensive treatment by Assertive Community Treatment (ACT) teams was compared to standard case management programs and found to be superior on 10 of the 13 criteria measured, in addition to being more effective in implementing substance abuse treatment (Teague, Drake, & Ackerson, 1995). In a study that compared ACT treatment and group therapy to controls (Bond, McDonel, Miller, & Pensec, 1991), the authors found few advantages for either treatment program compared to controls. Although there was modest evidence for improvement in alcohol and drug problems for clients in the groups compared to controls, there were no changes for ACT clients on these variables, suggesting that the ACT program as implemented in this study had relatively little impact on these domains. The authors recommended that treatment approaches for the SMD population be combined, capitalizing on the advantages of different modalities, and they suggested combining the two approaches examined in this study.

Drake (1996) recommended that treatment for the substance-abusing SMD population be integrated and longitudinal, utilizing stages of recovery. He emphasized that the process of recovery occurs over years rather than weeks and suggested a differential approach, e.g., patients with bipolar disorder are more interested and would benefit more from self-help groups than would schizophrenics. Ridgely and Jerrell (1996) stated that counselors who treat this population, in addition to acquiring adequate specialized training and consultation, be motivated to work with these very difficult and high-risk clients and have sufficient time to devote to them. They emphasized that extenuated periods of treatment are necessary for these clients who are subject to frequent relapse and strongly deny mental and substance abuse disorders.

## Offenders Mandated to Treatment

Several studies confirmed the fact that persons mandated to treatment fare as well or better than those who come to treatment of their own accord (e.g., Hirschel & Keny, 1990; Hoffmann, Ninonuevo, Mozey, &

Luxenberg, 1987; Vito, 1989; Watson, Brown, Tilleskjor, Jacobs, & Pucel, 1988). Jolin and Stipak (1992) found that electronically monitored home-confinement clients who received substance abuse treatment had lower recidivism when compared to monitored clients without treatment or those on work release. They concluded that electrically monitored home-confinement programs with concurrent drug treatment warrant further consideration as sentencing options for substance abusers.

To summarize the recurrent themes and main points of this diverse section then, chemical dependency is a chronic, not an acute condition and recovery is a slow, cyclical process. Therefore the value of using abstinence as the sole outcome goal is questionable, since its occurrence is unlikely, especially in early treatment. Retention in treatment, aftercare, and 12-step programs is critical to recovery and more frequent and intense services seem to work best. Cognitive-behavioral treatment, including skill training, is effective with most populations and socially oriented, supportive and nonconfrontational interventions produce more positive outcomes. Family dynamics impact severity of substance abuse and recovery potential. Persons with histories of abuse and other dysfunctional family interactions fare worse, as do those with more severe psychiatric and substance abuse problems.

## GENDER AND RACIAL DIFFERENCES IN SUBSTANCE ABUSE TREATMENT OUTCOMES

### Gender

While the basic nature of addictive processes is similar for both men and women, there are physiological, sociocultural, and psychological sex differences in the course and symptoms of addiction according to Blume (1996). Among them are the following:

1. Women begin drinking, in general, and abusive drinking at a later age than men, but present for treatment at approximately the same age and with the same severity of symptoms as men. This more rapid course of the illness in women is called "telescoping."

2. Alcoholic women drink much less than alcoholic men but suffer the same impairment. Studies indicate that women average 4.5 ounces of absolute alcohol per day compared to 8.2 ounces for men. One reason proposed for this difference is that women tend to rely more on the use of other sedatives in addition to alcohol. As women age, tolerance for alcohol and other drugs decreases and consumption is less but adverse health and social consequences remain the same.

3. Women entering treatment for alcoholism are more likely to have

significant others who are addicted or to be divorced or separated. Men entering treatment are more likely to have significant relationships with nonaddicted persons.

4. The onset of substance abuse is more likely to be related to a stressful event for women than for men.

5. Women are more likely to be dually diagnosed than men and to experience much more depression.

6. Women who are chemically dependent attempt suicide more frequently than addicted men. In alcoholic women, the rate of attempted suicide was 4 times that of nonalcoholic women and twice as frequent in their 20s as in their 40s. This age difference was not observed in nonalcoholic suicidal women.

7. Family problems and health concerns (including mental health) are the prime motivators for entering treatment among addicted women. For men, job and legal problems (especially DUIs) are more prevalent.

8. Alcoholic women entering treatment are more likely to have histories of prescription drug abuse (e.g., tranquilizers, sedatives, and amphetamines) than men but less likely to have histories of illicit drug abuse.

9. Women who commit homicide are more likely to be alcoholic than other women and also to have co-occurring personality disorders.

In treating women substance abusers, attention should be given to determining past history of physical or sexual abuse, possible prescription drug abuse, evaluation and treatment of family members, substance abuse education, child care needs, and low self-esteem according to Blume (1996). The author stated that outcome studies on treatment of chemically dependent women indicated that males and females in the same treatment program for alcoholism tend to do equally well. This was substantiated by several other authors, e.g., Duckert (1987); Kosten, Gawin, Kosten, and Rounsaville (1993); McCrady and Raytek (1993); Nathan and Skinstad (1987). Fewer studies have been done on other substances and results are equivocal. McCrady and Raytek (1993) reported most studies found no difference between males and females in outcome based on inpatient vs. outpatient treatment.

Studies predicting favorable outcome for women in treatment indicated that social factors played an important role, including number of life problems and supportive relationships. A social network that did not encourage substance use by women was a major factor in positive treatment outcome. Other predictors of favorable outcome included age (<35 or >50), being divorced or separated, possessing traditional feminine traits and moral standards, and having no sexual dysfunction according to Blume (1996).

Predictors of poorer treatment outcome for women included marital problems prior to treatment, dysfunctional relationships with significant others, few primary relationships prior to treatment, multiple life problems, history of delirium tremens, loss of control over drinking, early onset of alcoholism, lack of employment, and diagnosis of antisocial personality disorder (McCrady & Raytek, 1993).

Schneider et al. (1995) described the differences in the drinking careers of men and women, stating that the lifetime prevalence of alcohol abuse/ dependence in the United States is about 13% with men being five times as likely as women to have this diagnosis. Men are much more likely than women to receive treatment and studies involving women are fairly scarce in the literature.

Gender differences mentioned by the authors in addition to "telescoping" referred to above, were that for women most heavy drinking occurred in middle life, while for men it began in early adulthood. Problem drinking for women generally began as the result of social situations (e.g., dysfunctional relationships) or adverse events such as death or loss, while men began drinking to moderate negative affect such as boredom, low self-esteem, or tension. Men tended to go directly into treatment for help with their addiction problems, but women usually sought help initially from their personal physician or a psychiatrist. Women were also 1.5 to 2 times more likely than men to experience alcohol-related mortality. In their review of treatment outcome, Schneider et al. (1995) found that group therapy worked better for men while individual therapy and educational programs were more helpful for women.

Women alcoholics were more likely than men alcoholics to have experienced childhood family difficulties according to Mutzell (1994). These included having an alcohol and drug-abusing parent, parents with nervous problems, attempted suicide by a parent, and serious schisms in the family. Kingree (1995) also examined effects of family support among other variables, in determining gender differences in substance abuse treatment. Women reported less self esteem and family support, more self-blame and parental blame than men. Wallen (1992) found that women were more likely than men to report a sexual abuse history, indicate more emotional distress, and be more willing to seek help for emotional problems.

Several studies discussed differential outcome variables, treatment needs of women, and problems encountered by women in treatment. Schneider et al. (1995) found that for men, being married was associated with less relapse, but for women it was a risk factor for relapse. There was less risk of relapse for women with fewer years of problem drinking, but with men less risk was associated with more years of problem drinking. Women who stayed in treatment for the entire program had greater relapse rates. The authors suggested this may be due to lack of confidence in ability to recover leading to longer retention in treatment, or to the fact that the emphasis was on group rather than individual therapy and women fare better in individual treatment. Also noted was the fact that since the center in this study treated mostly male patients, it did not serve the women's needs well.

Rounsaville et al. (1987) found significant interactions in the relationship between diagnosis and treatment outcome for men and women. Having an additional diagnosis was associated with poorer outcome for men, but having a diagnosis of major depression was associated with a better outcome in women.

The importance of addressing the heterogeneous nature of women in treatment due to generational and age effects was stressed by Harrison and Belille (1987). Specialized treatment service needs for women included assertiveness groups, self-esteem workshops, women-only therapy groups, groups on parenting, sexuality, and life planning skills, as well as onsite gynecological and reproductive health care according to Nelson-Zlupko, Dore, Kauffman, and Kaltenbach (1996), but few treatment services provide these due to lack of awareness or financial resources. In their study assessing gaps in women's treatment services, five major themes emerged: (1) Individual counseling seemed to be the single most important service in determining treatment retention; (2) Sexual harassment was often present in conventional drug-treatment programs; (3) Child care was central in the recovery of women with children; (4) Women's needs and experiences were not addressed in most co-ed treatment groups; (5) Even if specialized services were provided, their effectiveness was diminished in treatment settings which failed to support and promote women.

## Race

### African-Americans

Since the passage of the Anti-Drug Abuse Act in 1986, efforts to study drug abuse in special populations have increased, but to date there is little information in the literature on the relationship between ethnicity and drug use and treatment outcome. Surveys indicated that an estimated 3.2 million African-Americans used illicit drugs in the past year and 1.7 million African-Americans used an illicit drug in the past month of the survey. African-American males between the ages of 12 and 35 were more likely to have used illicit substances than white males of the same age range. This was especially true regarding cocaine usage; 1.4% of African-American males over age 35 used cocaine compared to 0.2% of white males of that age. The percentage of males of both races between the ages of 12 and 17 who used an illicit substance in their lifetime, the past year or past month, however, was equal. While the rates of cocaine and marijuana use by African-Americans in the past month were higher than for whites, the lifetime rates of marijuana and cocaine use were higher among whites (John, Brown, Jr., & Primm, 1996).

Issues that needed to be addressed on the subject of substance abuse treatment of African-Americans were pointed out by John et al. (1996) and Foulks and Pena (1995). One of the most salient issues was the heterogeneous nature of this population. John et al. stated: "The African-American subpopulations present a diverse multicultural community. Fundamentally there are at least three cultural subgroups: (1) African-Americans who are descendants of African slaves and who were actually born in the United States. (2) African-Americans who are descendants of African slaves of the Caribbean and who migrated to the United States. (3) African-Americans who were born in Africa and migrated to the United States. Within this subgroup there are a multitude of different cultures depending on the originating African Country" (p. 699). The unique characteristics of each of these subcultures became important when the research concerned racial matching of patient and therapist. Foulks and Pena illustrated this point with the following example: "A Jamaican-American therapist of Rastafarian tradition and Indian and Nigerian descent may share few cultural values with a 'black patient' whose father is light skinned and whose mother is Irish Catholic" (p. 616). The authors stated that distal factors such as skin color, declared ethnic identity, language spoken, and religion are not as important in patient/ therapist matching as the proximal indicators of mutual values, behaviors, beliefs, and attitudes. Better outcomes were achieved when demographic variables such as marital and socioeconomic status of patient and therapist were matched.

Due to the variety of African-American subcultures, the issue of subject selection becomes important. In a comparative study, if subjects are not randomly chosen, selection bias may confound results. Also, reliable responses to substance abuse surveys may be influenced by the fact that a disproportionate number of African-Americans are incarcerated for drug-related crimes and this may result in reluctance to respond truthfully.

Foulks and Pena (1995) stated that explanations for substance use and abuse in the African-American community that focus solely on psychological factors may be inadequate and reductionistic. Racial differences cited in the prevalence of crack cocaine use "become non significant if one controls for social and environmental factors by stratifying the data into neighborhood risk sets" (p. 610). The authors stated that with the African-American cocaine abusers they studied, the number, type, and severity of social and family problems were more etiologically important than psychopathology per se. They discussed the demoralization and dysphoria brought about by poverty and racial oppression and how those factors may be associated with substance use and abuse. They recommended therapeutic interventions that were sensitive to effects of ethnicity and the client's sense of well-being.

National Institute on Drug Abuse (NIDA) data indicated that African-Americans and Hispanics were three times more likely than whites to receive substance abuse treatment. While some have argued that treatment models and theories of addiction are based on middle-class whites, and that causes of addiction for African-Americans are different requiring different treatment, the outcome literature so far indicates that African-Americans benefit as much from existing treatment as other groups. Community structure surrounding the treatment was more important in influencing outcome than ethnic status and variables such as pretreatment employment and type of treatment were more important in several studies (Foulks & Pena, 1995).

According to John et al. (1996), factors associated with substance abuse by African-Americans included undereducation, unemployment, underemployment, hopelessness, dysfunctional families, and other indices of poverty. None of these factors however, have been unequivocally determined to be causal and, in fact, some or perhaps all may be the result of substance abuse. The authors stated that ". . . Prevention and treatment programs do provide services for African-Americans. Most of these programs are neither described or evaluated in the published literature. The utilization by African-Americans of prevention and treatment programs and the effectiveness of these programs is largely unknown" (p. 704).

Two studies that did appear in the literature, however, indicated the following results: Pavkov, McGovern, Leone, and Geffner (1992) compared psychiatric symptomology between African-American and Caucasian adults in an inpatient substance abuse treatment center. They found that although both groups were equivalent in amount and frequency of usage, African-American alcoholics used significantly more substances in addition to alcohol than Caucasians. African-Americans reported higher levels of somatization, obsessive-compulsive behavior, depression, hostility, paranoid ideation, psychoticism, and stress. The staff assessed African-Americans as exhibiting lower levels of global functioning compared to Caucasians. Kendall, Sherman, and Bigelow (1995) examined the relationships among race, sex, age, and psychiatric symptoms between African-American and Caucasian polysubstance abusers. They found a significant effect only for race. Caucasian subjects reported significantly more psychiatric symptoms than African-American subjects. The authors suggested that racial differences be considered in treatment resource provision and planning.

## Hispanic Americans

Many of the issues considered above in regard to substance abuse treatment of African-Americans are repeated for the Hispanic American culture. The Hispanic population is also heterogeneous with subcultures of Mexican Americans, Puerto Ricans, and Cuban Americans. Language barriers and lack of sociocultural understanding create major problems in substance abuse treatment of Hispanic Americans according to Ruiz and Langrod (1996). They stated, "It is also apparent that treatment programs designed and operated by 'Anglo' professionals have not developed adequate cultural components and sensitivity in programming to attract lower socioeconomic Hispanics" (p. 705). Non-Spanish-speaking staff who do not know specific sociocultural issues faced by Hispanic addicts hinder effective treatment, and governmental regulations and policies interfere with acceptance of treatment programs, e.g., compulsory urine testing required in methadone maintenance programs conveys an implicit message of disbelief of the patient's word. This may be offensive to the Hispanic's sense of dignity, which is culturally salient and highly defended.

In lifetime use of illicit drugs, Hispanics have a lower rate (31.2%) than African-Americans (33.5%) and Whites (38.9%). In comparison to the population in general, however, they have a slightly higher lifetime rate for use of crack and heroin, according to the National Household Survey on Drug Abuse conducted by NIDA and the Substance Abuse and Mental Health Services Administration (1994).

As is the case with women and African-Americans cited above, well-conducted treatment-outcome studies on Hispanic substance abusers are lacking. Studies from the 1970s and 1980s show equivocal results according to Ruiz and Langrod (1996). One study indicated that most Mexican Americans treated for heroin addiction relapsed after discharge, and refused postdischarge social casework services. Another study found Hispanics to have the highest rates of dropout and expulsion from treatment, as well as the lowest rates of completion. Other studies found that positive outcome resulted from client/counselor agreement on appropriateness of services such as appraisal of the client's problems and most effective approaches in dealing with them. The authors concluded by stating that currently, most of the non-Hispanic treatment staff are unprepared to treat the Hispanic population in terms of: "(a) Spanish language ability, (b) comprehension of the Hispanic substance abuser's socioeconomic background, and (c) awareness of the negative impact on service effectiveness, treatment outcome, and, even more importantly, on prevention strategies" (p. 711).

In summary, well-conducted outcome studies on special populations are lacking, so it is unknown whether outcomes would be improved if programs were more sensitive to gender or ethnic issues. What is evident from existing studies is that treatment can be effective for these populations. An overall theme in the literature was the heterogeneous nature of these populations, indicating that one-size-fits-all programming is not appropriate. Women experience a more rapid course of decline from substance abuse than men, a process known as "telescoping." Social factors are extremely salient for women substance abusers, and generally they have experienced more depression and abuse than men. For African-Americans, it is more important for clients and therapists to share mutual values, beliefs, behaviors, and attitudes than skin color. Hispanics face barriers to treatment that include language differences and lack of sociocultural understanding.

It is unknown at this point whether or not outcome for these populations would be improved if these issues were addressed in program planning and treatment. The universal plea in the literature, however, was to develop programs with these differences in mind in order to determine their impact on outcome.

## CONCLUSIONS AND IMPLICATIONS

The literature overwhelmingly supports the fact that treatment works if it is of sufficient duration and outcome goals are realistically and appropriately set. It is important to note that chemical dependency is a chronic, not an acute, condition and recovery can be a slow, cyclical process. For this reason, abstinence as the sole outcome goal may be unrealistic, especially early in a person's treatment history. Retention in treatment is the best predictor of success, with a minimum of approximately 6 months, and cognitive-behavioral treatment, including skill training, is effective with most populations.

Comorbidity and symptom severity are related to poorer outcome, with depression, antisocial personality disorder, and drug use other than the drug of choice being the most common comorbid conditions. Persons with comorbid disorders are difficult and costly to treat and require lengthy and specialized programs. Research on special populations such as women and ethnic minorities is scarce, but indications are that customary treatment regimens are effective with these groups.

Since effective treatment of substance abuse is such a multifaceted area requiring a multipronged attack, it is imperative that persons needing treatment do not slip through the cracks of the public system. In order to insure that this doesn't happen, there must be collaboration among supporting agencies such as mental health boards, drug and alcohol boards, and the criminal justice system. These agencies, on both state and local levels, should ensure that necessary funds are available to provide effective treatment. Utilizing court involvement to maximize treatment compliance is an effective tool to keep substance abusers in treatment long enough to enhance successful outcome probabilities.

Public policy generally endorses punishment as a deterrent to substance abuse. Research indicates that treatment is more clinically effective and more cost-effective than imprisonment. Increasing public awareness of this fact is necessary so that funds may be made more readily available for treatment as an alternative to jail. The current drug court movement is a step in this direction.

Adoption of standards for outcome measurement other than just abstinence should be encouraged to facilitate comparison of research results. This would lead to identification of the most effective treatments. There should also be agreement on appropriate instruments for outcome measurement to facilitate comparison.

Since the best predictor of successful outcome for substance abuse treatment is length of stay, managed care limiting of services is contraindicated for this population. Awareness of the special problems inherent in treatment of substance abusers should be increased and treatment needs of this population must be reconciled with managed care limitations.

Finally, research on subgroups of substance abusers such as minorities, those with comorbid disorders, and women should be increased with special attention given to the specific needs of each population. It is encouraging that knowledge of the complexity of substance abuse treatment is expanding and treatment philosophies are becoming less punitive and more supportive as the public sector gains awareness of the issues involved.

## REFERENCES

Alexander, M. J. (1996). Women with co-occurring addictive and mental disorders: An emerging profile of vulnerability. *American Journal of Orthopsychiatry, 66*, 61–70.

Blow, F. C., Cook, C. L., Booth, B. M., & Falcon, S. P. (1992). Age-related psychiatric comorbidities and level of functioning in alcoholic veterans seeking outpatient treatment. *Hospital & Community Psychiatry, 43*, 990–995.

Blood, L., & Cornwall, A. (1996). Childhood sexual victimization as a factor in the treatment of substance misusing adolescents. *Substance Use & Misuse, 31*, 1015–1039.

Blume, S. G. (1996). Women: Clinical aspects. In J. H. Lowinson, P. Ruiz, R. B. Millman, & J. G. Langrod (Eds.), *Substance abuse: A comprehensive textbook, third edition*, (pp. 645–654). Baltimore, MD: Williams & Wilkins.

Bond, G. R., McDonel, E. C., Miller, L. D., & Pensec, M. (1991). Assertive community treatment and reference groups: An evaluation of their effectiveness for young adults with serious mental illness and substance abuse problems. *Psychosocial Rehabilitation Journal, 15,* 31–43.

Booth, B. M., Yates, W. R., Petty, F., & Brown, K. (1991). Patient factors predicting early alcohol-related readmissions for alcoholics: Role of alcoholism severity and psychiatric comorbidity. *Journal of Studies on Alcohol, 52,* 37–43.

Booth, P. G., Dale, B., Slade, P. D., & Dewey, M. E. (1992). A follow-up study of problem drinkers offered a goal choice option. *Journal of Studies on Alcohol, 53,* 594–600.

Braucht, G. N., Reichardt, C. S., Geissler, L. J. Bormann, C. A., Kwiatkowski, C. F., & Kirby, Jr. M. W. (1995). Effective services for homeless substance abusers. *Journal of Addictive Diseases, 14,* 87–109.

Brower, K. J., Blow, F. C., Hill, E. M., & Mudd, S. A. (1994). Treatment outcome of alcoholics with and without cocaine disorders. *Alcoholism, Clinical & Experimental Research, 18,* 734–739.

Burling, T. A., Seidner, A. L., Salvio, A., & Marshall, G. D. (1994). A cognitive-behavioral therapeutic community for substance dependent and homeless veterans: Treatment outcome. *Addictive Behaviors, 19,* 621–629.

Burnam, M. A., Morton, S. C., McGlynn, E. A. Petersen, L. A., Stecher, B. M., Hayes, C., & Vaccaro, J. V. (1995). An experimental evaluation of residential and nonresidential treatment for dually diagnosed homeless adults. *Journal of Addictive Diseases, 14,* 111–134.

Caplehorn, J. R. M. (1994). A comparison of abstinence-oriented and indefinite methadone maintenance treatment. *International Journal of the Addictions, 29,* 1361–1375.

Carroll, K. M. (1996). Relapse prevention as a psychosocial treatment: A review of controlled clinical trials. *Experimental & Clinical Psychopharmacology, 4,* 46–54.

Carroll, K. M. , Nich, C., & Rounsaville, B. J. (1995). Differential symptom reduction in depressed cocaine abusers treated with psychotherapy and pharmacotherapy. *Journal of Nervous & Mental Disease, 183,* 251–259.

Carroll, K. M., Power, M. D., Bryant, K. J., & Rounsaville, B. J. (1993) One-year follow-up of treatment-seeking cocaine abusers: Psychopathology and dependence severity as predictors of outcome. *Journal of Nervous & Mental Disease, 181,* 71–79.

Clopton, J. R., Weddige, R. L., Contreras, S., Fliszar, G. M., & Arredondo, R. (1993). Treatment outcome for substance misuse patients with personality disorder. *International Journal of the Addictions, 28,* 1147–1153.

Colon, I., & Massey, R. K. (1988). Patient attitudes and beliefs as predictors of treatment outcome in detoxification: A pilot study. *Alcoholism Treatment Quarterly, 5,* 235–244.

Comtois, K. A., & Ries, R. K. (1995). Sex differences in dually diagnosed severely mentally ill clients in dual diagnosis outpatient treatment. *American Journal on Addictions, 4,* 245–253.

Condelli, W. S., & Hubbard, R. L. (1994). Relationship between time spent in treatment and client outcomes from therapeutic communities. *Journal of Substance Abuse Treatment, 11,* 25–33.

Desmond, D. P., & Maddux, J. F. (1996). Compulsory supervision and methadone maintenance. *Journal of Substance Abuse Treatment, 13,* 79–83.

Desmond, D. P., Maddux, J. F., Johnson, T. H., & Confer, B. A. (1995). Obtaining follow-up interviews for treatment evaluation. *Journal of Substance Abuse Treatment, 12,* 95–102.

Dickey, B., & Azeni, H. (1996). Persons with dual diagnoses of substance abuse and major mental illness: Their excess costs of psychiatric care. *American Journal of Public Health, 86,* 973–977.

Doyle, H., Delaney, W., & Tobin, J. (1994). Follow-up study of young attendees at an alcohol unit. *Addiction, 89,* 183–189.

Drake, R. E. (1996). Substance use reduction among patients with severe mental illness. *Community Mental Health Journal, 32,* 311–314.

Drake, R. E., Mueser, K. T., Clark, R. E., & Wallach, M. E. (1996). The course, treatment, and outcome of substance disorder in persons with severe mental illness. *American Journal of Orthopsychiatry, 66,* 42–51.

Duckert, F. (1987). Recruitment into treatment and effects of treatment for female problem drinkers. *Addictive Behaviors, 12,* 137–150.

Dunn, G. E., Ryan, J. J., Paolo, A. M., & Van Fleet, J. N. (1995). Comorbidity of dissociative disorders among patients with substance use disorders. *Psychiatric Services, 46,* 153–156.

Emrick, C. D., & Hanson, J. (1983). Assertions regarding effectiveness of treatment for alcoholism. *American Psychologist, 38,* 1078–1088.

Etheridge, R. M., Hubbard, R. L., Anderson, J., Craddock, S. G., & Flynn, P. M. (1997). Treatment structure and program services in the Drug Abuse Treatment Outcome Study (DATOS). *Psychology of Addictive Behaviors, 11,* 244–260.

Fals-Stewart, W., Birchler, G. R., & O'Farrell, T. J. (1996). Behavioral couples therapy for male substance-abusing patients: Effects on relationship adjustment and drug-using behavior. *Journal of Consulting & Clinical Psychology, 64,* 959–972.

Finney, J. W. (1995). Enhancing substance abuse treatment evaluations: Examining mediators and moderators of treatment effects. *Journal of Substance Abuse, 7,* 135–150.

Fisher, M. S., & Bentley, K. J. (1996). Two group therapy models for clients with a dual diagnosis of substance abuse and personality disorder. *Psychiatric Services, 47,* 1244–1250.

Fletcher, B. W., Tims, F. M., & Brown, B. S. (1997). Drug Abuse Treatment Outcome Study (DATOS): Treatment evaluation research in the United States. *Psychology of Addictive Behaviors, 11,* 216–229.

Floyd, A. S., Monahan, S. C., Finney, J. W., & Morley, J. A. (1996). Alcoholism treatment outcome studies, 1980–1992: The nature of the research. *Addictive Behaviors, 21,* 413–428.

Foulks, E. F., & Pena, J. M. (1995). Ethnicity and psychotherapy: A component in the treatment of cocaine addiction in African Americans. *Psychiatric Clinics of North America, 18,* 607–620.

Friedman, A. S., Terras, A., & Kreisher, C. (1995). Family and client characteristics as predictors of outpatient treatment outcome for adolescent drug abusers. *Journal of Substance Abuse, 7,* 345–356.

Gainey, R. R., Wells, E. A., Hawkins, J. D., & Catalano, R. F. (1993). Predicting treatment retention among cocaine users. *International Journal of the Addictions, 18,* 487–505.

Gambert, S. R. (1996). The elderly. In J. H. Lowinson, P. Ruiz, R. B. Millman, & J. G. Langrod (Eds.), *Substance abuse: A comprehensive textbook, third edition* (pp. 692–699). Baltimore, MD: Williams & Wilkins.

Gregson, R. A. M., & Taylor, G. M. (1977). Prediction of relapse in men alcoholics. *Journal of Studies on Alcohol, 38,* 1749–1760.

Harrison, P. A., & Belille C. A. (1987). Women in treatment: Beyond the stereotype. *Journal of Studies on Alcohol, 48,* 574–578.

Hartmann, D. J., Wolk, J. L., & Sullivan, W. P. (1995). State-wide self-report of treatment effectiveness: Promise, pitfall, and potential. *Alcoholism Treatment Quarterly, 13,* 45–57.

Helzer, J. E., & Pryzbeck, T. R. (1988). The co-occurrence of alcoholism with other psychiatric disorders in the general population and its impact on treatment. *Journal of Studies on Alcohol, 49,* 219–224.

Higgins, S. T., & Bickel, W. K. (1993). Treating cocaine abusers. *Hospital & Community Psychiatry, 44,* 1007.

Hird, S., Khuri, E. T., Dusenbury, L., & Millman, R. B. (1996). Adolescents. In J. H. Lowinson, P. Ruiz, R. B. Millman, & J. G. Langrod (Eds.), *Substance abuse: A comprehensive textbook, third edition* (pp. 683–692). Baltimore, MD: Williams & Wilkins.

Hirschel, J. D., & Keny, J. R. (1990). Outpatient treatment for substance-abusing offenders. *Journal of Offender Counseling, Services & Rehabilitation, 15,* 111–130.

Hitchcock, H. C., Stainback, R. D., & Roque, G. M. (1995). Effects of halfway house placement on retention of patients in substance abuse aftercare. *American Journal of Drug & Alcohol Abuse, 21,* 379–390.

Hoffmann, J. A., Caudill, B. D., Koman, J. J., Luckey, J. W., Flynn, P. M., & Hubbard, R. L. (1994). Comparative cocaine abuse treatment strategies: Enhancing client retention and treatment exposure. *Journal of Addictive Diseases, 13,* 115–128.

Hoffman, J. A., Caudill, B. D., Koman, J. J., & Luckey, J. W. (1996). Psychosocial treatments for cocaine abuse: 12-month treatment outcomes. *Journal of Substance Abuse Treatment, 13,* 3–11.

Hoffmann, N. G., & Miller, N. S. (1992). Treatment outcomes for abstinence-based programs. *Psychiatric Annals, 22,* 402–408.

Hoffmann, N. G., Ninonuevo, F., Mozey, J., & Luxenberg, M. G. (1987). Comparison of court-referred DWI arrestees with other outpatients in substance abuse treatment. *Journal of Studies on Alcohol, 48,* 591–594.

Hser, I-Y., Anglin, M. D., & Powers, K. (1993). A 24-year follow-up of California narcotics addicts. *Archives of General Psychiatry, 50,* 577–584.

Hubbard, R. L. (1997). Evaluation and outcome of treatment. In J. H. Lowinson, P. Ruiz, R. B. Millman, & J. G. Langrod (Eds.), *Substance Abuse: A Comprehensive Textbook, third edition* (pp.499–511). Baltimore, MD: Williams & Wilkins.

Hubbard, R. L., Craddock, S. G., Flynn, P. M., Anderson, J., & Etheridge, R. M. (1997). Overview of 1-year follow-up outcomes in the Drug Abuse Treatment Outcome Study (DATOS). *Psychology of Addictive Behaviors, 11,* 261–278.

Jacobsen, L. K., & Kosten, T. R. (1989). Naloxone challenge as a biological predictor of treatment outcome in opiate addicts. *American Journal of Drug & Alcohol Abuse, 15,* 355–366.

John, S., Brown, Jr., L. S., & Primm, B. J. (1996). African Americans: Epidemiologic, prevention and treatment issues. In J. H. Lowinson, P. Ruiz, R. B. Millman, & J. G. Langrod (Eds.), *Substance abuse: A comprehensive textbook, third edition* (pp. 699–705). Baltimore, MD: Williams & Wilkins.

Jolin, A., & Stipak, B. (1992). Drug treatment and electronically monitored home confinement: An evaluation of a community-based sentencing option. *Crime & Delinquency, 38,* 158–170.

Jones, B. E., & Katz, N. D. (1992). Madness and addiction: Treating the mentally ill chemical abuser. *Journal of Health Care for the Poor and Underserved, 3,* 39–45.

Joseph, H., & Paone, D. (1996). The homeless. In J. H. Lowinson, P. Ruiz, R. B. Millman, & J. G. Langrod (Eds.), *Substance abuse: A comprehensive textbook, third edition* (pp. 733–743). Baltimore, MD: Williams & Wilkins.

Kashner, T. M., Rodell, D. E., Ogden, S. R., & Guggenheim, F. G. (1992). Outcomes and costs of two VA inpatient treatment programs for older alcoholic patients. *Hospital & Community Psychiatry, 43,* 985–989.

Kendell, J. C., Sherman, M. F., & Bigelow, G. E. (1995). Psychiatric symptoms in polysubstance abusers: Relationship to race, sex, and age. *Addictive Behaviors, 20,* 685–690.

Keso, L., & Salaspuro, M. (1990). Inpatient treatment of employed alcoholics: a randomized clinical trial on Hazelden-type and traditional treatment. *Alcoholism: Clinical & Experimental Research, 14,* 584–589.

Kingree, J. B. (1995). Understanding gender differences in psychosocial functioning and treatment retention. *American Journal of Drug & Alcohol Abuse, 21,* 267–281.

Kofoed, L., Kania, J., Walsh, T., & Atkinson, R. M. (1986). Outpatient treatment of patients with substance abuse and coexisting psychiatric disorders. *American Journal of Psychiatry, 143,* 867–872.

Kosten, T. A., Gawin, F. H., Kosten, T. R., & Rounsaville, B. J. (1993). Gender differences in cocaine use and treatment response. *Journal of Substance Abuse Treatment, 10,* 63–66.

Kosten, T. R., Rounsaville, B. J., & Kleber, H. D. (1987). Predictors of 2.5-year outcome in opioid addicts: Pretreatment source of income. *American Journal of Drug & Alcohol Abuse, 13,* 19–32.

Leshner, A. I. (1997). Introduction to the Special Issue: The National Institute on Drug Abuse's (NIDA's) Drug Abuse Treatment Outcome Study (DATOS). *Psychology of Addictive Behaviors, 11,* 211–215.

McCrady, B. S., & Raytek, H. (1993). Women and substance abuse: Treatment modalities and outcomes. In E. S. Lisansky Gomberg & T. D. Nirenberg (Eds.), *Women and substance abuse* (pp. 314–338). Norwood, NJ: Ablex Publishing Corporation.

McKay, J. R., McLellan, A. T., & Alterman, A. I. (1992). An evaluation of the Cleveland criteria for inpatient treatment of substance abuse. *American Journal of Psychiatry, 149,* 1212–1218.

McLellan, A. T., Woody, G. E., Luborsky, L., O'Brien, C. P., & Druley, K. A.

(1983). Increased effectiveness of substance abuse treatment: A prospective study of patient-treatment "matching." *Journal of Nervous & Mental Disease, 171,* 597–605.

McLellan, A. T., Grissom, G. R., Brill, P., Durell, J., Metzeger, D. S., & O'Brien, C. P. (1993). Private substance abuse treatments: Are some programs more effective than others? *Journal of Substance Abuse Treatment, 10,* 243–254.

McLellan, A. T., Luborsky, L., O'Brien, C. P., Barr, H. L., & Evans, F. (1986). Alcohol and drug abuse treatment in three different populations: Is there improvement and is it predictable? *American Journal of Drug & Alcohol Abuse, 12,* 101–120.

Means, L. B., Small, M., Capone, D. M., Capone, T. J., Condren, R., Peterson, M., & Hayward, B. (1989). Client demographics and outcome in outpatient cocaine treatment. *International Journal of the Addictions, 24,* 765–783.

Mejta, C. L., Nayler, C. L., & Maslar, E., M. (1994). Drug abuse treatment: Approaches and effectiveness. In J. A. Lewis (Ed.), *Addictions: Concepts and strategies for treatment* (pp. 59–81). Gaithersburg, MD: Aspen Publishers, Incorporated.

Miller, L. (1991). Predicting relapse and recovery in alcoholism and addiction: Neuropsychology, personality and cognitive style. *Journal of Substance Abuse Treatment, 8,* 277–291.

Miller, N. S., Belkin, B. M., & Gibbons, R. (1994). Clinical diagnosis of substance use disorders in private psychiatric populations. *Journal of Substance Abuse Treatment, 11,* 387–392.

Miller, N. S., & Hoffmann, N. G. (1995). Addictions treatment outcomes. *Alcoholism Treatment Quarterly, 12,* 41–55.

Miller, W. R. (1992). The effectiveness of treatment for substance abuse: Reasons for optimism. *Journal of Substance Abuse Treatment, 9,* 93–102.

Montgomery, H. A., Miller, W. R., & Tonigan, J. S. (1995). Does Alcoholics Anonymous involvement predict treatment outcome? *Journal of Substance Abuse Treatment, 12,* 241–246.

Moos, R. H., & Moos, B. S. (1995). Stay in residential facilities and mental health care as predictors of readmission for patients with substance use disorders. *Psychiatric Services, 46,* 66–72.

Mutzell, S. (1994). Alcoholism in women. *Early Child Development & Care, 101,* 71–80.

Nace, E. P., & Davis, C. W., (1993). Treatment outcome in substance-abusing patients with a personality disorder. *American Journal on Addictions, 2,* 26–33.

Nathan, P. E., & Skinstad, A-H. (1987). Outcomes of treatment for alcohol problems: Current methods, problems and results. *Journal of Consulting & Clinical Psychology, 55,* 332–340.

Nelson-Zlupko, L., Dore, M. M., Kauffman, E., & Kaltenbach, K. (1996). Women in recovery: Their perceptions of treatment effectiveness. *Journal of Substance Abuse Treatment, 13,* 51–59.

Ojehagen, A., Skjaerris, A., & Berglund, M. (1988). Prediction of posttreatment drinking outcome in a 2-year out-patient alcoholic treatment program: A follow-up study. *Alcoholism: Clinical & Experimental Research, 12,* 46–51.

Ojehagen, A., Berglund, M., & Moberg, A. L. (1994). A 6-year follow-up of alcoholics after long-term outpatient treatment. *Alcoholism, Clinical & Experimental Research, 18,* 720–725.

Oppenheimer, E., Sheehan, M., & Taylor, C. (1990). What happens to drug misusers? A medium-term follow-up of subjects new to treatment. *British Journal of Addiction, 85,* 1255–1260.

Osher, F. C. (1996). A vision for the future: Toward a service system responsive to those with co-occurring addicting and mental disorders. *American Journal of Orthopsychiatry, 66,* 71–76.

Ouimette, P. C., Ahrens, C., Moos, R. H., & Finney, J. W. (1997). Posttraumatic stress disorder in substance abuse patients: Relationship to 1-year posttreatment outcomes. *Psychology of Addictive Behaviors, 11,* 34–47.

Ouimette, P. C., Finney, J. W., & Moos R. H. (1997). Twelve-step and cognitive-behavioral treatment for substance abuse: A comparison of treatment effectiveness. *Journal of Consulting & Clinical Psychology, 65,* 230–240.

Pavkov, T. W., McGovern, M. P., Leone, J. S., & Geffner, E. S. (1992). Psychiatric symptomatology among alcoholics: Comparisons between African Americans and Caucasians. *Psychology of Addictive Behaviors, 6,* 219–224.

Piotrowski, N. A., Clark, H. W., & Hall, S. M. (1994). Treatment research with crack-cocaine-dependent male veterans: The efficacy of different recruitment strategies. *American Journal of Drug & Alcohol Abuse, 20,* 431–443.

Poldrugo, F., & Forti, B. (1988). Personality disorders and alcoholism treatment outcome. *Drug & Alcohol Dependence, 21,* 171–176.

Putt, C. (1996). *Relationship of pre-existing levels of hostility and aggression to substance abuse and psychiatric symptom severity.* Unpublished doctoral dissertation, Kent State University, Kent, OH.

Ravndal, E., & Vaglum, P. (1994). Self-reported depression as a predictor of dropout in a hierarchical therapeutic community. *Journal of Substance Abuse Treatment, 11,* 471–479.

Rawson, R. A., Shoptaw, S. J., Obert, J. L., McCann, M. J., Hasson, A. L., Marinelli-Casey, P. J., Brethen, P. R., & Ling, W. (1995). An intensive outpatient approach for cocaine abuse treatment: The Matrix model. *Journal of Substance Abuse Treatment, 12,* 117–127.

Richard, A. J., Montoya, I. D., Nelson, R., & Spence, R. T. (1995). Effectiveness of adjunct therapies in crack cocaine treatment. *Journal of Substance Abuse Treatment, 12,* 401–413.

Ridgely, M. S., & Jerrell, J. M. (1996). Analysis of three interventions for substance abuse treatment of severely mentally ill people. *Community Mental Health Journal, 32,* 561–572.

Robertson, E. C. (1992). The challenge of dual diagnosis. *Journal of Health Care for the Poor and Underserved, 3,* 198–207.

Rohrer, J. E., Vaughan, M. S., Cadoret, R. J., & Carswsell, C. (1996). Effect of centralized intake on outcomes of substance abuse treatment. *Psychiatric Services, 47,* 1233–1238.

Rosenheck, R., Massari, L., Astrachan, B., & Suchinsky, R. (1990). Mentally ill chemical abusers discharged from VA inpatient treatment, 1976–1988. *Psychiatric Quarterly, 61,* 237–249.

Roth, A., & Fonagy, P. (1996). *What Works for Whom?: A Critical Review of Psychotherapy Research* New York: The Guilford Press.

Rounsaville, B. J., Dolinsky, Z. S., Babor, T. F., & Meyer, R. E. (1987). Psychopathology as a predictor of treatment outcome in alcoholics. *Archives of General Psychiatry, 44,* 505–513.

Rounsaville, B. J., Kosten, T. R., Weissman, M. M., & Kleber, H. D. (1986). Prognostic significance of psychopathology in treated opiate addicts: A 2.5-year follow-up study. *Archives of General Psychiatry, 43,* 739–745.

Ruiz, P., & Langrod, J. G. (1996). Hispanic Americans. In J. H. Lowinson, P. Ruiz, R. B. Millman, & J. G. Langrod (Eds.), *Substance abuse: A comprehensive textbook, third edition* (pp. 705–711). Baltimore, MD: Williams & Wilkins.

Schneider, K. M., Kviz, F. J., Isola, M. L., & Filstead, W. J. (1995). Evaluating multiple outcomes and gender differences in alcoholism treatment. *Addictive Behaviors, 20,* 1–21.

Sheehan, M. F. (1993). Dual Diagnosis. *Psychiatric Quarterly, 64,* 107–134.

Simpson, D. D., Joe, G. W., Broome, K. M., Hiller, M. L. Knight, K., & Rowan-Szal, G. A. (1997). Program diversity and treatment retention rates in the Drug Abuse Treatment Outcome Study (DATOS). *Psychology of Addictive Behaviors, 11,* 279–293.

Smith, E. M., North, C. S., & Fox, L. W. (1995). Eighteen-month follow-up data on a treatment program for homeless substance abusing mothers. *Journal of Addictive Diseases, 14,* 57–72.

Sobell, L. C., & Sobell, M. B. (1989). Treatment outcome evaluation methodology with alcohol abusers: Strengths and key issues. *Advances in Behavior Research & Therapy, 11,* 151–160.

Sobell, M. B., Sobell, L. C., & Gavin, D. R. (1995). Portraying alcohol treatment outcomes: Different yardsticks of success. *Behavior Therapy, 26,* 643–669.

Stephens, R. S., Wertz, J. S., & Roffman, R. A. (1993). Predictors of marijuana treatment outcomes: The role of self-efficacy. *Journal of Substance Abuse, 5,* 341–354.

Stockfisch, R., Galanter, M., & Lifshutz, H. (1995). Trends in dual-diagnosis patients. *American Journal of Addictions, 4,* 356–357.

Stockwell, T., Bolt, L., Milner, I., Russell, G., Bolderston, H., & Pugh, P. (1991). Home detoxification from alcohol: Its safety and efficacy in comparison with inpatient care. *Alcohol and Alcoholism, 26,* 645–650.

Stoddard, C. E., & Thompson, D. L. (1996). Alcohol and the elderly: Special concerns for counseling professionals. *Alcoholism Treatment Quarterly, 14,* 59–69.

Strain, E. C., Stitzer, M. L., Liebson, I. A., & Bigelow, G. E. (1993). Methadone dose and treatment outcome. *Drug & Alcohol Dependence, 33,* 10–117.

Substance Abuse and Mental Health Services Administration. (1994). National Household Survey on Drug Abuse, Population estimates 1993. *DHHS publication no. (SMA) 94–3017.*

Teague, G. B., Drake, R. E., & Ackerson, T. H. (1995). Evaluating use of continuous treatment teams for persons with mental illness and substance abuse. *Psychiatric Services, 46,* 689–695.

Timko, C., Moos, R. H., Finney, J. W., & Moos, B. S. (1994). Outcome of treatment for alcohol abuse and involvement in Alcoholics Anonymous among previously untreated problem drinkers. *Journal of Mental Health Administration, 21*, 145–160.

Tomasson, K., & Vaglum, P. (1995). A nationwide representative sample of treatment-seeking alcoholics: A study of psychiatric comorbidity. *Acta Psychiatrica Scandinavica, 92*, 378–385.

Vaillant, G. E. (1983). *The natural history of alcoholism.* Cambridge, MA: Harvard University Press.

Vito, G. F., (1989). The Kentucky Substance Abuse Program: A private program to treat probationers and parolees. *Federal Probation, 53*, 65–72.

Wallen, J. (1992). A comparison of male and female clients in substance abuse treatment. *Journal of Substance Abuse Treatment, 9*, 243–248.

Waltman, D. (1995). Key ingredients to effective addictions treatment. *Journal of Substance Abuse Treatment, 12*, 429–439.

Watson, C. G., Brown, K., Tilleskjor, C., & Jacobs, L., & Pucel, J. (1988), The comparative recidivism rates of voluntary- and coerced-admission male alcoholics. *Journal of Clinical Psychology, 44*, 573–581.

Weinstein, C. S., & Shaffer, H. J. (1993). Neurocognitive aspects of substance abuse treatment: A psychotherapist's primer. *Psychotherapy, 30*, 317–333.

Wells, E. A., Peterson, P. L., Gainey, R. R., Hawkins, J. D., & Catalano, R. F. (1994). Outpatient treatment for cocaine abuse: A controlled comparison of relapse prevention and Twelve-Step approaches. *American Journal of Drug & Alcohol Abuse, 20*, 1–17.

Wilens, T. E., Prince, J. B., Biederman, J., Spencer, T. J., & Frances, R. J. (1995). Attention-deficit hyperactivity disorder and comorbid substance use disorders in adults. *Psychiatric Services, 46*, 761–763.

Wolk, J. L., Hartmann, D. J., & Sullivan, W. P. (1994). Defining success: The politics of evaluation in alcohol and drug abuse treatment programs. *Journal of Sociology & Social Welfare, 21*, 133–145.

Woody, G. E., McLellan, A. T., Lubursky, L., & O'Brien, C. P. (1986). Psychotherapy for substance abuse. *Psychiatric Clinics of North America, 9*, 547–562.

Wright, J. D., & Devine, J. A. (1995). Factors that interact with treatment to predict outcomes in substance abuse programs for the homeless. *Journal of Addictive Diseases, 14*, 169–181.

# 3

# The Case of "Paul"

## Loreen G. Rugle and E. Thomas Dowd

### INTRODUCTION

Paul is a 35-year-old white male who looks somewhat young for his age on first appearance. He is divorced but is living with his ex-wife and their two children, a son age nine and a daughter age six. He is currently employed in construction, but his job is in jeopardy due to absences from work and recent arguments with the foreman. He presented with a request for treatment for relapse of alcohol and cocaine use. He reported drinking two six packs of beer a day and smoking $500.00 worth of cocaine per week. He has also been smoking marijuana four to five days per week and occasionally taking Valium for sleep disturbances (approximately once a week). This pattern is consistent with his past history of substance dependence and use. He reported a history of alcohol dependence since the age of 15 and became addicted to heroin in the army while stationed in Europe in the early 1980s. However, he has not abused opiates since his discharge from the military in 1984. He did IV cocaine for about one year after his discharge from the service but switched to smoking cocaine. He has experimented with a variety of drugs since adolescence, including LSD, PCP, amphetamines, and qualuudes, but has not consistently used or abused these drugs. He has a history of six DUIs and attended court mandated AA meetings for a year in the late 80s following an arrest for DUI. He decreased his drinking and drug use at that time but reported at most two or three weeks of total abstinence at any one time. He has spent time in local jails three times following arrests for DUIs with the longest time being three weeks.

He has completed three prior detoxifications. Upon admission to his first detoxification, he reported drinking 18–24 beers per day along with several shots of whiskey, smoking 5–6 grams of cocaine three to four times per week and using Valium (20mg) daily. At the time of that admission, he acknowledged significant marital problems, with his wife threatening separation if his substance use continued. Paul also risked losing his job as the foreman of a construction crew. He had no acute medical problems. He did report a head injury at age 16 following a fight at school and being unconscious for several hours at that time. Paul was discharged from detox with diagnoses of alcohol and cocaine dependence and a recommendation was made that he enter a 28-day residential treatment program. However, he did not enter a treatment program following this detoxification, stating that he would try Alcoholics Anonymous and thought he could maintain abstinence in this manner without additional treatment. He also stated that he needed to return to work to maintain his job and provide for his family. He did not keep subsequent outpatient aftercare appointments.

Paul began drinking beer one week after leaving the detoxification unit. He was admitted for detoxification a second time five months after his initial detoxification. His alcohol and cocaine use were at levels comparable to those when he was first admitted five months earlier, although he was using Valium only two or three times a month. His wife had taken their two children and returned to live with her parents after Paul had become physically violent, shoving her into a wall during an argument over his continued substance use. He had lost his foreman's position due to intoxification while on the job. He was receiving unemployment insurance checks and had significant unstructured time on his hands, which he stated contributed to increased substance use. Following this second detox, Paul entered a residential treatment program, acknowledging that he had made a mistake by not doing so earlier.

Paul described his substance use more completely during this second detox episode. He indicated that he only used cocaine if he had been drinking heavily first. He obtained Valium from his wife who had obtained a prescription from her physician for anxiety. At this time he admitted that he had not been completely sober for more than one week for the past 15 years.

Initial psychological assessment of Paul included an MMPI, the NEO Personality Inventory (NEO-PI), the Beck Depression Inventory (BDI), the Beck Hopelessness Scale (BHI), the Barratt Impulsivity Scale, and the Spielberger State-Trait Anger Scale. The MMPI was valid and within normal limits. Highest scales were 2 (T68), 4 (T67), 3 (T67), and 1 (65). This profile is shown in Figure 3.1.

The NEO-PI factor scores were as follows: Neuroticism, very high; Extraversion, average; Openness, low; Agreeableness, very low;

# MMPI PROFILE

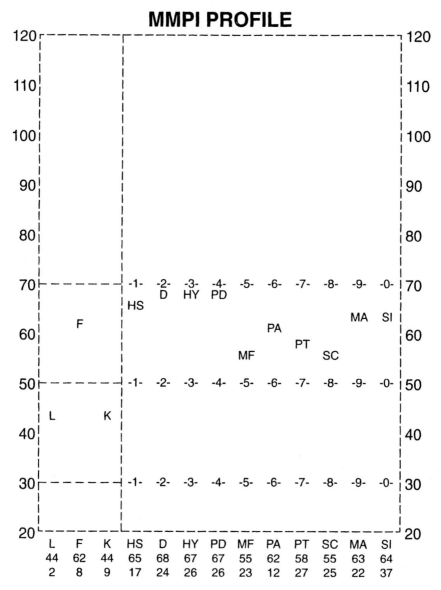

**FIGURE 3.1**   MMPI profile for Paul.

Conscientiousness, very low. A complete profile, including facet scores for all factors, is shown in Figure 3.2.

Paul was high on Impulsivity when compared to both normals and substance abusing comparison groups; his total score being 62 compared with 49.40 for the instrument norm group, 52.85 for a cocaine-abusing

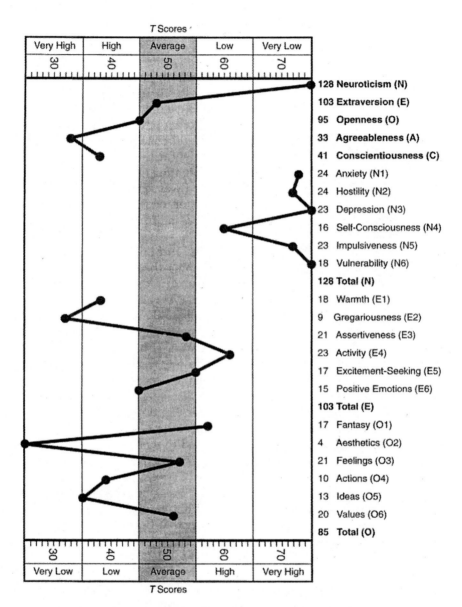

**FIGURE 3.2**   NEO Personality Inventory profile for Paul.

sample, and 55.10 for an alcohol-abusing sample. His trait anger scores were at the 97th percentile and his style of expressing anger openly rather than controlling or bottling up anger was at the 99th percentile. His BDI score was 21, indicating a moderate-severe level of depression. His BHI score was 10, indicating a moderate level of hopelessness.

# PSYCHOSOCIAL HISTORY

Paul was the third of six children, with an older brother and sister, one younger brother, and two younger sisters. Both parents worked when Paul was a child and he recalled the house often being chaotic. His father worked the day shift and his mother worked evenings. His older brother, who was four years older than Paul, was often left in charge when his father would go out drinking and would either let all the siblings do what they wanted or become angry and violent with them. Paul reported that there was a great deal of arguing and fighting among the siblings as they grew up. His father was an alcoholic and was verbally and physically abusive of the children at times, with his anger focusing more on the two oldest siblings. However, Paul recalled that he frequently was beaten with his father's belt if he were caught doing something he wasn't supposed to, if his brother told his father that he had not done his chores, or if he happened to be the nearest child when his father was in a bad mood.

Paul remembered that his father did not drink as much during the weekends when his mother was also home. Weekends were often pleasant, especially when Paul was younger. The family went for rides in the country, had cookouts, or attended amusement parks. Occasionally, his father would take Paul and his older brother fishing and these were remembered as special times. During these family weekends, Paul recalled his father as being happy and, if he got angry, his mother was usually able to smooth things over. As Paul got older, his father began to drink more on the weekends and his parents began fighting more.

Paul described his mother as a gentle, loving person who had been a lot of fun when he was a child. She returned to work after his youngest sibling was born and subsequently she always seemed tired and had little time or energy for the children.

Paul remembered his older sister and him breaking up one particularly violent fight between his older brother and his father. His brother was 17 at the time and left home permanently after that fight. After his brother left, Paul felt that he caught much more of his father's anger and abuse. Paul ran away frequently during that period, often staying with friends for weeks at a time. He reported that he always felt guilty when he did this, worrying about what was happening to the younger children. After his older brother left home, his older sister was rarely home in the evenings and became pregnant at age 18, dropped out of high school, and got married.

Paul described a history of difficulty in school. He repeated third grade and quit school in the eleventh grade when he was told he would have to take summer classes or repeat that grade. He had a history of skipping school, beginning in junior high, and described school as always being a struggle. He enjoyed practical classes like shop and felt that he was always good at working with his hands. He developed a very positive relationship with a shop teacher who was able to get him a job working with a construction company after school and during summers. Paul stated that working made him feel good about himself and he enjoyed being "one of the guys." He began drinking beer while working on construction sites, since he felt the other workers had really accepted him the first time they offered him a beer. He also enjoyed the sense of freedom earning his own money gave him.

Paul did not participate in organized sports in school. As early as elementary school, he preferred working at odd jobs (e.g., cutting the neighbor's grass, delivering newspapers) rather than participating in after-school activities. He had a few close friends but was always embarrassed to bring his friends over to his house because he did not know if his father would be drunk.

On the advice of his former shop teacher, Paul joined the army after leaving school. He stated that he had not liked the discipline of the service and felt very lonely when he was stationed in Europe. His parents divorced while he was overseas and he received a letter from his mother apologizing for all the pain the children had gone through. Paul had been drinking heavily even prior to entering the service and had begun using opiates. Shortly before returning to the States, he was diagnosed with hepatitis which prompted his discontinuing IV opiate use.

Paul was honorably discharged from the army after two years and returned home to live with his father briefly. His father had stopped drinking and had been regularly attending AA meetings. Paul himself was drinking and using cocaine heavily at this point and his father told him he could not stay with him because of this. He had obtained a job with the construction company for which he had worked throughout high school and within a year was promoted to foreman. He also began dating a girl he had dated in high school whom he had always liked a great deal. Her father was also an alcoholic and he felt she had understood him and his problems at home when they were in high school. She was attending a local community college, intending to obtain a degree in elementary education. After she became pregnant, they decided to get married. Paul was making good money at his job and they were able to quickly purchase a small house.

During this time, Paul and his older brother (who also worked in construction) began to be drinking and drugging buddies. His older sister had moved with her husband and daughter to Montana, had become Jehovah's Witnesses, and Paul had only limited contact with them. His younger sister was living with his mother and completing college. One younger brother had joined the navy and the other was living with his father and completing high school. During this time, Paul saw both his parents occasionally. He was able to develop a relationship with his father who, according to Paul, was working a very strong AA program and in retrospect was attempting to make amends to his children. He began going fishing again with his father, but his father insisted that Paul not drink or drug while they were fishing. Eventually Paul found this too difficult to manage and they had diminished contact as his drinking and drug use progressed.

After Paul's first child was born, his wife went to work as a secretary and his mother babysat for them. His wife and mother developed a very close relationship and, at this point, Paul felt his life was going well in spite of his increased substance use. He stated that he denied any substance abuse problems even after getting his first DUI, when his daughter was about a year old. He ignored the concerns of his parents and wife who tried to warn him about his drinking and drugging. After their second child was born, Paul stated that he felt his wife had less and less time for him. She did not return to work and he felt increasing financial pressures. He did not tell her how much money he was spending on his regular cocaine use. His wife began having trouble sleeping and her physician prescribed Valium, which Paul also began using and subsequently abusing. There were more arguments at home and Paul began staying out later and later "with the crew" after work. He stopped going to church since on Sunday he was usually sleeping off a Friday and Saturday night binge.

At work Paul had taken pride in his reputation as a hard, conscientious worker and in the fact that he was tough but reasonable and fair with his crew. As his substance abuse progressed, he began arriving late on job sites and leaving early to go drinking. He became increasingly irritable with his men and would become irrationally angry and verbally abusive when confronted with errors that were often his responsibility. The owner of the construction company, who had a very good relationship with Paul, expressed his concern about the changes in his attitude and behavior.

As mentioned previously, after his third DUI, he began attending AA and cut back on his drinking and drug use. His marital conflict initially subsided but, as his drinking and drug use returned and indeed exceeded previous levels, conflict increased until Paul entered treatment.

Paul initially had difficulty with written assignments in therapy and needed significant assistance in completing them. He had difficulty tolerating emotional interactions in group therapy, becoming frustrated and angry when others in the group were discussing highly emotional topics or when group interactions seemed too intense or confusing for him. He would get "wound up" during group sessions and stated that he did not see what good this was doing him; "talking about all this only makes me feel worse." He described his feelings during group therapy as having a "knot in my stomach."

Later, Paul began to be more expressive in group therapy. He completed a written autobiography, during which he was quite emotional and tearful at times, particularly around his violent behavior and his concern for its impact on his children. His affect became less angry and depressed during the remainder of treatment. Paul also participated in AA and reported enjoying the meetings and "getting a lot out of them." His wife participated in family groups and attended Al-Anon. He and his wife met with his counselor. Paul's weekend pass prior to discharge went well. He spent the weekend with his wife and children. They attended church, spent time with other family members, and went on a picnic. Although Paul and his wife had agreed in counseling not to rush back into living together, at the end of this weekend his wife had agreed to immediately move back in with him.

Paul's discharge plan included weekly aftercare, attending daily AA meetings, and taking antabuse. His wife planned to continue attending Al-Anon. Paul planned to attend church on a weekly basis, and he and his wife planned to conduct daily meditations (from the 12 step daily mediation book) together each morning.

## POSTTREATMENT HISTORY

After his previous therapy, Paul attended aftercare for six weeks and then gradually his attendance became sporadic, although he attended AA regularly and had obtained a sponsor. He did not have any dirty urines. Urges and dreams of drinking and drug use occurred several times per week but were becoming somewhat less frequent, and he felt antabuse was helping him avoid the first drink. He missed several weeks of aftercare group and, when he was called by his counselor, he stated that everything was going well. He was still attending AA regularly, work was very busy, and he felt he was doing well enough to discontinue aftercare and spend more time with his family.

## CURRENT PRESENTING PROBLEM

As indicated initially, Paul presented again for treatment six years after completing his first residential treatment program. Following his first treatment, he remained completely abstinent for approximately nine months. He had been attending AA regularly and reported doing well, but he had decreased the number of meetings attended first to two per week, then one per week. He attributed this to feeling he was doing well and also to longer work hours during the summer. He had discontinued taking antabuse shortly after discontinuing aftercare. He then began going out on Friday evenings with his crew to have a few beers. He stopped attending AA meetings and told himself he would be able to handle a couple of beers on a Friday night. He quickly returned to using cocaine as well on his Friday nights out. His wife continued attending Al-Anon meetings and expressed her concerns but generally did not nag him about his drinking or drug use. Within six months, he was close to his old level of substance use, marital conflicts were occurring more frequently, and job problems were occurring again. He lost his job when he felt one of his crew members was questioning his judgment; he punched him and walked off the job.

At this point, he became concerned about his behavior and, with encouragement from his father and sponsor, returned to AA. This began a pattern of periods of abstinence of four to ten months alternating with periods of relapse of two days to several months. He was able to find employment, though repeatedly lost jobs during this five and one-half year period due to temper outbursts, problems with attendance, and intoxication at work. Incidents of domestic violence had occurred and his wife had divorced him a year ago. During the past year, he had not been able to maintain more than two days of sobriety at a time. He continued to attend AA meetings sporadically and had regular contact with his sponsor.

Recontacting his therapist was prompted by a weekend episode with his ex-wife, with whom he was still living. During that episode, he had been intoxicated and had become angry that she would not allow him to take the children for the day. He became violent and struck her in front of the children. He reported that the look of fear in his children's eyes and their unwillingness to come near him after this happened had shocked him and he realized he needed more help than AA could provide. His sponsor had been recommending professional help for some time, but he had denied this need. He was also close to losing his current job and was quite concerned about his future potential for being hired by any construction company in the area if he lost this job, since he had created a very bad reputation for himself recently.

Paul was tearful and shaky during the meeting. He was frightened that he would not be able to maintain any sobriety. However, he was hesitant to enter a residential program since he did not think his employer would continue his employment if he missed additional work.

All chapter authors organized their responses to this case by answering the following questions:

I. Please describe your treatment model in no more than 3–4 double spaced pages.

II. What would you consider to be the clinical skills or attributes most essential to successful therapy in your approach (1–2 pages)?

III. It is important to the goals and mission of this volume that you answer each of the following questions regarding the case material. Please limit your response to each question to no more than two double-spaced pages (500 words).

1. What would be your therapeutic goals for this patient? What are the primary goals and the secondary goals? Please be as specific as possible.

2. What further information would you want to have to assist you in structuring this patient's treatment? Are there specific assessment tools you would use (i.e., data to be collected)? What would be the rationale for using those tools?

3. What is your conceptualization of this patient's personality, behavior, affective state, and cognitions?

4. What potential pitfalls would you envision in this therapy? What would the difficulties be and what would you envision to be the source(s) of the difficulties?

5. To what level of coping, adaptation, or function would you see this patient reaching as an immediate result of therapy? What would the long-term result be subsequent to the ending of therapy (i.e. prognosis for adaptive change)?

6. What would be your time line (duration) for therapy? What would be your frequency and duration of the sessions?

7. Are there specific or special techniques that you would implement in the therapy? What would they be?

8. Are there special cautions to be observed in working with this patient (e.g., danger to self or others, transference, counter-transference)? Are there any particular resistances you would expect and how would you deal with them?

9. Are there any areas that you would choose to avoid or not address with this patient? Why?

10. Is medication warranted for this patient? What effect would you hope or expect the medication to have?

11. What are the strengths of the patient that can be used in the therapy?

12. How would you address limits, boundaries, and limit-setting with this patient?

13. Would you want to involve significant others in the treatment? Would you use out-of-session work (homework) with this patient? What homework would you use?

14. What would be the issues to be addressed in termination? How would termination and relapse prevention be structured?
15. What do you see as the hoped-for mechanisms of change for this patient, in order of importance?

# 4

# A Psychodynamic Approach to Treatment

*Richard Hirschman and Michael Foster*

## I. THE TREATMENT MODEL

Freud's psychoanalytical theory (Freud, 1917/1973) has been the seminal building block of psychodynamic treatment, with its emphasis on specific and circumscribed psychodynamic processes, such as primitive drives and constricted id, ego, and superego functions resulting from conflict. More recent theoretical formulations have broadened the scope of psychodynamic treatment (e.g., Bloom, 1997; Gabbard, 1994; Gustafson, 1995a) with such issues as deficits of psychic structure, internal representations of "objects," ego functions, individuation (Bloom, 1997; Gabbard, 1994), real and false self (Masterson, 1988), dilemmas (Gustafson, 1995b), and interpersonal processes (Bugental, 1987; Elkind, 1992; Wachtel, 1993). Many of these formulations recently have been incorporated into short-term psychodynamic treatment (e.g., Bloom, 1997; Budman, 1981; Horowitz et al., 1984). Short-term treatment typically lasts for 20 sessions or less with the therapist and client focusing on a limited number of issues and specific goals (Bloom, 1997). Short-term psychodynamic treatment could be used when: 1) There are significant and circumscribed intrapsychic issues related to the symptomatology, such as, in this case, drug abuse and impulse control. 2) There are significant and circumscribed intrapsychic issues that are not otherwise addressed by other components of a multi-modal treatment. 3) There is limited access to long-term psychodynamic therapy. 4) The client does not have major psychopathology, such as schizophrenia. What follows immediately is a discussion of some of the central components of a generic psychodynamic model as used within the context of short-term treatment, with reference to a client with symptoms of drug abuse and impulse control. (See Frances, Franklin, & Borg, 1994 and Gabbard, 1994 for further information about longer-term psychodynamic treatment for substance abusers.)

Typically, psychological and behavioral problems result from a varying mix of motivating and conflictual factors, such as, environmental, developmental, cognitive, and emotional. Psychodynamic treatment is appropriate to the extent that significant antecedent events and conflicts, and current psychic representations of them are complicit in the current problematic behavior, or that behavior has significant "stand alone" conflictual psychological elements and psychic representations not directly yoked to the past. Other factors may require different treatments. For example, an adolescent who abuses drugs out of ignorance of its consequences or because his or her friends are doing it may benefit from treatment that also has educational components. Likewise, some learned, maladaptive, and circumscribed behaviors are most effectively changed with behavioral treatments, which, indirectly might also affect the negative, affective and cognitive concomitants of the behavior. Of course, outcome data regarding specific etiological-behavioral links for a given client should be evaluated when choosing short-term psychodynamic therapy or, for that matter, any type of therapy. (See Miller & Brown, 1997 for a review of treatment outcome studies for substance abusers, and other chapters in this book and Galanter & Kleber, 1994 for descriptions of other treatments for substance abusers.)

In order for past and current intrapsychic conflicts and psychic representations to serve as fodder for the therapy process in the short-term, the client must regard them as important. Clients can "carve up" their lives in different ways and may choose to ignore the importance of their own psychic history and current dynamically derived intrapsychic conflicts. For example, some clients may interpret their psychological problems existentially, such as, how to deal with their mortality or how to understand the meaning of their existence beyond their culturally and socially determined roles. Other clients may understand their psychological problems in terms of isolated symptoms in circumscribed contexts and expect symptom relief without much psychological exploration. Yet other clients may understand their psychological problems as externally driven, such as, by social or political factors and be unwilling to engage in a process of self-exploration even for a relatively brief period of time if, for example, other people, social systems, or ideologies are the perceived culprits.

Not only may some clients *perceive* intrapsychic conflicts and psychodynamic representations as irrelevant to their well-being, their psychological discomfort *realistically* may be a function of factors other than intrapsychic, such as, a lack of one or more basic resources (e.g., food, clothing, shelter, or nurturance) necessary for psychological adaptation and physical survival. To the extent that a client understands his or her psychological discomfort in terms of a lack of basic resources, and this is a consensually validated assessment of how things are, then psychodynamic therapy might not be the only treatment of choice or perhaps not even a choice at all. On the other hand, a client's nonintrapsychic views of himself or herself may actually represent a resistance to participate in the psychodynamic process, in order to avoid exposure to more psychic pain. Distinguishing between a client's resistance and a justified lack of focus on psychodynamic issues often is difficult for the therapist, particularly in short-term treatment.

Just as each client has a unique way of understanding his or her life, he or she also brings to therapy varying degrees of ability to think abstractly about himself or herself and to experience the connections and patterns holistically. We are referring here to the ability of clients to make connections among their psychological representations and behaviors, or to see patterns in their own behaviors that have antecedent or dispositional roots. Certainly in the early stages of psychodynamic therapy, the therapist may try to catalyze this type of self-exploration and emphasize its importance. However, leaving resistance and defense aside for the moment, a given client still may not be capable of this type of self-exploration even if he believes intrapsychic representations and antecedent events are important for self-understanding. Someone who is unable to experience and actively process the cognitive and affective elements of his current situation or the cognitive and affective connections between his history and current circumstances will not be able to take advantage of psychodynamic therapy, particularly in the short-term. For psychodynamic therapy to be effective, intrapsychic representations must have as much potency and potential for being recognized by the client as easier to perceive external elements, such as symptoms, do.

Even if a client is capable of abstract self-analysis, significant intrapsychic elements, such as motivators, distortions, and regulators of intrapsychic conflict, must be consciously available. Depending on how traditional one's view is of psychodynamic theory, these elements typically are unconscious or perhaps less inaccessible, just below the conscious "surface." For dealing with relatively circumscribed problems and maintaining goals in short-term psychodynamic therapy, it must be assumed that these elements are to some extent accessible or could become accessible during the therapy process. Also, the psychodynamic process is made easier to the extent that awareness of nonrepressed, relevant motivators occurs simply as a function of a shift in attention and a supportive therapeutic ambiance.

To the extent that a client values her psychodynamic explanations for self-understanding and her intrapsychic world is rich and potentially available for self-exploration, psychodynamic therapy may catalyze insight for that client. Insight is the awareness of the cognitive and affective components of intrapsychic life, particularly as they relate to the client's interpersonal matrix. Presumably, greater understanding of oneself is better than less understanding, unless of course that understanding comes at too high a price to permit adaptive functioning, such as, by the tempering of defenses that typically keep the client's maladaptive behavior in check.

In addition to the affective and cognitive relief that a client may experience through greater self awareness, he may be better able to exercise control over his maladaptive behavior and may have more choices on how to alter it. The assumption here is that symptoms are driven and shaped by intrapsychic forces and intrapsychic protective mechanisms, and to be insightful about them potentially gives the client behavioral options that would not be present without the insights. The primary goal of the therapy process would be how the client's new or existing insights could lead to constructive behavioral changes. Stretching the point a bit, a knowledgeable mechanic is better able to fix a car engine, assuming he knows how to lift the hood to see the engine, than someone who does not know how to lift the hood and who knows little or nothing about the mechanics of a car.

## II. ESSENTIAL CLINICAL SKILLS AND ATTRIBUTES

To implement the above model requires the therapist to be skillful and knowledgeable about psychodynamic theory, about specific aspects of the psychodynamic process, and to have many of the skills relevant to success with most therapies. Perhaps one important generic attribute for the therapist to have is theoretical flexibility. Paul's case could be conceptualized using many different psychodynamic perspectives including, for example, drives, ego, object relations or dilemmas. The therapist may need to form several different conceptualizations in order to present interpretations that are valid and amenable to Paul's therapeutic story, his experience, and his willingness to do therapeutic work.

Because of the complexity of psychodynamic theory, the therapist also needs to be skillful in generating hypotheses and testing them within a quasiscientific context. By this we mean that the therapist offers a hypothesis, allows the client to work with it therapeutically and thereby accumulates evidence as to whether the hypothesis is helpful to the client. A client's failure to use a hypothesis constructively may mean that the hypothesis is irrelevant or perhaps that the hypothesis is relevant but that the client is not yet able to work with it. Therefore, being able to recognize a client's resistance to engage in constructive therapeutic work also is an important quality for the therapist to have, in order to distinguish between an irrelevant hypothesis and a hypothesis that might be viable and relevant for future work, but at the moment is too threatening.

As is generally true of therapists of all theoretical orientations, another important quality for the psychodynamically oriented therapist is the generic ability to form a therapeutic alliance with the client, i.e., the belief by therapist and client that they are both committed to working toward the goal of helping the client develop constructive solutions to his problems. Some important qualities of the therapist that help catalyze this process are genuineness, warmth, and empathy. Empathy is a particularly important quality in determining patient outcome (Miller & Brown, 1997).

A psychodynamically oriented therapist also needs to be skillful in recognizing and interpreting the interactions between himself or herself and the client as well as recognizing and interpreting the client's perceptions of the the client's world outside of the therapy. The ability to do the latter is a generic skill necessary for all therapists. However, the ability to do the former is often more difficult because it requires the therapist to divert attention away from the content as it is presented by the client, and pay attention to the characteristics of how something is said, the subtleties of interaction between therapist and client, and the meaning of the content as it might reflect something about the therapist-client relationship.

In that regard, one of the more important therapist-client processes from a psychodynamic perspective is transference. In a broad sense, transference refers to attitudes and feelings that develop by the client regarding the therapist, that may be derived from attitudes and feelings the client has for current or historically significant people in his life. These attitudes and feelings may be positive and perhaps may imbue the therapist with the "authority" to temporarily help the client cater to his positive side, as others may have done for him. On the other hand, negative transference may impede the therapy process. Careful and sensitive analysis of the transference process is necessary, but it may be particularly difficult to do in short-term psychotherapy.

## III. THE CASE OF "PAUL:" 15 CLINICAL QUESTIONS

*1. What would be your therapeutic goals for this patient? What are the primary goals and the secondary goals?*

As mentioned above, the focus of short-term psychodynamic therapy is to facilitate the client's development of insight about the intrapsychic forces that drive his current behavior. For Paul, this focus would be adapted at first to support the most obvious and immediate goals which are to help him abstain from drugs and prevent relapse, and to be able to exercise more control over his anger, frustration, and impulses. In order to maximize reaching these goals, it is likely that the short-term psycho-dynamic therapy with Paul would be one component of a comprehensive, multi-modal approach in which his abstinence from drugs would be the first order of business. In that regard, some other possible treatment components to consider for him are: AA, medical treatment, behavior therapy, and nonconfrontational group therapy (Gabbard, 1994).

If we consider insight as a goal, the actual intrapsychic issues that Paul might be encouraged to explore would largely be based on the therapist's conceptualization of how Paul's intrapsychic forces are affecting his life. One potentially important intrapsychic issue for Paul is the conflictual nature of his behavior, i.e., his impulses to be abusive, aggressive, irresponsible, and self-indulgent as his father had been, and at the same time, to be an upstanding, moralistic, and protective individual who abhors his father's negative traits. One event that immediately precipitated Paul coming to treatment was his shock at his children's fearful reaction to him. The meaning of that event and the power of that particular event to act as a catalyst for Paul seeking treatment is perhaps related to his perceptions of his conflictual relationship with his own father. In other words, Paul may have been driven to treatment because the reaction of his children brought the conflicts with his own father to the fore, and his normal protective mechanisms collapsed under the weight of those conflicts. Those conflicts may be ripe for therapeutic interpretation and work and, to the extent they are relevant, Paul should benefit from increased insights about them.

Another treatment goal for Paul might be for him to process and change his use of maladaptive protective responses for conflict management, such as, his use of drugs to temper his negative affective states, his impulsive acting-out for cathartic relief, and perhaps his belief that he can modulate his use of drugs. During treatment, he may have to be gradually weaned from using these responses in "knee jerk" fashion, with the hope that, in the long-term, he will find more appropriate and permanent substitutes for them. In this regard, self-insight into his affect, conflicts, and protective mechanisms might help relieve some of the psychological pressure he is experiencing. Perhaps early in the therapy process, the therapist might serve as a resource for Paul to develop less self-destructive coping strategies, with the hope that eventually he would internalize them or, via insight, discover his own adaptive substitutes.

As part of this process, Paul would need to be more fully aware of the cyclic nature of his behavior and what he jeopardizes by engaging in acting-out behavior and drug abuse. More specifically, Paul's tendency to relapse after previous treatments may be due partly to his inability to fully internalize and remind himself that he risks losing that which he values, such as, abstinence from drugs, healthy intimacy with his ex-wife and children, and consistent and positive job performance. The therapist "sides with" these positive forces in the hope that Paul will more fully internalize them so that they can more effectively compete, in a psychological sense, with his tendencies to engage in repetitious and maladaptive coping. The goal here would be to help him avoid a cyclic process in which unprocessed recovery facilitates future relapse. Much like using a balance sheet, Paul potentially will be more able to choose alternative behaviors to the extent that he has heartfelt insight about the losses as well as the "gains" of his maladaptive behavior and how the losses and "gains" are intertwined with his psychodynamic issues. Outside of the therapy, perhaps he will be most able to experience and apply these insights during periods of abstinence when he is capable of realistically experiencing his choices, and during periods of anticipation of drug use or acting-out behaviors when the conflict of choice may be most pressing.

In addition to increasing Paul's awareness of the intrapsychic causes of his addictive behavior and acting-out, another goal of psychodynamic therapy with him would be to facilitate his ability to identify, label, and verbalize his intrapsychic affective and cognitive states within the therapy sessions (Gabbard, 1994). To the extent that this ability can be fostered in Paul, perhaps he would be more able to recognize his maladaptive feelings and thoughts outside of therapy sessions and therefore be able to utilize more positive solutions rather than rely on the affective tempering qualities of drugs or the use of acting-out behaviors for cathartic relief of anger or rage. If Paul's abuse of drugs is partly a defense against his experience of confusing negative and perhaps even positive affective states, then clarifying, labeling, and discussing his affect within the therapy session might reduce his tendency to respond in "knee jerk" fashion to confusing and unpleasant states.

Other related therapeutic goals for Paul would be to strengthen his ego functioning (Frances, Franklin & Borg, 1994) partly by creating a supportive therapeutic atmosphere and emphasizing his strengths, and to increase his superego functioning partly by emphasizing firm boundaries for his behavior. Inconsistent parenting and a chaotic childhood environment may have thwarted his ability to internalize and utilize checks on his impulsive behavior. The therapist temporarily may assume ego and superego functions by setting limits, boundaries, and sanctions on his behavior, and reinforcing his positive abilities to cope. Hopefully, some of these functions would be internalized by Paul partially as a function of a positive transference and the overall therapeutic process.

*2. What further information would you want to have to assist you in structuring this patient's treatment? Are there specific assessment tools you would use, (i.e., data to be collected)? What would be the rationale for using those tools?*

At times during Paul's past therapy experiences, he was guarded about what he revealed. It would be helpful to know the extent to which the information he revealed in the current case report is accurate and undistorted. Toward this end, interviews could be conducted with his ex-wife, children, and other members of his family; in addition, corroborating information could be obtained by requesting objective records from legal, employment, and educational sources. Also, in past therapy sessions, Paul was capable of being insightful. More detailed accounts of his past therapy experiences might help in determining which specific techniques made him less defensive and more open, and the pitfalls that prevented him from being open.

The use of projective tests, such as, the Rorschach or TAT, might help clarify Paul's psychological problems and dispositional tendencies. His data from the MMPI were unrevealing, but his data from the NEO-PI suggested some possible problems he may have, such as, 1) feelings of depression, hopelessness, and other negative affects; 2) overt expression of anger; 3) impulsivity; 4) conventional and perhaps restricted views and affects; 5) egocentrism; and 6) casualness in implementing goals. In addition to the possibility of providing further conceptual and diagnostic information about him and clarifying the potency of some of his dispositional tendencies, his responses to the ambiguity of a projective test might provide information about how he would respond to the ambiguous and abstract elements of psychodynamic therapy.

Regarding the need for specific information, of particular importance is Paul's past and current relationship with his father, since he may be imitating aspects of his father's negative style. Also, to the extent that Paul identifies with his father, more information about his father's positive characteristics potentially could be used therapeutically to help Paul experience and perhaps incorporate those positive characteristics in his own psychological design. Since Paul apparently had a good relationship with his shop teacher in school, more information about that teacher similarly might be used by Paul as he is more able to identify with positive aspects of significant others.

Equally important is the extent to which Paul has social support and what he can do to maximize it for himself in the future. In the past, his periods of healthy functioning may have been modulated by his level of social support, although we do not know if this occurred. Interviews with his father, mother, ex-wife, siblings, and children perhaps would reveal this information and the extent to which others are committed to him now and in the future. In addition to the obvious aspects of Paul's behavior that make it more or less difficult for others to offer him support, perhaps there also are more unobtrusive behaviors that others have noticed that he could modify to increase his interpersonal intimacy.

Additional information about his ex-wife might be helpful in another sense. It is unclear if she is perhaps a resource for Paul or complicit in his drug abuse behavior, or both at different points in time. Her father was an alcoholic and, as Paul believes, this may have increased her sensitivity to Paul's problematic upbringing and drug abuse problems. On the other hand, dealing with Paul's problems perhaps has provided her with secondary gains necessitated by her own socialization. Since at one point her prescribed Valium was a drug source for Paul, further information is needed about her drug use and how it may or may not intertwine with his problems.

Although the case report contains descriptive information about the negative events of Paul's life, such as skipping school, divorce, drug use, family and job problems, there is little information about Paul's current thoughts and feelings about these events and his recollections of how he phenomenologically experienced them at the time. More specific information to be obtained would include: 1) his thoughts and feelings at the time of the events; 2) his attempts at problem-solving solutions that worked and solutions that did not work; and 3) his current understanding of the precipitating events of his maladaptive behavior. Also, perhaps there are instances he could recall that demonstrate his successful avoidance of problems; he may have incorrectly evaluated or distorted his previous successes at positive coping, which, if clarified, might be helpful to him in the future. All of this information, if used therapeutically, might help him to understand the repetitious nature of his behavior and those psychological forces that continue to undermine his attempts to bring out his best side.

*3. What is your conceptualization of this patient's personality, behavior, affective state and cognitions?*

For most of his adult life Paul has been a substance abuser. He may be unwittingly duplicating the drug abuse patterns of his father as he tries to psychologically identify with him, in perhaps the only way he knows. Furthermore, his drug use may serve as self-medication (Gabbard, 1994) for anxiety occurring in anticipation or as a result of his need to psychologically relieve himself via outbursts of anger or impulsivity. He may be trying to maintain his daily functioning by creating a drug state that seems "normal" for him because of the drugs' palliative effects on feelings generated by his areas of conflict. Problems for Paul arise when his impulsivity or anger "breaks through." It is at that point that perhaps he is most aware that taking drugs does not allow him to maintain equilibrium and to function adequately in areas that he values, such as his family and job. He seems somewhat insightful about his own failures, such as his inability to control his negative affective states by his self-medicating strategies, and he is insightful and motivated for treatment when these failures are tangible, such as when his children fear him or when his job is in jeopardy. Similarly, his drug use may reduce anxiety associated with painful self-deprecating emotions, such as, guilt or low self-worth that result from his anger, impulsivity, drug abuse, or failure to meet interpersonal and work obligations. Perhaps his drug use may also be euphoric for him, although we have little evidence at this point for that being a primary motivating factor. Although we are being somewhat inferential, it would not be surprising if Paul is depressed, although we would need more information to get an accurate read of the type and extent of his potential mood disorder.

Conflicts that generate challenges to Paul's positive view of himself as a competent and worthwhile person might be particularly threatening. Examples might be threats to his sense of being a good worker and a good father and the satisfaction he obtained from the interpersonal aspects of his job. Although we do not know the specific conflicts that typically have occurred between Paul and his ex-wife, it is fair to assume that at least some of them concern Paul's roles as mate, father, and provider.

As mentioned before, Paul may be in conflict about issues concerning his father and the likelihood that he will repeat his father's mistakes. Paul came from a dysfunctional family, particularly regarding his father's behavior, and it is difficult to know the extent to which the family dynamics during his upbringing keyed him to the issue of repeating his father's mistakes later in life. Although his father's drinking behavior was dysfunctional, it was somewhat predictable. His father generally was sober on weekends, perhaps also inoculating Paul with a sense of the ambiance of healthy family interactions. Nevertheless, the lack of consistency in those positive family experiences and witnessing his father's drinking and outbursts may have generated in him insecurity, anger, and difficulty in incorporating appropriate behavioral boundaries and rules, and moral sanctions. In turn, these difficulties may have planted the seeds for his anxiety and maladaptive coping as an adult.

Although the MMPI does not reveal any negative dispositional patterns, nevertheless Paul's problems are longstanding and repetitive. However, he has some strengths. For example: 1) He values his role in his family, particularly as a father, and seems to care about his children. 2) Ever since his experience in shop class, he has taken pride in being able to work with his hands. 3) He values himself as a hard, conscientious worker who related to those he supervised in a balanced and fair manner. The fact that he was put in a position of responsibility on the job and, at least for awhile, had an excellent relationship with the owner of the company, also reflects well on his interpersonal abilities and perhaps his ability to be receptive to authority. 4) Sporadically, he has been able to maintain periods of sobriety during which he functions as an adequate family member and worker. 5) He enjoys the company of men and being "one of the boys." This quality is positive to the extent it involves Paul having a sense of community and healthy mutual interdependence and does not involve more stereotypic, macho-type behaviors, such as excessive drinking. 6) He was able to experience some relief in one therapy encounter by openly discussing his problems. Perhaps this behavior is a predictor of how he can function in future therapy encounters.

Overall, Paul has been dysfunctional most of his adult life, but seems capable of periods in which he can function interpersonally and vocationally in a moderately healthy manner. His primary behavioral problems are drug abuse, and impulsively acting-out his anger and frustration. These behaviors may provide him with temporary relief from anxiety and perhaps depression that may have its origins in his early family experiences. Although he has some personal strengths, they are, at this point, insufficient to overcome his longstanding problems.

*4. What potential pitfalls would you envision in this therapy? What would the difficulties be and what would you envision to be the source(s) of the difficulties?*

Given Paul's spotty ability to be open in therapy, sensitivity by his therapist to his receptivity for insight is critical. The therapy easily could become derailed to the extent that the therapist pushes too hard for openness or is too accepting of resistance. Also, Paul's motivation in therapy may wax and wane. He has developed maladaptive strategies that provide some temporary relief and it may be difficult for him to wait on, via treatment, strategies that may not work as well, even in the short-term. His commitment to therapy and his concomitant progress may be positively affected by his ability to internalize controls, promoted by the therapist, over his drinking and acting-out behavior. Much skill would be needed by the therapist to allow Paul to internalize controls without him becoming overly dependent on the therapist.

Given the longstanding and cyclic nature of Paul's problems, it also would not be surprising if some of his problems reoccur or if new problems arise during the therapy. As such, the therapist would have to guard against counter-transference reactions, such as being disappointed or frustrated by Paul's lack of progress. Likewise, for a variety of reasons previously mentioned, Paul may have difficulty in being insightful, which also could elicit a counter-transference reaction by the therapist. To minimize such reactions, the therapist should realistically and periodically evaluate his reactions to Paul and actively monitor Paul's capabilities to benefit from the psychodynamic process.

Perhaps the most important potential pitfall is the possibility that Paul's work in therapy and the insights that result from it might further trigger his need to self-medicate with drugs or increase his feelings of anxiety or depression with a concomitant risk of suicidal behavior. More specifically, Paul may have regrets or guilt feelings about past transgressions that might become more prominent for him in the therapy process, which, in turn, might further overwhelm his self-protective capabilities. The therapist should carefully monitor Paul's affective state, drug use, and the pace of the therapy in order to shift the therapy process or activate other components of the multi-modal treatment approach as needed to minimize a downturn for him.

*5. To what level of coping, adaptation, or function would you see this patient reaching as an immediate result of therapy? What result would be long-term subsequent to the ending of therapy, (i.e., the prognosis for adaptive change)?*

Generally, the extent to which significant behaviors and motivating factors in a person become habitual and crystallized over a long period of time affects that person's prognosis. Paul's is no exception and because of his long problematic history, his prognosis is guarded. We would expect moderate improvement for him in the long-term. His psychological dynamics seem to have childhood roots. He has sought relief from the adult manifestations and transformations of his earlier problems and conflicts by adopting constant and maladaptive coping strategies during most of his adult life.

There is evidence that Paul can sustain relatively brief periods of healthy functioning. Therefore, it would not be surprising if he were able to make significant short-term gains in therapy that would appear to be indications of long-term potential gains. To maximize long-term gains, there should be regular follow-up sessions and multi-modal treatment. During the follow-up sessions, at the fist sign Paul is "slipping," the appropriate components of the multi-modal treatment should be resumed. Perhaps follow-up, psychodynamic sessions could be used to help him examine areas of slippage as well as newly developed constructive strategies of abstinence and impulse control. Careful follow-up monitoring of his affective state and potential suicidality also would be necessary.

Long-term changes resulting from therapy may be undermined by Paul's lack of social support. As mentioned earlier, it is unclear if his ex-wife is a resource. He does not appear to have any close friends, although more information about this area would be helpful. His most constructive allies might be his father, who has stopped drinking, his mother, his siblings, and ex-substance abusers he met at AA. It is unclear the extent to which past conflicts with his father might get in the way of Paul having a relationship with him or the extent to which Paul already has developed intimacy or could develop intimacy with others, such as members of AA. It would not be surprising if Paul has other longstanding dispositional problems limiting his ability to be intimate, above and beyond the interpersonal problems caused by his substance abuse and poor impulse control.

Overall, Paul's maladaptive functioning has existed for most of his adult life with some periods of relief from it. It is a matter of how long changes in him can last. The most important immediate goal of therapy is to eliminate Paul's reliance on drugs. Without that change, progress in other areas, such as vocation and family, would be limited. He should be capable of abstinence, at least in the short-term. However, given his history, abstinence is less likely to occur in the long-term without rigorous follow up in a multi-modal treatment context. Being somewhat optimistic, we expect Paul to be regularly employed and not have his job be in jeopardy because of drug abuse or impulsivity. He appears to be a good worker when the conflictual elements of his character do not take over. Likewise, we expect him to resume a positive role as a family member, particularly as a father. Also, we expect him to be able to control his anger and impulsivity, or find socially acceptable methods to diffuse them. It is difficult to predict if a consistent and positive shift in his behavior can occur in the long-term. Given his history, the most likely possibility is more tumultuous cycles of poor adaptation and recovery.

*6. What would be your timeline (duration) for therapy? What would be your frequency and duration of the sessions?*

Although we would expect Paul to gain some insight into important psychodynamic issues within the 20-session short-term therapy time line, we do not believe that this treatment by itself is sufficient to maximize adaptive changes in him. We would hope that during the 20 sessions, Paul might experience some cathartic relief, become more skillful in identifying his affective states, incorporate some more adaptive controls over his impulsive behavior, explore specific issues of self-worth, and be in a better position to weigh the tradeoffs of how he is and how he would like to be. However, given his extensive problematic history, his profile of recurrent episodes of substance abuse and acting-out is not likely to disappear. Because of the possibility he might develop more significant depressive symptoms, follow-up with a multi-modal treatment team is a necessity. A once-a-month or an as-needed follow-up regimen of psychodynamic treatment could be instituted for Paul, particularly if there is previous progress in using psychodynamic treatment with him.

*7. Are there specific or special techniques that you would implement in the therapy? What would they be?*

We already have discussed our general model of how short-term psychodynamic therapy could be used in treating Paul. During therapy, he should be allowed to tell his story at his own pace, attend to circumscribed aspects of himself that heretofore were too painful to address, and develop substitutes for the self-medicating effects of drugs and the cathartic relief from his acting-out behaviors. Generally, these goals are more likely to occur to the extent the therapist is skillful in establishing a therapeutic alliance with Paul and in catalyzing alternative coping strategies, such as via a positive transference or by helping him to label and understand his affective "triggers." In addition, Paul has a long history of prematurely terminating treatment. Discussions about this issue and how it relates to his current treatment might include informal, verbal, therapeutic contracts, and explanations about the psychodynamic therapy process, including expectations of likely feelings, time frame, goals, and resistance.

*8. Are there special cautions to be observed in working with this patient, (e.g., danger to self and others, tranference, counter-tranference)? Are there any particular resistances you would expect and how would you deal with them?*

It is unlikely that Paul would express physical hostility and impulsivity toward the therapist. There is little evidence that Paul responds to authority with physical aggression, even when confronted with bad news. Nevertheless, he has a history of impulsively acting-out toward others when he is challenged, such as becoming physically violent toward his ex-wife when she questioned him about his substance abuse. Given that the therapy with him, at times, might be challenging, the therapist should take typical precautions to maximize his or her own physical safety, such as, conducting the therapy in a nonisolated environment, physically positioning himself during the therapy to maximize his physical safety and establishing firm boundaries and rules for permissible behavior for Paul. Perhaps of greater concern is the need to establish procedures for Paul's safety if his depression, anxiety, or feelings of inadequacy become worse. The specifics of what Paul would be told to maximize his physical safety would depend on the availability of other resources in the area. Generally though, the therapist should have a "contract" or a promise with him that, if he intends to harm himself or others, he will seek out those other resources if the therapist is unavailable. Similarly, there should be ongoing monitoring during the therapy of his suicidal thoughts and/or plans, intentions to harm others, and level of impulse control.

*9. Are there any areas that you would choose to avoid or not address with this patient? Why?*

The balance between exploration and support is critical given Paul's psychological vulnerabilities and the possibility that depression and anxiety could exacerbate the situation as he becomes more insightful. Areas to be avoided, at least early in therapy before a therapeutic alliance has been established, are those that he is unable to easily incorporate and work with as part of the therapeutic dialogue. With the information available to us in the case study, it is difficult to determine which issues those might be, other than those that perhaps focus on his self-devaluation. As we discussed earlier in the chapter, in short-term therapy, the focus is circumscribed. The dialogue in Paul's therapy would not drift far from the links among his psychodynamic processes, impulsivity, substance abuse, and his failures to cope.

*10. Is medication warranted for this patient? What effect would you hope or expect the medication to have?*

We would generally advise against medication for Paul's anxiety and depressive symptoms, at least until some therapeutic progress occurs, because of his long history of abusing drugs, including Valium, to self-medicate. It is a pattern we would like to break. Paul had some success with antabuse and perhaps its use might be considered (as well as anti-depressant medication if warranted, later in the therapy) by the medical members of the multi-modal treatment team who obviously would make the final determination about drug treatment.

*11. What are the strengths of the patient that can be used in therapy?*

Although we have covered this topic earlier, here we will highlight some essential elements of it. Paul's recognition of his need to change is perhaps his most significant strength. (It is the maintenance of previous positive changes that have been problematic for him.) Also, he has not relinquished his beliefs about what he values, such as being a good father, a competent worker, a fair person, and a potential non-substance abuser. However, it is common for those who are depressed or are substance abusers to lose sight of what is potentially good in life and therefore to not be motivated to use their strengths to establish goals that might make them happier. If Paul's superego functions are overpowering (Gabbard, 1994), it may be even more difficult for him to use his strengths positively without experiencing guilt. Perhaps there are people in Paul's life, such as his ex-wife, who might make the journey toward positive goals easier. Others, at times, have experienced Paul as likable and competent. Another resource for him might be religion via the church. There is evidence that he periodically attended church, but we are not informed in the case study about his religious commitments or the extent to which any particular church or its members elicited his devotion.

*12. How would you address limits, boundaries and limit setting with this patient?*

As mentioned earlier, rules of limits and boundaries would be established primarily to try to control Paul's substance abuse and his potential to hurt himself and others, such as his ex-wife. The rules would be monitored by the therapist and other members of the multi-modal treatment team, and informal "contractual" agreements regarding the limits and boundaries might be formed as necessary, as a contingency of therapy. Paul also would be informed that as the therapy progresses, he might experience periods of negative feelings about the issues discussed and that it would be expected that he would turn to the therapist and other members of the treatment team for help rather than rely on his previous self-medicating strategies and relief from acting-out his impulses. In that regard, an informal "contractual" agreement and discussions with him about his commitment to therapy might help.

*13. Would you want to involve significant others in the treatment? Would you use out-of-session work (homework) with this patient? What homework would you use?*

Paul's difficulties are not restricted to or limited by specific situations or individuals. Rather his difficulties and maladaptive coping strategies seem to be triggered by the situation at hand and the concomitant psychological threats that situation may arouse in him. Paul has a lot to deal with on his own and should be seen in individual therapy. However, later, perhaps he might be seen in therapy with his ex-wife, if it appears that their relationship will continue and Paul is ready to work on those problems unique to their relationship.

*14. What would be the issues to be addressed in termination? How would termination and relapse prevention be structured?*

The time line for termination in short-term psychodynamic therapy is, to some extent, arbitrary with the limiting factors being the circumscribed issues and goals relevant to the problem at hand. Implicit in the therapy is the idea that once the relevant circumscribed issues are discussed therapeutically and there is some evidence that those discussions have or have not helped achieve certain behavioral goals, then the therapy process would terminate. Limiting the number of sessions to 20 or less is an incentive both for the therapist and Paul to focus on the circumscribed psychodynamic issues and behavioral goals defined early in the therapy process. Perhaps there might be a renegotiation between the therapist and Paul to extend the process if progress is imminent or relevant but unresolved issues are still being addressed.

As we mentioned earlier, with Paul's problems being extensive and chronic, follow-up treatment is a necessity. At the very least, perhaps monthly sessions with him should occur, primarily to deal with new problems and potential relapse. Paul may have a continual need to understand his motivations to abuse drugs and impulsively act out in new situations. Assuming some progress was made during psychodynamic treatment, he may have to explore new situations as they occur, from whatever new perspectives he gained during the treatment, to avoid his "knee-jerk" responses that, heretofore, provided him with cathartic or self-medicating relief. As part of relapse prevention, perhaps Paul and his therapist could define situations which would obligate him, in an informal, contractual sense, to see the therapist. For example, one such situation might be his intent to meet friends at a bar after a significant period of abstinence. Overwhelming feelings of anger, frustration, guilt, or self-devaluation also might trigger a contractual visit to the therapist.

*15. What do you see as the hoped-for mechanisms of change for this patient, in order of importance?*

Given the complexity of Paul's dispositional tendencies to abuse drugs and act impulsively, and the likelihood that these behaviors probably are caused by many different factors, it is hard to be precise about the mechanisms of change that we expect for him. Earlier in the chapter, we presented some potential links among his psychodynamic makeup and behavior. More generally, from a psychodynamic perspective, to understand why one does what one does is a prerequisite for changing one's behavior. However, it would be naive and empirically incorrect for us to assume that this process is the only way in which behavior change occurs. We see the human condition more holistically, such that behavior and psychological states interact and affect one another, and that one directional loop may predominate over the other as a function of dispositional or situational context, particularly when problems are complex and longstanding, as is the case for Paul. As such, we believe that Paul's best chance for psychological relief is multi-modal treatment. Perhaps the psychodynamic component of his treatment would catalyze adaptive behavioral changes in him that are functionally and directionally determined by intrapsychic forces. It would be a significant accomplishment for Paul if that were to occur

## REFERENCES

Bloom, B. L. (Ed.). (1997). *Planned short-term psychotherapy* (2nd ed.). Boston: Allyn and Bacon.

Budman, S. H. (Ed.). (1981). *Forms of brief therapy.* New York: Guilford Press.

Bugental, J. F. T. (1987). *The art of the psychotherapist.* New York: W. W. Norton.

Elkind, S. N. (1992). *Resolving impasses in therapeutic relationships.* New York: Guilford Press.

Frances, R., Franklin, J., & Borg, L. (1994). Psychodynamics. In M. Galanter & H. D. Kleber (Eds.), *Textbook of substance abuse treatment*. Washington, D. C.: American Psychiatric Press.

Freud, Sigmund, (1973). *Introductory lectures on psychoanalysis* (J. Strachey, Trans., J. Strachey & A. Richards, Eds.) New York: Penguin. (Original work published in 1917).

Gabbard, G. O. (1994). *Psychodynamic psychiatry in clinical practice. The DSM-IV edition*. Washington, D.C.: American Psychiatric Press.

Galanter, M., & Kleber, H. D. (Eds.). (1994). *Textbook of substance abuse treatment*. Washington, D. C.: American Psychiatric Press.

Gustafson, J. P. (1995a). *Brief versus long psychotherapy*. Northvale, NJ: Jason Aronson.

Gustafson, J. P. (1995b). *The dilemmas of brief psychotherapy*. New York: Plenum Press.

Horowitz, M., Marmar, C., Krupnick, J., Wilner, N., Kaltreider, N., & Wallerstein, R. (1984). *Personality styles and brief psychotherapy*. New York: Basic Books.

Masterson, J. F. (1988). *The search for the real self. Unmasking the personality disorders of our age*. New York: Free Press.

Miller, W. R., & Brown, S. A. (1997). Why psychologists should treat alcohol and drug problems. *American Psychologist, 52*, 1269–1279.

Wachtel, P. L. (1993). *Therapeutic communication: Principles and effective practice*. New York: Guilford Press.

# 5

# Behavioral Systems Approach

## *Douglas H. Ruben*

Advances in behavioral systems approaches to substance abuse treatment frequently face the proverbial question: What is so different about this intervention? Is it a recycled version of orthodox behavior therapy mixed with elements of cognitive therapy? Or, is it a disguise for Milan-based family systems theory overhauled in behavioral language? These are good questions. Essentially, how does using the word "systems" distinguish one therapy from another therapy?

Conceptually the term "systems" has a ubiquitous meaning: It refers to a holistic series of interrelated events that surround human behavior. As this chapter will show, interrelated events become measurable predictors of addiction and psychopathology when they are effectively *integrative in a field continuum* (Morris, 1982; Ruben, 1984, 1986). "Field-integrative" thinking shifts the mindset of practitioners from *behavioral* to *interbehavioral*. *Behavioral* refers to clinical focus on specific, tangible responses such as alcohol intake, IV-cocaine use, or aggressive outbursts. *"Inter"* refers to events occurring *"in between"* responses and surrounding environment and causally responsible for response outcomes. Interactive events studied may precipitate, accompany, or follow addictive behaviors and are clinically significant to etiology and treatment (Ruben, 1990).

Identifying and treating these variables are the subject of this chapter, which addresses a systems behavioral intervention with the client in question. First, we examine basic tenants of this unusually innovative behavioral strategy. Second, guidelines are offered for implementing the systems approach given the client's presenting symptoms.

## I. THE TREATMENT MODEL

### Operational Principles of Behavioral Systems Approach

Defining parameters of any natural science begins with a basic question: *Where's the proof?* Systems behavioral therapy is fortunate in this respect since its body of research largely emanates from three sources. First is the extensive documented literature on applied and experimental analysis of behavior generated since the late 1950s. Laboratory and field applications using elementary principles of respondent and operant conditioning account for incontrovertible evidence of behavior-change methods for many pathological disorders. Behavioral methodology redesigned for addiction treatment is one example.

A second influence is J.R. Kantor's interbehavioral model touted as a "broader behavioral approach." It is broader because it eloquently incorporates other disciplines, such as psychiatry, philosophy, sociology, and chemistry (Kantor, 1959). Basically, the interbehavioral concept, in comparison to Skinner's conditioning models, removes *causality* from a significant role in the prediction of behavior. Functions of reinforcers and other controlling variables *correspond to* rather than *cause* modifications in human behavior. Kantor's unit of analysis in this respect consists of five generic factors: (1) the organism; (2) the stimulus; (3) media of contact; (4) setting factors; and (5) interbehavioral history. Where Skinner considers these factors microscopically reducible to be scientific, Kantor's argument is the antithesis. Reductionism distorts the complete and complex content of everyday life. Scientific analysis, then, *if it is truly behavioral,* would examine these constituents of a field as interactive parts of the whole (cf., Ray & Delprato, 1989; Morris, 1997).

A third contribution is human ecology. Traditionally regarded as "systems theory," human ecological theory studies interaction between living organisms and their environment. No living organism exists in isolation. The basic unit from which research principles emerge results from the complex interplay of living and nonliving elements within the *ecosystem.* Think of ecosystems as one large interdependency between physiological-biological, human-built, and social-cultural settings. In family study, ecosystem approaches such as, for example, social exchange theory, can efficiently illuminate variables in parent-child relationships. Parents may disperse or withhold unique response contingencies regarding love, status, information, money, goods, and services.

Resources in ecosystems also can be multivariate. Givers and receivers of resources are explainable by similar principles that explain responders of operant and respondent conditioning and organisms within an interbehavioral field. In fact, overlapping language and methods of analysis among all three systems—ecosystems, behavioral systems, and interbehavioral systems—account for a burgeoning discipline of learning theory called *Ecobehavioral model* (Ruben, 1992a; 1993b).

Accordingly, now the psychological field is larger and the entire system closely resembles kinetic energy in machinery. There are no singular units of action per se but rather the synthesis of many larger aggregates of action. In family addiction, for example, such multiple factors considered as interdependent and operationally definable may include the abused substance, neglect or mistreatment of children, family sabotage of recovery progress, deterioration of job or economy, and legal ramifications. While these components may sound similar to other treatment models— and rightly they should—here the difference lies in using *an expanded behavioral orientation.*

## II. ESSENTIAL CLINICAL SKILLS AND ATTRIBUTES

Intuitively, the reader may figure a practitioner of behavioral systems theory inevitably must have "behavioral clinical training." This, assumingly, consists of basic knowledge of conditioning principles, reinforcement contingencies, effects of punishment, and advanced background in cognitive, emotional, and verbal behavior. So, too, awareness of Kantor's interbehavioral paradigm and eclectic models of human ecology may round out the clinician's arsenal.

Equipped with behavioral technology, practitioners are in good shape, but are not yet ready for applications to addictionology. As with most behavioral disorders, treating providers must possess one quality over and above their training to effectively assess and treat patients: namely, *the ability to teach.* Different from many approaches, behavioral systems theory focuses on *construction* of new behavior. Skill development and new functional, adaptive behaviors are byproducts of viewing therapy as:

1. equivalent to training.
2. continuous rather than isolated to the treatment session.
3. preventive; relapse prevention is an immediate part of training.
4. naturalistic; it does not appear as therapy to the casual observer.
5. multidisciplinary; it entails intercommunication with fields of medicine, social work, rehabilitation, business, and consumerism.
6. constructive; it emphasizes alternative behavioral patterns to replace those patterns of the client prone to psychological and physical dependency (cf., Delprato & McGlynn, 1986).

Competent behavioral systems practitioners are teachers first, and therapists second. They develop highly perceptive skills at sorting relevant from irrelevant variables and, as teachers, must be effective communicators of their observations using basic clinical skills in empathy, reflection, and rapport-building. However, establishing therapist-client rapport is not essential to imparting behavior change; clients can change without liking the change-agent. What is essential are positive interpersonal skills. Simple as this seems, decades of graduating behavior therapists have lacked crucial interpersonal skills with the public and may appear cold, unemotional, and rigidly intolerant to patient failures. However, described as "teachers," behavioral systems practitioners replace their scientific rigor with warmth and recognition of their fallibility.

## III. THE CASE OF "PAUL": 15 CLINICAL QUESTIONS

Presented is a 35-year-old, recently divorced, male Caucasian temporarily employed in construction and showing extensive polydrug abuse history. Primarily identified are alcohol, marijuana, and cocaine dependency tracing back to adolescence. Recreational abuses includes LSD, PCP, amphetamines, and Quaaludes. Progressive stages of addiction show impulsivity, blackouts, short durations of abstinence, repeat offense of DUILs, several failed detoxifications, and psychosocial repercussions including divorce, job jeopardy, and diminished family involvement. Developmentally, he is an adult child of a violently aggressive, alcoholic household causing him continuous guilt and anxiety and distorting his concept of family normalcy.

Given these variables, here is how a behavioral systems therapist approaches the client in question.

*1. What would be your therapeutic goals for this patient? What are the primary goals and the secondary goals? Please be as specific as possible.*

Recidivism is an obvious, but only one among many, pathologically disturbing variable targeted for treatment. To assuredly prevent recidivism, behaviors in the family and client causing readdiction must be identified and labeled as primary goals. Drug-inducing patterns (urges), compulsive behaviors, job and life instability, and aggressive behavior, for example, receive instant attention. However, eliminating impulsivity and drug cravings, and stabilizing life routines is half the intervention. The other half is eliminating defective substitutes that may prevent relapse but are ephemeral; for example, drinking eight cups of coffee, smoking three packs of cigarettes, eating three candy bars daily, overexercising, increasing frequency of sexuality, and other "new" compulsive habits.

Given that treatment lasts an average of 3 to 5 months, long-range goals include the following:

1. Decrease and control impulsivity in all activities apart from drug urges. This includes reduction in physical pace of action, decision making, and distractibility. Skills taught include relaxation, constructive use of idle time, and interrupting urges by understanding the "urge curve" and delays of self-gratification.

2. Decrease and control drug-related urges by eliminating all substitutes or newly compulsive behaviors. Skills taught include allowing body to feel calm, sedated, and not always anxious without using foods, OTC drugs, overconsumption of liquids (tea, coffee, pop, etc.), sugars, and distracting activities of equal compulsion (e.g., collector hobbies, gambling, etc.).

3. Decrease and control anger and aggressive outbursts. Skills taught include assertiveness, elimination of conflict-avoidance behavior, acceptance of mistakes in self and others, and modification of distorted, irrational beliefs.

4. Increase non-drug-using verbal behavior and social discussion. Skills taught include community service at anti-drug agencies such as MADD (Mothers Against Drunk Drivers), attendance at social or cultural functions not involving alcohol (church, synagogue, PTA, AA, etc.). Pro-recovery statements also taught for discussion around client's peers and family.

5. Recovery inoculation skills. These skills include self-motivating steps of progress when faced with loved ones who reject the client's progress or unknowingly sabotage his efforts. Skills help to prevent collapse of improvement in the absence of family validation.

*2. What further information would you want to have to assist you in structuring the patient's treatment? Are there specific assessment tools you would use (i.e., data to be collected)? What would be the rationale for using these tools?*

Discernment of target behaviors may begin intuitively and even be confirmed through client self-reports and reports by family members. However, behavioral systems is an empirical science relying on data collection as evidence for presuppositions. Pools of measurable data gathered in normal research would be ideal; concurrent response counts, duration measures, frequency tabulations, and diaries of interactive stimulus-response events ultimately represent the best baseline rates.

But that is utopia. In clinical practice, realistic limitations prevail such as managed care sessions restrictions, attrition rates, shortage of agency funding, and ethical caveats that rule out fancy data recording methods. Alternatively, psychometric testing might be considered, for example, *MMPI-2, Taylor-Johnson Temperament Analysis*, and standardized checklists such as *Michigan Alcoholism Screening Test, MacAndrew Alcoholism Scale* (within MMPI-2), and *Adult Child of Alcoholic Behavior Profile*. In Paul's case, high MMPI infrequency scores suggest moderate malingering and denial of faults. A more thorough battery elucidating tendencies for fabrication and deception may be *the Computerized Assessment of Response Bias* or *Word Memory Test.*

Employing traditional psychometrics combined with self-reported, family-reported, and agency-reported data, one can expect to glean the following sources of behavioral information:

1. What is the frequency of alcohol and drug abuse?
2. With whom and in what setting does the person use drugs?
3. What is the longest and shortest period of abstinence and why?
4. What is the client's disposition prior to, during, and after drug-use?
5. How are these dispositions (response patterns) similar to childhood patterns?
6. In what other ways does the client satisfy urges (impulses) beside polydrug use? In other words, what are preexisting substitutes for non-drug use?
7. In what ways does the family or others (peers, co-workers, etc.) unknowingly enable reinforcement of the client's impulses (for drugs or other needs)?
8. What are behavior patterns of each critical family member in response to the client's routine (inebriated) and nonroutine (sober) behaviors?
9. What skill deficits are pronounced in client's history? That is, what psychosocial skills never properly developed?
10. What skill excesses are pronounced in client's history? That is, what psychosocial skills overdeveloped and became intense and life-interfering?
11. Is the client involved in any setting or group where his drinking or impulsive behaviors are regarded as normal?
12. What medical or organic defects impede functional or social activities historically or currently precipitating alcohol and drug use? That is, does the client suffer an illness or disease self-medicated by substance abuse?
13. How do family members react when client is abstinent and in recovery?
14. What recurrent factors derail client's recovery and cause recidivism?
15. What therapies, legal interventions, or other resources has client undergone in drug-cessation efforts? Court-ordered abstinence, for instance, may result from investigations by Friend of the Court and Child Protective Services.
16. How have intrafamily disturbances previously interfered with

healthy recovery and prognostically exacerbated addiction? For example, has the client or his significant partner ever committed sexual, physical, or verbal abuse (domestic assault, CSC)? Do they inescapably attend family social functions endorsing alcohol or polydrug use?

*3. What is your conceptualization of this patient's personality, behavior, affective state, and cognitions?*

A behavioral systems perspective overlaps initially with radical behavioral perspectives. Each position carefully assesses stimulus-response interconnections in the environment of the human organism. Envisioning variables, however, may differ for behavioral systems, since data is accepted about childhood history, biological predispositions, and intermingling family and medical contingencies.

In other words, traditional (Skinnerian) therapists ask *what is the frequency, duration, and intensity of stimulus-response contingencies and the rules governing these contingencies?* These rules may deal with cognitions, emotions, and different states of deprivation. Behavioral systems therapists also ask these questions. But they further ask, *what is it about the frequency, duration, and intensity of all the important stimulus-response interactions that cause a continuum of dysfunctional behavior from childhood to adulthood?* System behaviorists typically look at thoughts, feelings, cognitions, states of deprivation, organic, and cultural variables, but over a longer period of time crossing many dimensions of the client's stimulus field.

In Paul's case, behavioral systems therapists may wonder why Paul's ex-wife lives with him and its potential impact: Does her cohabitation have an untoward influence on the client's recidivism? Is she submissively codependent? Is she, herself, a polydrug abuser or suffering acute anxiety, depression, or other debilitating disorder preventing her independence? Replies of "Yes" to any of these questions makes her a suspicious variable computed into the behavioral systems formula. Assessment of her own contingencies and interrelationship to Paul's target behaviors equally is vital to preintervention planning,

Conceptually speaking, systems behaviorists view Paul this way: He exhibits a history of anticipatory anxiety and inhibition later released as eruptive anger to avoid and escape conflict. Influences of Traumatic Brain Injury (TBI) are suspect. Following hostile outbursts, severe rule-governed statements arise about shame, suicidality, depression, and drug use. Client also exhibits history of using stimulant-acting drugs (including alcohol) to (a) maintain high-arousing visceral sensations perceived as "being in control" and "normal;" and (b) to counter periods of paralyzing depression, helplessness, and anxiety over being manipulated, hurt, and codependent on other people.

Sedative-acting drugs (cannabis, opiate synthetics, etc.) act to self-medicate rising anxiety and enable moderate adjustment to daily functional routines. Finally, chronic interpersonal deficits, low frustration tolerance to failure, and inconsistent family support detrimentally limit his relapse-prevention efforts.

*4. What potential pitfalls would you envision in this therapy? What would the difficulties be and what would you envision to be the source(s) of the difficulties?*

Pitfalls in systems behavioral therapy resemble problems affecting most treatment interventions (Ruben, 1993a). Consider the following warning signs of therapy derailment with Paul:

## Client Obstacles
Paul may rapidly progress in treatment and feel overconfident; he may substitute a new addiction for a prior one; engage in avoidance and escape behavior; engage in risky behaviors (e.g., new jobs, capital ventures, sky-diving, etc.); dislike the therapist or therapy; or get defiantly defensive and deteriorate his support system.

## Therapist Obstacles
Paul's recurrency and early termination of therapies suggests a history of "provider impediments." Providers unknowingly may impede progress in several ways: lack of training in substance abuse and family discordance; pace of therapy moves too rapidly; insensitivity to Paul's emotional fragility; implicit trust of Paul's overconfidence and recovery motivation; "enabling," not "directing" opportunities for Paul's growth. All of these hurdles seriously limit analysis of field events and can disrupt Paul's treatment progress.

## Family Obstacles
Behavioral systems is leery of the assumption that family members automatically embrace the addict's recovery. Abused and neglected families may be very apprehensive about Paul's recovery. They may inadvertently sabotage it in six ways: (1) distrust Paul's abstinence and expect relapse; (2) overprotect and disable Paul to succeed; (3) create exaggerated expectations about Paul's complete personality transformations after recovery; (4) express resentment and anger; (5) resist change to avoid changing their own habits; and (6) excessively change their behaviors and confuse Paul (Ruben, 1993b).

*5. To what level of coping, adaptation, or function would you see this patient reaching as an immediate result of therapy? What result would be long-term subsequent to the ending of therapy (i.e., prognosis for adaptive change)?*

Readdicted polydrug abusers with a multiplicity of deficits, excesses, and defective social contingencies challenge the most astute therapist of any orientation. In behavioral systems, the challenge is equally tough. Prognostically, Paul's chance of sustained recovery remains dangerously low unless structured interventions produce consistent change; change not only in abstinence and drug-free contingencies, but also in revising his interpersonal approach to families and friends.

*6. What would be your time line (duration) for therapy? Would would be your frequency and duration of sessions?*

Duration of therapy ideally is longer than many managed care programs or third-party payers allow. Traditionally, behavioral therapies are among the few providers who rallied behind the clarion call to cut back on session length. Sessions largely range from 6 months to 1 year. Comprehensive sessions scheduled twice weekly, and assuming the cooperation of family, may reduce duration of sessions to 6 months. Transitions from weekly to biweekly or monthly appointments entirely depend on evinced abstinence as reported and corroborated by family members, also seen in therapy, and interagency communication (e.g., with probation officer, AA check-in sheets).

*7. Are there specific or special techniques that you would implement in the therapy? Would would they be?*

Therapy is multicomponental, meaning that it moves along sequentially in a series of progressive, skill-learning components or steps. Steps contain a prescribed number of new skills taught using different interventions within the session and designed for transfer outside the session. Measurably demonstrated skills that meet criteria in one step prompt new steps to commence, until all the steps are completed. Naturally, incremental steps are not always possible if two or more steps warrant attention simultaneously, but this rarely disrupts the overall scheme of treatment.

Stepwise learning in this respect has two goals. First, it allows close monitoring of Paul's progress relative to clearly defined skills in contrast to drug-abusing or other bad habits. Second, it stimulates motivation for behavior change as Paul observes salient improvements in his life. In behavioral systems, multicomponental steps include (cf. Ruben, 1992b): *cues and urges, belief systems, social skills, life-style restructuring, marital and family skills, employment skills, community resources, and relapse prevention.*

## Cues and Urges

In this component, emphasis is on the fact that abstinence is not due to willpower, but instead depends on learned counter-reactions to highly susceptible conditions. Cues triggering Paul's urges for anger, drug reuse, impulsivity, and job termination, for example, are isolated and systematically desensitized whereby Paul can face them without risk of unwanted responses.

### Belief Systems

Paul's perspectives on drinking and drug abuse appear fraught with irrational or distorted thinking, engendered from childhood, from current situations, or from his family and social relationships. Combining Rational-Emotive Therapy with behavioral systems, treatment steps include, first, dispelling impure inferences, and asking questions to discover facts about assumed behaviors; second, instructional steps to interrupt obsessions and replace them with problem-solving skills; third, solutions are inserted as new "rule-governed behaviors" guiding Paul's choice of action in home, work, and social situations.

### Social Skills

Retraining of Paul's social skills essentially replaces his interpersonal deficits and fears. Areas covered include:

A. Basic assertiveness;
B. Confrontation, assertiveness;
C. Problem-Solving/Decision making;
D. Dating and initiation skills in social settings;
E. Negotiation skills (for managers in industry);
F. Compromise skills (for couples);
G. Interview skills.

### Life Style Restructuring

Major changes in Paul's daily routine are crucial to abstinence or drug use reduction. His repetitive habits around which defective thinking and responses occur remain the anchors or "reinforcers" sustaining his dysfunctional integrated-field of behavior. To change these, Paul needs to learn to:

1. Change his work schedule;
2. Change his transportation schedule;
3. Change his social activities;
4. Change his family and spouse contact;
5. Change his medication (antabuse) schedule;
6. Change his eating and mealtime schedule;
7. Change his sleep schedule;
8. Change his use of idle time;
9. Change his tendency for avoidance and escape.

## Marital and Family Skills
In this component, attention is drawn to clearly defined stressors between Paul's ex-wife and himself, including Paul's misguided criteria in selecting new dating partners.

## Employment Skills
Here, focus is entirely on redefining and changing Paul's (1) stressful performance at work; (2) abrupt or anticipated unemployment; (3) conflict relationships between worker and supervisor; and (4) job ambiguity.

## Community Resources
Part of Paul's therapy involves referral to appropriate agencies in the community that ensure a "natural" transfer of sobriety or drug-free life style beyond the therapeutic session. Referrals typically are to five services. These include: (1) medical, (2) social, (3) legal, (4) vocational, and (5) educational agencies.

## Relapse Prevention
Paul's final component in therapy is maintenance of skills learned in short-term therapy. Actually, "relapse prevention" steps are ongoing from onset of therapy as life style restructuring alters contingencies of the client's natural environment.

*8. Are there special cautions to be observed in working with this patient (e.g., danger to self or others, transference, counter-transference)? Are there any particular resistances you would expect and how would you deal with them?*

Behaviorally translated, "transference" may refer to *codependency of contingencies producing or sustaining drug recovery.* Paul's undertaking of a treatment replacing his old habits with healthy habits forces him to rely heavily on a therapist's guidance. Acquiring new life style habits that feel awkward typically panic addictive-disordered clients accustomed to their routines. Naturally, Paul eagerly expects directive feedback on his abstinence trials and social-interpersonal changes. Therapist feedback given positively but excessively, such as nightly by telephone or e-mail, may relieve Paul's rising anxieties but also reinforce his unwanted dependency on the therapist. Reciprocally, addiction therapists ingrained with the philosophy of reassuring Paul through each behavior-change obstacle may be inadvertently reinforcing two contingencies. One is Paul's overdependency. The second is the therapist's underlying vicarious need to avoid seeing Paul relapse and feel responsible for misguided interventions.

In nondirective therapies, client-therapist cohesion is fundamental to positive behavior outcome and consequently risks this codependency contingency phenomenon. Directive, behavioral systems approaches are not immune to this problem either, but they might handle Paul's desperate pleas for guidance differently. Focus in each stepwise component, instead, is upon *self-regulation*. Paul rapidly develops a personal behavioral repertoire not only for creating drug-altering responses but also for troubleshooting obstacles produced by these healthy responses that can potentially reverse progress. He learns, for example, to identify, isolate, discuss, and attempt to ameliorate persistently disturbing cues (e.g., job stress, fatigue, depression); he becomes his own therapist, relying upon himself for emergency answers and reaffirmation of constructive steps taken to resolve the problems. Self-regulatory steps for Paul's addictions shift control away from overhelping therapists and back to Paul. This efficiently allows Paul to view therapy as educational and facilitative rather than as an umbilical chord onto which he must hold tightly in order to be drug-free. Paul grows dependent on himself, not externally upon therapy or therapists, at each stage of intervention.

*9. Are there any areas that you would choose to avoid or not address with this patient? Why?*

Target responses identified in behavioral systems methodology largely remain *corporeal*. They are currently or potentially physical, measurable, observable, or reducible as multiple units within a larger stimulus field. This includes the gamut from human feelings to human thoughts. However, excluded as irrelevant to analysis are such reified constructs as ego, unconsciousness, libido, hierarchy of self, and transcendental states. The assumption is that patterns described by these labels are translatable into more scientific, behavioral systems terminology. Libido, for example, may be translatable into impulsivity; this coalesces with Ma scales on Paul's MMPI-2 showing above average hypomania; weak impulse control predictably implies high-risk of recidivism.

*10. Is medication warranted for this patient? What effect would you hope or expect the medication to have on him?*

Interdisciplinary input in therapy is essential to behavioral systems. Medical adjuncts such as rehabilitation or prescriptive medicines are not viewed as encumbrances on interventions; rather, they intricately enable treatment of variables concurrently or sequentially important to clinical target behaviors such as anger and polydrug addiction. For example, antabuse may be initially useful for Paul, while restructuring his life style patterns and introducing drug-free perceptions. Likewise, low-dosage and short-durations of BuSpar for anxiety may facilitate conflict-resolution skills without Paul being debilitated by fears and need for avoidance.

Traditionally, behavior therapists rejected medications as masking learnable symptoms and thereby undermining necessary behavior change.

Holistically, this is not the case. Behavioral systems therapists treat bio-behavioral influences and are receptive to medicinal catalysts to make treatment more effective.

*11. What are the strengths of the patient that can be used in therapy.*

Client-directed input is a powerful measure of behavior change. Paul's reaffirming incentives to be different and reattempts at therapy point to two strengths employable in his program. First, he is insightful. Paul undeniably recognizes his shortcomings as life-intrusive and has been receptive to changing his habits. Secondly, Paul experienced pride and wishes to restore it. His ambition at work, in parenting, and toward drug recovery reached a temporary plateau for nine months during which, while abstinent, he adjusted effectively. Consequently, returning to this plateau is realistically achievable given his capabilities.

*12. How would you address limits, boundaries, and limit-setting with this patient?*

Limits and boundaries again imply ambiguous or reified concepts typically omitted in behavioral systems treatment. However, that does not exclude the phenomena to which they refer. Redefined in Paul's case, boundaries and limits may pertain to awareness and acceptance of Paul's deficits and excesses, and choices for self-growth within which he can set and meet realistic expectations. The job of the behavioral systems therapist is to advise guidelines clarifying these expectations and which methods will effectively and rapidly help Paul along the way.

*13. Would you want to involve significant others in the treatment? Would you use out-of-session work (homework) with this patient? What homework would you use?*

Viewing therapy as a behavioral system, partners in treatment typically go beyond the boundaries of therapist-patient and private office. Outside these confines are nuclear or extended family members deeply invested in Paul's recovery and eager to participate in his process. When data is collected, they can assist in varying ways to report or submit proof of behavior patterns both in initial assessment and during the course of intervention. Examples of data-recording in Paul's case include:

1. Diary of Paul's alcohol and drug intake for 1 week compiled by ex-spouse and nine-year-old son. Diary to include frequency of intake, types of alcohol consumed (beer, wine, mixed drinks), drugs consumed (marijuana, pills, etc.), and disruptive or sedative behavior after alcohol and drug use. Diary used randomly during different stages of treatment.

2. Biweekly reports from community service agency for whom Paul is

volunteering. Report reflects Paul's anti-drug discussions and proselytiz-
ing pro-abstinence among other people in the agency office.

3. Paul's self-reports structured as entries in daily diaries or on audiotape covering:

    a. Reasons for aborting efforts.

    b. Degree of shame, embarrassment, hostility, imposterism, or other
       reactions suffered when deliberately trying new behavior or
       resisting temptations for alcohol, drugs, or other impulses.

    c. Fears of new behavior patterns and losing old identity. A com-
       mon complaint in transforming old to new behaviors is odd
       feelings of impersonalization. This indicates if Paul is afraid to
       become somebody new and abandon habits of control know
       since childhood.

    d. Untreated factors influencing therapy which pose serious threats
       to recidivism of drinking, drug use, anger, or other compulsions.
       Examples include unanticipated DUIL convictions (jail time), job
       loss, family death, religious conversions, and formation of inti-
       mate relationships.

    e. Organic factors recently or recurrently arising causing pain, dis-
       comfort, or disabling attempts at behavior change. Data may reveal
       OTC or prescriptive drugs Paul takes for, say, chronic lower-back
       pain. Naturally, unregulated dose increments in, for example,
       vicadon and extra-strength Tylenol with codeine may rebuild
       tolerance and increase Paul's rate of recidivism.

*14. What would be the issues to be addressed in termination? How would
termination and relapse prevention be structured?*

Therapy concludes following a structured relapse-prevention component and maintenance steps. Relapse prevention includes transfer of (1)
skill training and (2) programmed relapse.

## 1. Skill-Training

At this point in therapy, focus is upon assuring adaptive skills transfer
and maintenance in high-risk drug-using situations.

(a) *Transfer and maintenance of skills.* Transfer refers to learned skills
occurring in all the important places in the client's world. Paul's assertiveness skills, for example, may be strong at home but weak at work.
Therapists should identify where skills are not "transferring" and direct
efforts to correct this.

Once learned, "implanting the skills" involves (a) teaching Paul how
to solicit feedback; (b) teaching spouse or significant other how to attend
to progress or positive steps in Paul's behavior; and (c) teaching Paul
what positive and desirable consequences to expect for recovery steps.

## 2. Programmed Relapse

Make Paul aware that sobriety or abstinence is a learned process and that control over urges and cues and other emotional or behavioral factors *increases the probability of* but does not guarantee total prevention.

Maintenance steps are the final steps to closure of therapy. In Paul's case, recovery must measurably meet three criteria. First, his abstinence is generalizable across the current and potential stimulus field. Second, nondrug behaviors not only have replaced drug-using behaviors but effectively are generating natural, positive contingencies. Third, bio-behavioral, employment, or other factors impinging on drug-using behaviors are under control.

### Abstinence is Generalizable

Clear evidence appears over 6 months that Paul's drug-free and newly developed behaviors occur in low- to high-risk drug-using situations and equally occur in new places or with new people engaged in abstinence. Behavioral *potentials* occur when drug-free and healthy behaviors advance to particularly unique situations for which the client lacked any history of responding (e.g., attendance at church).

### Nondrug Behaviors Generate Positive Contingencies

This is when Paul regularly displays new skills that become intermingled in daily rituals, routines, and habits.

### External Factors Are Under Control

Stress inoculation from external factors such as job, family, and physical condition is conceivably possible when these conditions remain constant. However, in Paul's continuum of field events, variables are not static. Job loss, divorce, medical problems—each of these emotionally devouring obstacles can potentially sabotage new skills and reverse Paul's symptoms to baseline levels.

One measure to prevent regression is *adaptive skills* (Ruben, in press). Adaptive skills allow Paul the capability to be flexible, accept mistakes and disappointments, and recover quickly from unfulfilled expectations using problem-solving tools.

Overall, termination of therapy conveys to Paul that he has achieved skill mastery and runs a low risk of polydrug relapse. Therapy may be "over," but it is never completed permanently. Paul may wish to return in several weeks or during the following year for "refresher" sessions to fine-tune drug-free coping skills or to review his personal progress in light of unforeseen problems.

*15. What do you see as the hoped-for mechanisms of change for this patient, in order of importance?*

Paul's attainment of long-term abstinence is only a reasonable goal providing he learns and masters new skills in handling tempting situations. In behavioral systems, proof of change is not simply "R & R": *remove* bad behavior and *replace* it with good behavior. Lasting change also requires the underlying mechanism of *response covariation*, meaning that Paul's refusal to drink alcohol must involve response patterns that are similar to or overlap with his efforts to refuse other drugs. Self-relaxing under stress to avert drinking, for example, may also prevent drug use as well as volatile anger. Reducing visceral levels covaries with drug urges, drug-seeking behavior, and irritability; as one pattern decreases, so do the other patterns. That way, Paul's abstinence has broad and specific consequences for the rest of his field continuum.

In short, approaches to substance abuse based in behavioral systems principles have many empirical advantages over traditional behavioral and nonbehavioral approaches. Holistic field variables, covariation, interdisciplinary input, and behavior constancy of results rank highest among these gains. Treating the addiction covers Paul's entire drug-dependency status, from biological and cultural contingencies to response units, all viewed integratively as a field of behavior. In effect, the systems approach using multicomponental steps is a quantum leap to credibility for addiction specialists and for behavioral therapists looking to broaden their horizons.

## REFERENCES

Delprato, D. J., & McGlynn, F. D. (1986). Innovations in behavioral medicine. In M. Hersen, R. M. Eisler, & P. M. Miller (Eds.), *Progress in behavior modification, vol. 20* (pp. 67–122). Orlando, FL: Academic Press.

Kantor, J. R. (1959). *Interbehavioral psychology.* Chicago: Principia Press.

Morris, E. K. (1982). Some relationships between interbehavioral psychology and radical behaviorism. *Behaviorism, 10,* 187–216.

Morris, E. K. (1997). Reflections on contextualism, mechanism, and behavior analysis. *Psychological Record, 47,* 520–542.

Ray, R., & Delprato, D. J. (1989). Behavioral systems analysis: Methodological strategies and tactics. *Behavioral Science, 34,* 81–127.

Ruben, D. H. (1984). Major trends in interbehavioral psychology from articles published in the "The Psychological Record," *Psychological Record, 34,* 589–617.

Ruben, D. H. (1986). The interbehavioral approach to treatment. *Journal of Contemporary Psychotherapy, 16,* 62-71.

Ruben, D. H. (1990). Interbehavioral approach to treatment of substance abuse: A "new" systems model. *Alcoholism Treatment Quarterly, 7,* 47–61.

Ruben, D. H. (1992a). Behavioral systems approach. In C. E. Stout, J. L. Levitt, &

D. H. Ruben (Eds.), *Handbook for assessing and treating addictive disorders* (pp. 3–24). Westport, CT: Greenwood Press.

Ruben, D. H. (1992b). Treatment of alcohol and drug abuse. In C. E. Stout, J. L. Levitt, & D. H. Ruben (Eds.), *Handbook for assessing and treating addictive disorders* (pp. 165–180). Westport, CT: Greenwood Press.

Ruben, D. H. (1993a). Transition failures in alcohol and drug abuse treatment. In D. H. Ruben & C. E. Stout (Eds.), *Transitions: Handbook of managed care for inpatient to outpatient treatment* (pp. 115–134). Westport, CT: Praeger.

Ruben, D. H. (1993b). *Family addiction: An analytical guide.* New York: Garland Press.

Ruben, D. H. (in press). *I can stop drinking.* Ventura, CA: Newjoy Press.

# 6

# Cognitive Therapy of Substance Abuse

## Cory F. Newman and Christine L. Ratto

## I. THE TREATMENT MODEL

The cognitive model of substance abuse is not an etiologic model. Thoughts, per se, do not cause substance abuse. The causes of addictions are multivariate, including such contributing factors as heredity, cellular adaptation, neurotransmitter depletion, early modeling, peer pressure, socioeconomic disadvantage, excessive exposure to the drug culture, faulty attitudes about the effects of drugs and alcohol, exaggerated beliefs about personal control, and insufficient regard for oneself and one's health, among others. Rather, the cognitive model is an extremely useful heuristic tool through which to conceptualize the *maintenance* of substance use, and the tendency toward cyclical *relapse*. Further, the cognitive model highlights numerous *points of intervention* in order to break the chains of events and vicious cycles that are inherent in the addictive process.

We should emphasize that the cognitive model is not in opposition to psychobiological or 12-step models of substance abuse. Rather, these models can effectively complement each other, provided that the proponents of each approach demonstrate flexibility and open-mindedness toward common goals. For example, one of our clients reported that he found cognitive therapy's emphasis on skills such as communication, problem-solving, and rational reevaluation to be invaluable in improving his sense of mastery and pleasure in life, without having to resort to cocaine. At the same time, his 12-step support group provided him with his only set of "clean and sober, nonjudgmental" friends, and this was indispensable in reducing social high-risk situations. Further, he was taking an SSRI, which he claimed helped alleviate not only his concurrent depressive symptoms, but also dimmed his drug cravings.

Cognitive therapy is a highly active, directive, structured treatment, geared toward the client's acquisition of psychological skills in a time-effective manner. When applied to substance abuse (Beck, Wright, Newman, & Liese, 1993), cognitive therapy focuses on three main areas in order to help clients work toward the ideal goal of abstinence: (1) modifying their maladaptive beliefs about their drug-related behaviors, and the drugs themselves; (2) teaching them important life skills, so as to achieve satisfaction and higher self-efficacy without resorting to artificial "fixes;" and (3) changing clients' views about themselves, their lives, and their futures (the "cognitive triad," see Beck, 1976), so that they feel more hopeful, less helpless, and more respectful of themselves and others. Given the high prevalence of comorbidity associated with substance abuse, cognitive therapy's track record as an empirically supported treatment for depression and anxiety disorders makes it eminently suitable for utilization with a substance abusing population.

The cognitive model of substance abuse has been pictorially highlighted in the form of a seven-component flowchart, with the seventh step feeding back into the first (Fig. 6.1). Thus, the process of *maintenance* of substance abuse is inherent in the model. In addition, each of the seven components presents opportunities for therapeutic *interventions*, which will be described below. Although the seven components are presented in an orderly, linear sequence, causality may by bidirectional, cyclical, and the process of *relapse* can be triggered at any point in the chain. The following is a brief description of each of the seven components.

## 1. High-Risk Stimuli

This is the variable most commonly associated with relapse (Marlatt & Gordon, 1985); therefore, it is presented as the first step in the model. Such stimuli may be external or internal with respect to the substance abuser. External stimuli serve as "cues" for substance abuse, for example seeing "old drinking buddies," a beer advertisement, a pipe, or a hand-held mirror. Interventions involve careful planning to maximize avoidance of the "people, places, and things" associated with substance use.

Internal stimuli are the emotional or physiological states that either remind clients of times they have used in the past, or that stimulate a desire to use. Cognitive therapy is especially useful in teaching clients to learn ways to manage and cope with internal cues such as dysphoria, anxiety, guilt, anger, boredom, and physical malaise.

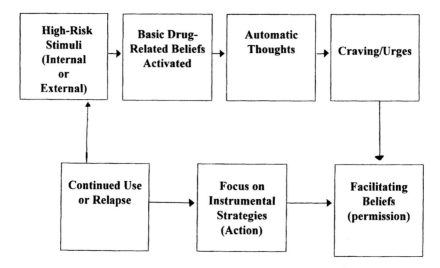

**FIGURE 6.1**    Cognitive model of substance abuse.

## 2. Maladaptive Beliefs About Drugs

These are the dysfunctional points of view that many substance abusers maintain about drugs and their use. Interventions include helping clients examine and modify such erroneous beliefs. For example, some clients will claim that they have been abstinent from alcohol, but then mention that they have been drinking beer. Upon closer examination, their distorted belief is that, "Beer isn't really alcohol." Similarly, cocaine abusers may believe that their snorting of the drug is "safe," because "only smoking and mainlining cocaine can make me addicted."

Another type of maladaptive belief involves an interaction between the substance abuser's views of the self, world, and future (the "cognitive triad"), and about the drugs themselves. For example, socially anxious substance abusers may believe that, "The only way I can face other people is if I'm high, therefore drugs and alcohol help me avoid being lonely." Similarly, a hopeless individual with low self-esteem may maintain that, "My life is going nowhere anyhow, so I might as well use drugs and die happy now."

Interventions focus heavily on changing these pernicious beliefs that perpetuate hopelessness, helplessness, and low self-efficacy, and therefore make clients vulnerable to ignoring future consequences for their substance abuse. Instead, clients learn to view themselves as having lives that are worth preserving for the long term, and that drugs counteract this goal.

## 3. Automatic Thoughts

These are the instantaneous ideas and images that clients get when their addictive beliefs are activated. Such thoughts often involve stereotypic exclamations such as, "Who cares?" or "Do it!" or "Party time!" or "What the f—k!" These thoughts serve to trigger increased craving, and propel the individual toward drug use. Therapists teach their clients to monitor and question these thoughts to become more aware of the effects of these thoughts on their physical sense of craving, and on their decision-making processes.

## 4. Cravings and Urges

These are the physiological sensations that cause discomfort, such that clients seek to use drugs in order to bring relief or to satisfy their "appetite." Chief interventions involve distraction and delay tactics, so that clients learn that cravings will subside on their own if not acted upon. Clients learn to engage in a wide variety of mastery and pleasure activities during the period of time in which they would have ordinarily acted on their urges to use drugs. Therefore, impulsivity is diminished, and alternative, pro-social behaviors are increased.

## 5. Permission-Giving Thoughts

This phenomenon is also known as "rationalizing." Here, clients who feel ambivalent about their drug use generate spurious arguments in order to tip the decision-making scales to permit themselves to use drugs. Interventions involve helping clients monitor thoughts such as, "One hit won't hurt," "I've been a good boy for six weeks, so I deserve to party now," and "I need to test my sobriety by seeing if I can handle a couple drinks." Clients are taught to examine these permission-giving thoughts, and to understand their seductive, deceptive nature.

## 6. Instrumental Strategies

These are the behavioral steps that users take to procure and use the substances. Examples include paging a drug supplier, going to a bar, borrowing money, and the like. An important intervention is to help clients structure their lives so that it is as inconvenient as possible to obtain the drugs, thus increasing the lag time between cravings and using. For example, clients can agree to keep no alcohol in their residences, to discard their beepers, and to have their paychecks go into their bank accounts via direct deposit. It is important that cognitive therapists elucidate the clients' thoughts and beliefs that are behind their reluctance to take such measures.

## 7. Using the Addictive Substances

Although this represents the seventh and final component in the model, it is not an "outcome" per se. Rather, it is a *process* in that the cognitive model does not view drug use as an all-or-none phenomenon in which the client reverts back to "square one" once the drug is used. Instead, each slip is seen as a new point on the client's decision-making continuum, and a potential, new high-risk situation that must be managed lest the cycle be repeated. Therefore, a major goal of cognitive therapy is to provide the clients with as many "tools" of self-assessment and self-help as possible to break the vicious cycle.

## II. ESSENTIAL CLINICAL SKILLS AND ATTRIBUTES

It is well-known that therapists' ability to communicate warmth, genuineness, and positive regard is central to their success in forming a productive alliance with their clients. This is true in working with substance-abusing clients. However, there are important caveats. For example, therapists of substance abusers must understand that their clients will be especially likely to minimize and underestimate their problems. Further, such clients may be more prone than non-substance-abusing clients to engage in outright lying to their therapists. Therefore, therapists must be extremely adept at assessing for inconsistencies in clients' self-reports, and for following up when clients' comments do not ring true. This requires that therapists be especially skilled in *confronting* their substance-abusing clients, yet still demonstrating caring and respect. This is an extraordinary balancing act, perhaps equaled only by therapists of clients suffering from borderline personality disorder, where good rapport must be matched with effective limit-setting.

In addition, therapists must be industrious, and conduct their sessions in a well-organized fashion. Cognitive therapists do not sit back and listen passively to their substance-abusing clients' tales. Instead, cognitive therapists question, probe, give feedback, instruct, and actively devise interventions and homework assignments. They structure their sessions so that important issues are addressed, even if clients do their best to sidestep them. If the session seems too easy, something is dreadfully amiss because the problems inherent in the lives of substance abusers are characteristically difficult to manage properly.

At the same time, therapists of substance abusers must be aware of their own tendency to "rescue" clients. It is essential that therapists not take an excessive proportion of the responsibility for the process of treatment and recovery. Rather, therapists must be skilled at avoiding the traps of co-dependency, some of the signs of which are: (1) feeling guilty and incompetent when resistant clients complain that "therapy isn't doing any good;" (2) becoming more and more active in response to the clients' becoming more and more apathetic; (3) being "nice" to clients by absolving them of the sorts of tasks (e.g., homework) that they would routinely expect from other clients; and (4) making excuses for their clients' maladaptive behaviors (e.g., defending their clients' repeated no-shows in supervision, or writing a bogus letter to the clients' employers to mitigate their absenteeism). In sum, *cognitive therapists must have a solid work ethic, and expect the same from their clients.* Low expectations rarely help anyone.

Therapists ideally should also be able to espouse high standards of client behavior without necessarily negatively judging the clients' character. For example, therapists should call their clients on maladaptive behaviors, such as lying and engaging in illegal activities or sexually hazardous behavior, without unduly shaming the clients or being harsh and punitive towards them. When therapists succeed in remaining aware of the clients' affective distress, it helps reassure the clients that they are being treated as *people*, not just as "bad drug abusers." Naturally, therapists should freely praise the clients when they engage in pro-social behavior, and when they earnestly engage in the demanding process of change.

Therapists of substance-abusers would do well to combine the qualities of high self-efficacy and high degree of faith in one's own reality-testing, along with relatively low levels of perfectionism (not to be confused with low standards). In other words, therapists need to be tolerant of difficulties and setbacks, for this is common in the treatment of the substance-abusing population.

From an academic standpoint, effective cognitive therapists possess the following skills: (1) the ability to weave the client's history of drug problems into a general developmental/psychological conceptualization; (2) good Socratic questioning techniques; (3) a solid understanding of the role of maladaptive beliefs in the maintenance of the drug-abuse problem; (4) attentiveness to the early warning signs of clients' premature disengagement from treatment; (5) a working knowledge of the "stages of change" model of addictions (Prochaska, DiClemente, & Norcross, 1992) so that motivational factors can be incorporated into the treatment; (6) organizational skills that maximize staying on task in session; and (7) facility in devising appropriate homework assignments, as well as other skills.

## III.  THE CASE OF PAUL: 15 CLINICAL QUESTIONS

*1. What would be your therapeutic goals for this patient? What are the primary and secondary goals?*

The primary goals of treatment have as much to do with *hope* and *safety* as they do with eliminating drug and alcohol use. For example, Paul reenters therapy in a demoralized state, believing that his family life and job security are acutely threatened, but not having confidence that he can maintain sobriety even though he has so much to lose. Indeed, Paul has a history of being underresponsive to the threat of negative consequences, and being inept at learning from past mistakes. He may believe that he has "tried everything" and is beyond help. With this level of hopelessness, Paul's dysphoria and helplessness may become exacerbated, resulting in his giving up on the process of therapy prematurely once again. In other words, before diving into a treatment plan, it is important to address whether Paul sees the *point* in trying therapy once again. The best treatment in the world is useless if the client's chair is empty.

Therefore, an important goal for the first session is to boost Paul's morale and make it clear that we (as his therapists) have not lost hope for him, even though we acknowledge that therapy will be very hard work. We can do this by overtly giving him the benefit of the doubt that he has learned some valuable lessons over the course of his life and repeated therapeutic experiences (including 12-step groups). After empathizing with his sense of despair (a better word than "fear," or "shame," which a "macho" male may not wish to acknowledge), we may tell him that, "Recovery is possible, if you commit yourself to changing, and if you can use all of the knowledge and experience you have gained over the course of your life and your treatments, in order to do it best this time." We may add, "Anybody can quit therapy; do you have that special something inside of you that will make you stick it out, even if it hurts?"

In addition, Paul's hazardous behaviors need immediate attention. His anger has bubbled over into acts of domestic violence. One of the primary goals of treatment is to do everything possible to minimize the likelihood of this behavior being repeated. In like fashion, Paul's history of sexually transmitted diseases, and reckless, impaired driving, must be addressed as part of the primary goal of increasing safety. In addition, although Paul does not threaten it overtly, his high level of hopelessness makes it prudent to assess for suicidality, and to deal with this as another high-priority issue.

Needless to say, Paul will assume that the goal of treatment is sobriety, and we largely agree. However, his current use of alcohol, cocaine, marijuana, and Valium is so extensive that it may not be possible to "go cold turkey" (assuming he were willing to entertain this goal) without inpatient, medical supervision. Yes, it is important for Paul to keep his job, and we must empathize with his fears of being fired if he takes time off for detoxification. On the other hand, how long do we expect him to keep his job if he *doesn't* give up his massive abuse of substances? The pros and cons of outpatient vs. inpatient treatment need to be addressed with Paul in the first session. At the very least, Paul's use of Valium necessitates a medical consultation.

Assuming that Paul decides to proceed with treatment, that his hope is rekindled, that he agrees to focus a great deal of therapeutic attention on his dangerous behaviors, and that he will commit to working toward sobriety, there are a number of secondary goals that we can pursue. For example, Paul needs to change his basic beliefs about himself, his life, his future, and drugs themselves. If he believes that he is fundamentally incompetent, we can look at his accomplishments, while sober, in the field of construction. If he believes that sobriety is impossible, we can examine the changes his father has undergone (at the same time, however, we must acknowledge Paul's anger toward his father for his past abuse). If he believes that the future is hopeless, we can ask him to reserve judgment until he has at least two years of sober living under his belt. If Paul thinks it is okay to drink "only a couple of beers," we can teach him to counteract this permission-giving belief with rational responses that support abstinence.

Other secondary goals of treatment are as follows: (1) learning how to relax in order to reduce anger, and to improve sleep without the need for chemical inducement; (2) using his time constructively, so that free time does not automatically lead to behaviors such as popping open a six-pack; (3) utilizing problem-solving skills, including planning, anticipating consequences, and harm reduction; (4) improving his communication skills, both at home and on the job; and (5) fostering relationships that do not revolve around drugs and alcohol. Taken together, this is a handful.

*2. What further information would you want to have to assist you in structuring this patient's treatment? Are there specific assessment tools you would use (i.e., data to be collected)? What would be the rationale for using these tools?*

As a matter of good, standard practice, we would want to obtain as many records of Paul's past treatments as possible, especially the more recent records. If possible, it would be useful to interview those closest to Paul, such as his ex-wife (who continues to have a relationship with him), and his father. However, this may be too risky at the start of treatment, as we may unwittingly trigger Paul's anger and mistrust, as well as unwittingly undermine his ex-wife's attempts to gain safe distance from him. Therefore, we would not exercise this option early in therapy. Later, after carefully weighing the pros and cons, we may respectfully broach this possibility to all parties.

Although Paul's MMPI scales were not outside of normal limits, it would be useful to perform an additional, structured clinical interview based on the Diagnostic and Statistical Manual, 4th Edition (American Psychiatric Association, 1994), both for Axis I (First, Spitzer, Gibbon, & Williams, 1994) and Axis II (First, Spitzer, Gibbon, Williams, & Benjamin, 1994). Further. we would utilize the Beck Depression Inventory (Beck,

Ward, Mendelson, Mock, & Erbaugh, 1961), the Beck Hopelessness Scale (Beck, Weissman, Lester, & Trexler, 1974), and the Beck Scale for Suicide Ideation (Beck, Kovacs, & Weissman, 1979), in order to assess for ongoing risk for self-harm.

Finally, although the psychometric data are lacking, it would be clinically useful to utilize three questionnaires developed by Fred Wright (see Beck et al., 1993) specifically to assess clients' *beliefs* about drugs, cravings, and relapse—the Beliefs About Substance Use, Craving Beliefs Questionnaire, and Relapse Prediction Scale (see appendix). Paul's responses to the items on these questionnaires would immediately cue us into some of our client's more extreme, dysfunctional beliefs that are part of his drug using cycle. These beliefs then would become targets of intervention.

*3. What is your conceptualization of this patient's personality, behavior, affective state, and cognitions?*

When evaluating the behavior and personality of a long-term substance abuser, there is a temptation to describe much of the problem in terms of narcissism (e.g., hedonism over all else) and sociopathy (e.g., he would "lie, cheat, and steal for drug money"). However, this is a classic "chicken and egg" problem—which came first, the drug-using behavior, or the narcissism and sociopathic behavior? The earlier the onset of the addictions, the more difficult to answer this question.

Clearly, Paul's behavior over the years has demonstrated a certain degree of self-absorption and disregard for societal norms. On the other hand, some of Paul's behaviors have provided a window into the positive potential of a life free of substance abuse. For example, Paul has at times been a very productive employee, he has shown empathy for his children, and he has voluntarily sought treatment (i.e., without court mandate). Paul's MMPI results do not indicate severe personality disturbance, therefore providing more evidence that his behavioral disturbances may be more the result of his drug use, rather than a cause.

Unfortunately, Paul's learning history is filled with trauma, neglect, poor role-modeling, and failure experiences. As a child, he witnessed domestic violence on a regular basis, and he was subject to harsh, arbitrary punishment from his alcoholic father. Further, his mother seems to have suffered from depression, and thus was less emotionally available than she might have been otherwise. As a result, Paul did not receive much positive regard, and he did not receive the sort of parental guidance and feedback that would teach him right from wrong. In such a bleak environment, one learns primarily how to survive the day, and to see things in black and white (e.g., "It's kill or be killed," and "Live it up today, because there's no tomorrow," and so on).

Paul also modeled his father's substance-abusing behaviors from an early age, thus incurring all of the typical lessons and consequences involved in being a slave to psychoactive chemicals. For example, Paul probably learned that drugs and alcohol were his only surefire way to avoid feeling emotional pain. However, this was only a temporary palliative, leading to further immersion into drug use, which entails its own painful consequences. Predictably, Paul failed miserably in school, finally dropping out. This was just one of many such experiences that surely crushed his self-esteem.

When a person suffers from low self-esteem, they sometimes overcompensate by acting out and adopting grandiose notions about themselves. Paul appears to be such a person. Using drugs such as cocaine would serve the purpose of making him feel strong, smart, and beyond harm. Unfortunately, they would also cause him to make disastrous decisions, to exacerbate his problems, and to stunt the kind of emotional growth that comes mainly from facing and meeting the challenges of life with a clear head. Thus, the cycle of drug use and low self-esteem became more and more ingrained, and impermeable to quick changes. In fact, Paul's main strategy when faced with difficulties was avoidance, such as when he dropped out of school, when he had difficulties in talking in group therapy, and when he would miss work.

The combination of low self-worth with compensatory grandiosity leads further to dysfunctional all-or-none views that are not conducive to therapeutic change. For example, Paul sometimes felt very ashamed of himself, probably believing that he was a failure, and as "bad" as his father. In a related vein, Paul probably learned to mistrust others, to expect that his needs would not be met, and that he did not have sufficient control over his life.

However, his history of treatment suggests that with a little success, he would flip to the opposite extreme, becoming convinced that he was in control and did not need further help. This overconfidence was a set-up for further relapses. Paul was unable to regulate or moderate his emotions, beliefs, and behaviors, a skill which is necessary in order to maximize success in "love and work."

A long history of drug intoxication also serves to blunt one's ability to introspect in an instructive way. This includes having difficulties in viewing one's own behavior objectively, reflecting upon one's own thinking process, or identifying emotions. These are serious obstacles to overcome in therapy. For example, Paul may be able to identify feelings of rage, and he is surely quite familiar with the feelings associated with drug-induced "rushes." However, he may be able to identify little else in his internal world. Therefore, it is noteworthy that he was able to see the fear in his children's eyes and to be affected by it. On the other hand, it seems that Paul is skilled at manipulating his ex-wife into getting back into his life, perhaps recapitulating his father's overpowering and demoralizing of Paul's mother. We would keep a close eye on how Paul views and behaves toward his ex-wife and children, as they are to be considered in harm's way until proven otherwise for a prolonged period.

*4. What potential pitfalls would you envision in this therapy? What would the difficulties be and what would you envision to be the source(s) of the difficulties?*

We have already touched upon some of the potential pitfalls in treatment, including: (1) Paul's difficulties in self-monitoring; (2) his hesitancy to think about or discuss painful clinical material; (3) his long history of "failed" treatments, thus leading to hopelessness and cynicism; (4) his mistrust of authority; and (5) the potential medical complications involved in doing outpatient work with someone who is heavily dependent on polysubstances. These obstacles would be more than enough, but there are others.

Paul has shown in the past that he has difficulty with homework assignments, especially of the written variety. Homework is a very important part of cognitive therapy, in that it teaches clients how to practice their new psychological skills "in the field," and leads to the clients' becoming their own therapists for the long run. At the same time, Paul is a high-school dropout. To subject him to written assignments may be a set-up to make him feel more ashamed, and more like a failure. Paul, rather than addressing these feelings and beliefs in session, is more likely to avoid them, perhaps dropping out of treatment altogether. Therefore, homework would have to be creatively crafted so that it would give Paul a higher chance of success, yet without seeming patronizing.

One such assignment might be for Paul to audiotape each therapy session, and to agree to listen to the entire tape when he would experience the urge to use drugs, *before* taking action to procure the drug. This would serve the function of giving Paul a period of reflective delay, while also passively reminding him of the issues he was dealing with in therapy. Further, if Paul were to hear himself on tape making pledges to behave more adaptively, it might stimulate enough cognitive dissonance to dissuade him from acting to satisfy his drug cravings.

Another problem concerns Paul's propensity for premature drop out, owing to inflated self-confidence as his compensatory strategy against shame and failure. The trick would be to convince Paul that staying in therapy was *smart*, a sign of *strength*, and the best way to make this treatment experience "different from all the others." As therapists, we would have to be very alert to signs that Paul had one or both feet out the door, and to address this in session. Similarly, if he were to be a "no-show" for a session, we would promptly try to contact him, and make a concerted effort to reengage him.

Other potential problems involve some of the factors that are common to the treatment of most chronic substance abusers. It would be difficult to keep Paul away from high-risk situations, as he undoubtedly had a well-established network of drug sources. Similarly, it would be a challenge to convince Paul that he could socialize without alcohol or drugs, especially since some of his fondest memories involve "bonding" with his construction buddies over a few postwork brews.

Another potential problem involves his ex-wife and children. Clearly, Paul wants to keep all of them in his life. This is understandable, and we have no problem empathizing with Paul on this matter. However, we cannot simply be blind advocates of this goal until such time as Paul's drug use and anger are under much greater control. Even then, we have a responsibility to help Paul rebuild his life, *irrespective* of how much he has contact with his ex-wife and children. This puts the therapists in a bind of loyalties, and may exacerbate Paul's sense of mistrust and hopelessness with regard to treatment. Therefore, our job would be to help Paul focus on how to "do right by them," even if it meant agreeing to keep some distance at this time. If Paul is capable of a degree of altruism, he may agree with this plan, though we would have to watch out for Paul's impulsive attempts to go see them. If, however, Paul continues to plead with us that he *needs* them at all costs and under all conditions, and gets angry at us for not understanding, then the problem is much worse.

*5. To what level of coping, adaptation, or function would you see this patient reaching as an immediate result of therapy? What result would be long-term subsequent to the ending of therapy (i.e., prognosis for adaptive change)?*

Assuming that Paul remains in therapy for a suitably long period and engages optimally in this process, we would expect him to achieve at least a brief period of sobriety. He would be willing to attend 12-step meetings regularly, to meet all of his responsibilities at work, and to be respectful of his ex-wife's boundaries. The question is, how long will this last, and will Paul learn sufficient self-help skills to cope with the daily grind of life, and yet continue to have hope for a sober, more fulfilling future?

We would expect that Paul's long-term prognosis would be guarded, but not hopeless. In order to maximize his chances of long-term maintenance of therapeutic gains, we would have to teach him a number of skills, including: (1) self-monitoring of thoughts, emotions, behaviors, and physiological cravings; (2) delay and distraction tactics in response to drug urges; (3) improved communication (perhaps facilitated by much in-session role-playing of key situations with co-workers and family); (4) rational reevaluation of his automatic thoughts, and beliefs (especially the core beliefs of incompetence and mistrust, as well as his permission-giving beliefs); (5) problem-solving; and (6) anxiety-reduction techniques, such as relaxation.

In order to maximize Paul's self-efficacy, we would help him to identify and utilize all of the tactics that he had used during past episodes of sobriety (however brief they may have been). In addition, Paul would have to learn not only how to maximize avoidance of external high-risk situations, but how to manage unavoidable *internal* high-risk stimuli (e.g., "drug dreams," emotional disappointment, and frustration). Paul would have to demonstrate significant changes in his beliefs about drugs and about himself, as well as the ability to modulate his emotions, behaviors, and thoughts, so that they were not all-or-none.

Long-term prognosis would improve to the extent that Paul views his "recovery" as being a lifelong task, which may or may not involve formal treatment along the way, but certainly involves ongoing practicing of self-help skills. Ideally, he would continue attending 12-step group meetings, eventually becoming a sponsor himself. He would have to learn to use relaxation techniques in response to anger and drug cravings, and to develop a repertoire of high mastery and pleasure activities that did not involve psychoactive substances. Perhaps most difficult of all, Paul would need to respect his ex-wife's wishes, in a way that his father failed to do with his mother. Arguably, this would benefit his kids greatly. Needless to say, these skills are not developed overnight. Much patience and many repetitions of therapy exercises are required.

*6. What would be your time line (duration) for therapy? What would be your frequency and duration of the sessions?*

We are assuming that Paul's therapy is neither subject to the dictates of a managed care contract, nor constrained by the standardization of a randomized clinical trial. Therefore, the question of the length of treatment, as well as the frequency and duration of sessions, is a collaborative issue between Paul and his therapist. Clearly, we cannot "dictate" to Paul how much therapy he should receive, especially with his history of mistrust of authority, and his "very low" Agreeableness score on the NEO Personality Inventory.

However, we can respectfully make a strong case to Paul that his level of desperation entering treatment, coupled with his chronic, longstanding problems, warrants fairly intensive and extensive care. It would be prudent for Paul to attend sessions twice per week for the standard "50-minute hour" per session. This would be frequent enough to monitor Paul's condition closely, and to begin teaching him some coping skills promptly, but not so frequent that he would become too dependent on therapy. In order to build an all-important social support system, we would suggest that Paul attend 12-step meetings every day, or at least on days on which he has no scheduled therapy session.

After approximately three months, provided that Paul is showing some improvements in his problems of substance abuse, hopelessness, and anger, we may suggest that Paul cut back to one session per week. It would be important to continue this arrangement faithfully for at least six months to a year. *Regularity* is the key. Paul needs to develop new, healthy, predictable *routines*, with therapy being one of his new activities. Missed sessions would be taken very seriously, and we would be inclined to assume that Paul's "no-shows" are signs of lapsing into drug use, unless proven otherwise. Therefore, we would aggressively pursue him if he failed to attend a session—not to criticize or accuse him, but to express concern and entreat him to reschedule as soon as possible. Once he returned to session, we would address the problem of his "therapy-threatening" behavior and its relationship to relapse.

Finally, therapy should not end abruptly. We believe that there should be a gradual weaning period. After a year, Paul (should he agree) could come to sessions every other week, and then once per month. We can see no compelling reason why *not* to have Paul come to see us on a quarterly basis (i.e., four times a year) over the course of a number of years, for booster sessions, and for brushing up on skills.

*7. Are there specific or special techniques that you would implement in the therapy? What would they be?*

The following techniques have been summarized in Beck et al. (1993) and are most effective in the context of a collaborative therapeutic relationship. Further, the *choice* of a specific technique, as well as its creative, individualized usage, is highly dependent on a solid case conceptualization (as described earlier).

We have hypothesized that Paul: (1) has core beliefs (or "schemas") of incompetence and mistrust; (2) becomes easily angered when his immediate goals are frustrated; (3) may be manipulating his ex-wife in order to prevent her from "abandoning" him; (4) has underdeveloped self-monitoring and problem-solving skills; (5) uses drugs and alcohol as a chief strategy in *avoiding* painful affect, upsetting thoughts, and burdensome responsibilities; and (6) tends to view things in all-or-none terms. Therefore, our interventions need to address these issues, in addition to helping Paul change his attitudes about drugs, and teaching him how to handle cravings.

In order to establish rapport, we need to show Paul that we are interested in him as a person, and not just invested in getting him off drugs or in "shrinking his head." We have to help him see how his particular developmental history ties into his current addictive behaviors, along with the concomitant sense of helplessness and despair. Additionally, it is a basic strategy in cognitive therapy to illustrate (using examples from the client's own life) how spontaneous thoughts and deeply held beliefs sometimes adversely affect behaviors and emotions in predictable ways.

The above serves as the foundation for our techniques. One such technique is an *activity schedule,* in which Paul would self-monitor the ways in which he utilizes his time. This helps to highlight ways in which he could use his time more effectively, so that he can have more of a sense of *mastery* (to counteract his sense of incompetence and helplessness). Later, this technique can be used to help Paul to *plan* activities that he might find enjoyable, but that would not involve drugs or alcohol.

Another important intervention is the *delay and distract* technique, in which Paul would respond to drug cravings by engaging in alternative, constructive, attention-consuming behaviors. This serves to weaken the link between cravings and drug-using behavior, teaches Paul that he is not necessarily a slave to his cravings, and creates a lag time between urges and using. Thus, Paul's urge has a chance to subside naturally (Paul's responses on the Craving Belief Questionnaire would shed light on whether he believes that his cravings can wane on their own). Further, he buys himself some time in which to make an active decision about whether or not to use drugs, rather than reacting impulsively. This fosters a functional sense of control.

Another important technique is *rational responding,* in which Paul would learn how to spot and modify problematic thinking patterns before they lead to a worsening of his affect and further dysfunctional behaviors. For example, we would teach Paul how to convert his all-or-none thinking into *rating scales.* If he catches himself saying, "It's pointless for me to try," he would change his self-statement to, "The odds are against me to succeed—on a scale of 0 to 10, my chances are a '2.'" Then, we would help Paul to expound on the hopeful and constructive things that comprise the "2," so that he does not quit, but rather applies some self-help skills.

A standard tool for doing rational responding is the *Daily Thought Record* (the *DTR*), in which clients practice recording key situations, emotions, automatic thoughts, constructive alternative thoughts, and outcomes. This technique requires practice and perseverance, so we would be willing to help Paul practice this in session. DTRs can be used to modify drug-related, dysfunctional thinking, as well as the problematic thoughts that are associated with dysphoria, anger, and other negative psychological reactions.

Although beyond the scope of this chapter, we would teach Paul the concepts of *problem-solving* (see Nezu, Nezu, & Perri, 1989). Other important techniques would focus on anticipating and recognizing *consequences* (e.g., the pros and cons of using and not using drugs, for now, and for the future, for Paul, and for his loved ones). We would teach Paul to utilize *relaxation and breathing control* in response to anger, anxiety, and drug urges. Additionally, in-session role-plays could be employed in order to help Paul with his communication and conflict-resolution skills. Any and all of the above can be used as part of therapy homework as well, though we are well aware that Paul's low self-efficacy and tendency to avoid would make this a hard sell. Still, we would gently persist.

*8. Are there special cautions to be observed in working with this patient (e.g., danger to self or others, transference, counter-transference)? Are there any particular resistances you would expect and how would you deal with them?*

As mentioned earlier, it may be hazardous to suggest that Paul go "cold turkey" from drugs and alcohol without medical supervision. We would be inclined to seek an outpatient medical consultation right at the start. Paul has already said that he would be disinclined to choose inpatient treatment, as he is afraid to jeopardize his job. We can empathize with this. On the other hand, it would important to weigh all options carefully before drawing any premature conclusions. For example, would Paul be allowed to take an unpaid leave? Would it be wise or realistic to suggest that Paul "wean" himself off his chemicals of choice, perhaps by eliminating the illicit drugs first, and working on the alcohol and Valium later? Would Paul agree to go the inpatient route if his substance use caused him to lose his job, and therefore there was no more job to preserve by insisting on outpatient treatment exclusively? These questions would have to be addressed.

We would expect Paul to be wary of us for some time, given that we are authority figures. However, we would not feel physically threatened by Paul, as his history of violent behavior is actually somewhat less extensive and serious than we might expect from a similar cohort of heavy drug users. Nevertheless, we would view him as a threat to his own family, given his history of domestic violence. Further, we would expect Paul to be a societal risk in terms of his tendency toward driving while impaired. Therefore, curbing Paul's actings-out toward his wife and his habit of drunk driving would be high priority issues very early in treatment. We would expect little resistance to the former problem, as this was the impetus for his seeking treatment at this time. However, we might encounter greater resistance to our focusing on the latter problem.

Paul is hypothesized to have an "incompetence" schema. Thus, as happened in earlier treatments, homework assignments could give rise to Paul's feelings of inadequacy. Perhaps we could encourage his cooperation with homework by doing predominantly nonwritten (i.e., no writing of prose) assignments and tasks at first. For example, he could agree to listen to a tape recording of the therapy session for "memory enhancement." In another vein, Paul could practice breathing control and relaxation techniques in response to his anger and drug cravings. Then, he could make numerical ratings of his levels of various emotional and physiological states. In addition, we could help Paul to generate mastery and pleasure activities, and encourage him to utilize these behaviors as alternatives to drinking and drugging. Under no circumstances would we shame him for failing to do his therapy homework. Instead, we would emphasize how homework could help Paul gain *more control* over his life, and empower him.

It is also important to anticipate a problem that is common with clients who have problems with addictions—namely, underreporting and lying. We cannot simply believe him when he says that he has been "clean" this week, if his concomitant attitudes and behaviors are not congruent. At the same time, it is unwise to harangue him as if he were on trial or in a confrontation group in a locked inpatient ward. We would have to show that our doubts are based on the knowledge that overcoming addictions is extremely hard work. Therefore, if progress seems too easy to be true, then something is amiss, and we must aim to help him get to the bottom of things. (See Beck et al., 1993 for a sampling of gentle, respectful ways to say the equivalent of, "I think you're lying".)

*9. Are there any areas you would choose to avoid or not address with this patient? Why?*

It would be tempting to avoid any number of problem areas, including Paul's domestic violence, his drunk driving, his unknown HIV (and other STDs) status, and exactly where he is getting his Valium. By avoiding these areas, therapists can delude themselves into thinking that it is neither their concern nor their responsibility. On the contrary, we cannot deliberately avoid any topic just to lighten our load. If we did, it would simply make it easier for Paul to continue to avoid things himself, and we would be "easy marks," not to mention less-than-stellar role-models for facing problems.

What we have to do is take care about the *manner* in which we bring these topics to the fore. It must be done respectfully and with somber concern, not with a judgmental tone. Periodically, we would ask Paul for feedback, to ascertain his thoughts and feelings about our comments. If Paul were to misconstrue our intent as flaunting our superiority, or authority, we would gently try to set him straight.

We would not avoid a topic of importance. This includes an inquiry into his HIV status. While it may seem that a past case of hepatitis was the extent of his STDs, we would strongly encourage a blood test just to be sure. In the meantime, we would have a serious discussion about the pros and cons of Paul's having sex with his ex-wife (we surmise that she is prone to submitting to his persuasions, and therefore is at risk in multiple ways).

*10. Is medication warranted for this patient? What effect would you hope or expect the medication to have?*

Although we would not rule out pharmacotherapy altogether, forever, we would be disinclined to recommend medication for this patient on an outpatient basis at this time. As an outpatient, Paul's use of medication would be largely unsupervised, and he does not seem to have the organizational, attentional, and motivational wherewithal to take medication as prescribed. Additionally, as long as Paul is still heavily into alcohol, and polysubstance use, introducing new chemicals into his body is a set-up for potentially harmful interactions. If we weigh the risks and benefits of medications for Paul, it is clear to us that the risks are significantly greater.

We are always in favor of the consideration of antidepressant medication when clients are deeply depressed, and perhaps suicidal. However, even when such clients are not abusing substances, the pros and cons of prescribing medication must be considered very carefully. In fact, it is standard practice to prescribe minimal amounts of medication to depressed clients, so as to reduce the risk of deliberate overdose. If we consider the fact that Paul already abuses other substances, the risk of overdose is increased. In order to treat Paul's depression with medication, we would argue that an inpatient venue would be most appropriate to start such a regimen.

Currently, Paul is abusing Valium. This is bad news, because such benzodiazepines serve to disinhibit people. This can only exacerbate his impulsivity. We would want to know how he got hold of the Valium. Did Paul stockpile it from a previous prescription? Is it a *current* prescription from an unsuspecting general practitioner (with whom we would want to communicate, given the proper release of confidentiality)? Is Paul bumming them off his ex-wife, or someone else? If he is using the Valium for sleep, we would try to convince him instead to use the breathing and relaxation techniques. If he using it for withdrawal symptoms, then there is even more evidence that he needs inpatient, medical supervision.

Having spelled out our concerns above, we should add that there are some medications we could consider (again, weighing the risks and benefits very carefully). For example, Antabuse could help Paul avoid alcohol, though it would require careful compliance from Paul in order to ensure nondangerous effectiveness. Further, there is some evidence that naltrexone can be used to "deaden" the effects of cocaine, in a similar fashion to opiates. If and when Paul has a period of sobriety, a trial of an anticonvulsant medication, such as Tegretol, may be indicated, as such agents have been used to curb anger outbursts that have a seizurelike quality. However, to reiterate, the use of pharmacotherapy seems very risky in Paul's *current* state.

*11. What are the strengths of the patient that can be used in the therapy?*

Paul has voluntarily sought treatment from us and admitted a problem, which is a positive sign. Paul's history of treatment has shown that he has gradually learned how to speak about himself and to engage more fully in the process of therapy. Paul has experienced some periods of time when he has been free of illicit substances (with a little less success in staying free of alcohol), and therefore we can ask him to draw from those times, to determine what tactics he utilized to help himself.

Paul seems to have the capacity for empathy, as demonstrated by his reaction of horror upon seeing the "look in his children's faces" when he hit their mother. If his MMPI is any indication, Paul does not suffer from underlying character pathology, thus offering hope that a period of abstinence could lead to marked improvements in behavior. As a case in point that hits very close to home, Paul's father has demonstrated the sort of positive metamorphosis that can occur if drugs and alcohol are out of the picture.

Paul is a skilled worker who seems to have what it takes to have a successful career in construction, provided that he is not impaired. He also enjoys activities such as fishing, which could potentially provide Paul with long periods of natural relaxation and stress-avoidance—but again, with the proviso that he is not using the time on the lake to get smashed or high.

*12. How would you address limits, boundaries, and limit-setting with this patient?*

Typically, we use the last 10–15 minutes of the first therapy session to talk about the "ground rules" for therapy, including legal issues, such as the limits of confidentiality. In order to facilitate good will, we would emphasize the therapist's responsibilities, such as returning daytime phone calls in a prompt fashion, having a back-up therapist (or other guidelines) for after-hours emergencies, working collaboratively with other professionals on the case, and treating the client as a unique individual, among others.

Then, we spell out some of the client's responsibilities, such as: (1) attending sessions as scheduled, on time, and in a sober state; (2) discussing disagreements with the therapist in a civil manner; (3) making a good faith effort to learn and practice the self-help techniques (i.e., homework); (4) giving accurate reports of what occurred between sessions (including drug use, acts of violence, and sexual behavior); and (5) agreeing to work toward personal change.

We would calmly state that we expect therapy to be hard work, but to be worthwhile for all parties. Our philosophy would be that all problems can be solved if there is cooperation between therapist and client. However, for the record, we would tell Paul that we would not proceed with a session if there were evidence that he was drunk or stoned. Further, under the above circumstances, we would expect him to find a way to get home *other* than driving himself.

As we would not expect Paul to physically lash out at the therapist, we would not focus on this potential situation as a matter of routine. However, if during the course of treatment Paul should demonstrate signs of marked anger toward the therapist, he would be told that threats of physical harm would lead to the cessation of treatment.

We do not expect that Paul would be the sort of client who would attempt to contact the therapist excessively between sessions, or the type of individual who would try to make the therapist into a personal friend. If anything, it is likely that Paul would be somewhat disengaged and avoidant, rather than overinvested and dependent. Still, we could note that while it is the role of the therapist to teach Paul the skills of self-help, it may be more the province of his 12-step sponsor and cohorts to address his everyday struggles with drug urges. Therefore, we would instruct Paul to attend 12-step meetings every day.

Perhaps the most troublesome issue regarding boundaries and limits that we believe is likely to occur has to do with "special favors." For example, Paul may want the therapist to write a letter that "excuses" him from work for reasons that are not entirely legitimate. Similarly, Paul may request that the therapist help him to convince his ex-wife to stay with him. Under such conditions, therapists have to have the courage to express their true clinical impressions, and to stand firm in the face of the client's attempts to cajole, guilt-trip, or intimidate. To give in to the client's demands in such cases is to set up a pattern whereby the client will use the therapist to do his bidding. It is far preferable to have a client abruptly terminate from therapy in a huff than to become the instrument of the client's manipulations.

*13. Would you want to involve significant others in the treatment? Would you use out-of-session work (homework) with this patient? What homework would you use?*

Whenever safe, and feasible, it is a good idea to involve the client's family and/or significant others in treatment. Such adjunct participants serve as "reality checks" regarding the client's self-report, as well as the client's chief source of all-important social support.

However, involving Paul's ex-wife or father—arguably the two most relevant of the cast of characters of his life—may *not* be safe practice.

Although Paul and his ex-wife are living together, there is no guarantee that the ex-wife is doing this out of a sense of free will. Many women have stayed with abusive partners out of fear that their lives would be in *greater* danger if they terminated their relationships.

There is some evidence that Paul is able to manipulate his ex-wife into staying in the relationship. By seeing them in session together, we run the risk of giving tacit legitimacy to Paul's having wheedled his way back into her life. On the other hand, it may provide us with the only window of opportunity for intervention into the problem of the violence in the relationship. This is a thorny dilemma! Perhaps we can learn more about the pros and cons of involving the ex-wife as therapy progresses. At the start of treatment, we may just leave her out of it.

It is also tricky as to whether we should involve Paul's father, assuming that the father would agree to participate (which is not at all certain). This is an emotionally loaded relationship, given the history of physical and emotional abuse perpetrated by the father. Nevertheless, ironically, the father may now be a good role-model for recovery, and a symbol of hope. If Paul were to see the rationale for involving his father in some sessions, and formulated a constructive agenda for those sessions, we would be inclined to offer the father an invitation to attend. This would probably occur *after* Paul had spent a few months learning a full range of cognitive therapy self-help skills.

The homework would be an important vehicle by which to teach Paul these all-important coping skills. As we have described earlier, we would encourage Paul to engage in self-monitoring, schedule activities that contribute to a sense of mastery and sober pleasure, utilize breathing control and relaxation, apply delay and distraction techniques, listen to audiotapes of the therapy sessions, and so on. We would expect Paul to be less than thrilled with the homework, but we would continue to assign it, explaining respectfully that we would want assignments "to be there for you when you decide that you will give them a shot."

*14. What would be the issues to be addressed in termination? How would termination and relapse prevention be structured?*

Termination should not take place abruptly, though we may have no say in the matter if Paul decides to drop out. In the past, this was a common mistake that Paul made, invariably setting himself up for a relapse because he was not skilled and well-practiced enough to be independent of treatment. Therefore, one of the most important tasks of the therapist is to spot early warning signs that Paul is losing interest in pursuing further sessions.

Perhaps we could ask Paul at the conclusion of each appointment what he believed he learned from the session, and what suggestions he would make for improving the level of helpfulness of the treatment. If Paul were to begin to cancel or miss appointments, it would be vital to contact him as soon as possible to address his misgivings about therapy. These strategies do not guarantee that Paul would stay for a full course of treatment, but they would increase the probability.

Assuming that Paul commits to treatment, we would eventually suggest that the frequency of sessions gradually be decreased. While he goes through this process of "weaning off" of therapy, he should continue to go to 12-step group meetings every day, as he has a history of ceasing to "work his program." As Paul's sessions with us switched toward a "booster" format, the increased periods of time between sessions would be conceptualized as natural behavioral experiments in dealing with the threats to his sobriety. However, we would emphasize that Paul should not try to "test" his sobriety. There are more than enough inevitable high-risk stimuli to contend with as part of everyday life without going to the extreme of *contriving* risks.

We would have no objections to Paul coming to see us for booster sessions, perhaps every three months, over the course of two or more years. Sobriety is a long-term issue, therefore, longitudinal follow-up treatment is highly desirable. We do not construe this as encouraging dependency on therapy. Rather, it is a prudent way in which to turn over most of the responsibility for maintenance over to Paul, while being available to give assistance in the future should the need arise.

*15. What do you see as the hoped-for mechanisms of change for this patient, in order of importance?*

Assigning an *order* of importance is very difficult, as the following factors interact and do not remain static over time. Therefore, we want to address as many of these factors as possible, so as to cover many bases, and produce positive feedback loops where vicious cycles once existed.

Many of the following mechanisms of change are common to all clients who seek treatment for substance. However, some are idiosyncratic to Paul, and the order of importance reflects this individualized approach to his treatment.

a. Increase Paul's sense of hope.
b. Help Paul reconceptualize his views of what effective treatment involves, including the learning of new skills, practicing those skills, and remaining committed to "working his program" for the long run.
c. Increase Paul's awareness of his internal dialogue, including his beliefs about drugs per se, his use of the drugs, and his core beliefs (schemas) about himself, his life, and his future. We would familiarize Paul with the seven-box model.

d. Paul would experience an increase in self-efficacy as a period of abstinence lengthened, and as he engaged in more activities that gave him a sense of accomplishment, or mastery.

e. Social support systems would strengthen, starting with the therapeutic relationship, and 12-step fellowship, and extending to family, co-workers, and everyday acquaintances in the world of functioning individuals.

f. Paul would begin to use his time more effectively, and thus would gain a better sense of purpose in life, as well as more sources of natural, positive reinforcement.

g. Paul would experience a reduction in physiological cravings for alcohol and drugs as his period of abstinence lengthened, thus leading to greater hope and a better sense of personal control.

h. Paul could gain the opportunity to explore some unresolved issues with his father, and may be able to make peace with losing his marriage. A solidly "recovered" addict does not need his sobriety to be a means to an end, such as winning back his wife. Sobriety is an end in itself, in that self-respect, with all of its psychological benefits, can emerge.

## REFERENCES

American Psychiatric Association. (1994). *Diagnostic and Statistical Manual of Mental Disorders* (4th Edition). Washington, D.C.: Author.

Beck, A. T. (1976). Cognitive therapy and the emotional disorders. New York: International Universities Press.

Beck, A. T., Kovacs, M., & Weissman, A. (1979). Assessment of suicidal intention: The Scale for Suicide Ideation. *Journal of Consulting and Clinical Psychology, 47*(2), 343–352.

Beck, A. T., Ward, C. H., Mendelson, M., Mock, J., & Erbaugh, J. (1961). An inventory for measuring depression. *Archives of General Psychiatry, 4,* 561–571.

Beck, A. T., Weissman, A., Lester, D., & Trexler, L. (1974). The measurement of pessimism: The hopelessness scale. *Journal of Consulting and Clinical Psychology, 42*(6), 861–865.

Beck, A. T., Wright, F. D., Newman, C. F., & Liese, B. S. (1993). *Cognitive therapy of substance abuse.* New York: Guilford Press.

First, M. D., Spitzer, R. L., Gibbon, M., & Williams, J. B. W. (1994). *Structured Clinical Interview for Axis-I DSM-IV Disorders.* Patient Edition (SCID-I/P, version 2.0). Biometrics Research Department, New York State Psychiatric Institute.

First, M. D., Spitzer, R. L., Gibbon, M., Williams, J. B. W., & Benjamin, L. (1994). *Structured Clinical Interview for DSM-IV Axis-II Personality Disorders* (SCID-II, version 2.0). Biometrics Research Department, New York State Psychiatric Institute.

Marlatt, G. A., & Gordon, J. R. (Eds.). (1985). *Relapse prevention: Maintenance strategies in the treatment of addictive behaviors.* New York: Guilford Press.

Nezu, A. M., Nezu, C. M., & Perri, M. G. (1989). *Problem-solving therapy for depression: Theory, research, and clinical guidelines.* New York: Wiley.

Prochaska, J. O., DiClemente, C. C., & Norcross, J. C. (1992). In search of how people change: Applications to addictive behaviors. *American Psychologist, 47,* 1102–1114.

# Chapter 6 Appendix*

- **Beliefs About Substance Use**
- **Craving Belief Questionnaire**
- **Relapse Prediction Scale**

* These forms were developed by Fred D. Wright, and appeared in Beck, Wright, Newman, & Liese, *Cognitive Therapy of Substance Abuse*. Copyright 1993 Guilford Publications. Reprinted with permission.

Name _____ Date: _____

## BELIEFS ABOUT SUBSTANCE USE (Wright)

Listed below are some common beliefs about drug use. Please read each statement and rate how much you agree or disagree with each one.

| 1 | 2 | 3 | 4 | 5 | 6 | 7 |
|---|---|---|---|---|---|---|
| Totally Disagree | Disagree Very Much | Disagree Slightly | Neutral | Agree Slightly | Agree Very Much | Totally Agree |

_____  1. Life without using is boring.

_____  2. Using is the only way to increase my creativity and productivity.

_____  3. I can't function without it.

_____  4. This is the only way to cope with pain in my life.

_____  5. I'm not ready to stop using.

_____  6. The urges/cravings make me use.

_____  7. My life won't get any better, even if I stop using.

_____  8. The only way to deal with my anger is by using.

_____  9. Life would be depressing if I stopped.

_____ 10. I don't deserve to recover from drug use.

_____ 11. I'm not a strong enough person to stop.

_____ 12. I could not be social without using.

_____ 13. Substance use is not a problem for me.

_____ 14. The urges/cravings won't go away unless I use drugs.

_____ 15. My substance use is caused by someone else (e.g., spouse, boyfriend/girlfriend, family member, etc.).

_____ 16. If someone has a problem with this, it's all genetic.

_____ 17. I can't relax without it.

_____ 18. Having this drug problem means there is something wrong with me.

_____ 19. I can't control my anxiety without using drugs.

_____ 20. I can't make my life fun unless I use.

Name _____ Date: _____

## CRAVING BELIEF QUESTIONNAIRE - CQ (Wright)

Please read the statements below and rate how much you agree or disagree with each one.

| 1 | 2 | 3 | 4 | 5 | 6 | 7 |
|---|---|---|---|---|---|---|
| Totally Disagree | Disagree Very Much | Disagree Slightly | Neutral | Agree Slightly | Agree Very Much | Totally Agree |

_____ 1. The craving is totally out of my control.

_____ 2. The craving is a physical reaction, therefore, I can't do anything about it.

_____ 3. If I don't stop the cravings they will get worse.

_____ 4. Craving can drive you crazy.

_____ 5. The craving makes me use cocaine.

_____ 6. I'll always have cravings for cocaine.

_____ 7. I don't have any control over the craving.

_____ 8. Once the craving starts I have no control over my behavior.

_____ 9. I'll have cravings for cocaine the rest of my life.

_____ 10. I can't stand the physical symptoms I have while craving cocaine.

_____ 11. The craving is my punishment for using cocaine.

_____ 12. If you have never used cocaine then you have no idea what the craving is like.

_____ 13. Since the craving is out of my control I should just sit and wait for it to go away.

_____ 14. The images/thoughts I have while craving cocaine are out of my control.

_____ 15. You can go insane from the craving.

_____ 16. The craving can make me lose control.

_____ 17. I do not have control over the causes of craving.

_____ 18. The craving makes me so nervous I can't stand it.

_____ 19. I'll never be prepared to handle the craving.

_____ 20. Since I'll have the craving the rest of my life I might as well go ahead and use cocaine.

_____    21. When I'm really craving cocaine I can't function.
_____    22. Either I'm craving cocaine or I'm not; there is nothing in between.
_____    23. There is no way to control the craving.
_____    24. If the craving gets too intense, cocaine is the only way to cope with the feeling.
_____    25. When craving cocaine it's O.K. to use alcohol to cope.
_____    26. I can't stand the panicky feeling when craving cocaine.
_____    27. The craving frightens me.
_____    28. The craving is stronger than my will power.

Name _____  Date: _____

## RELAPSE PREDICTION SCALE

As you know, there are many situations that can trigger an urge to use cocaine or crack. This scale has *two parts:* (1) to determine *how strong you think* the urges will be in certain situations and (2) what is the *likelihood that you will use* in these situations.

Listed below are several situations that might trigger strong urges to use cocaine or crack. Read each item and imagine yourself in that situation. In the first column, *Strength of Urges,* indicate how strong you think the urge will be. In the second column indicate the *Likelihood of Your Using* in these situations.

| 0 | 1 | 2 | 3 | 4 |
|---|---|---|---|---|
| None | Weak | Moderate | Strong | Very Strong |

|  | Prediction | |
|---|---|---|
|  | **Strength of Urges** | **Likelihood of Using** |
| 1. I am in a place where I used cocaine or crack before. | _____ | _____ |
| 2. Around people with whom I have previously used cocaine or crack. | _____ | _____ |
| 3. I just got paid. | _____ | _____ |
| 4. I see co-workers using. | _____ | _____ |
| 5. I am leaving work. | _____ | _____ |
| 6. It's Friday night. | _____ | _____ |
| 7. I am at a party. | _____ | _____ |
| 8. I am thinking of the last time I used. | _____ | _____ |
| 9. I start talking with someone about using. | _____ | _____ |
| 10. I feel bored. | _____ | _____ |
| 11. I feel great! | _____ | _____ |
| 12. I see a lover/ex-lover. | _____ | _____ |
| 13. I am having a drink. | _____ | _____ |
| 14. Best friend is offering some cocaine or crack. | _____ | _____ |
| 15. I feel sad. | _____ | _____ |
| 16. I see a prostitute. | _____ | _____ |

| 0 | 1 | 2 | 3 | 4 |
|---|---|---|---|---|
| None | Weak | Moderate | Strong | Very Strong |

|  | Prediction | |
|---|---|---|
|  | **Strength of Urges** | **Likelihood of Using** |
| 17. I am out looking for sex. | _____ | _____ |
| 18. I feel sexy. | _____ | _____ |
| 19. I remember how good the high feels. | _____ | _____ |
| 20. I feel angry. | _____ | _____ |
| 21. I feel stressed out. | _____ | _____ |
| 22. I feel guilty. | _____ | _____ |
| 23. I just used. | _____ | _____ |
| 24. I just broke my abstinence. | _____ | _____ |
| 25. I am getting ready for work. | _____ | _____ |
| 26. I am tired. | _____ | _____ |
| 27. I am frustrated. | _____ | _____ |
| 28. I see an anti-drug-use poster. | _____ | _____ |
| 29. I see a pipe. | _____ | _____ |
| 30. I am out gambling. | _____ | _____ |
| 31. I just had a "coke dream." | _____ | _____ |
| 32. I am watching sports. | _____ | _____ |
| 33. I am getting dressed up. | _____ | _____ |
| 34. I am under pressure at work. | _____ | _____ |
| 35. I am thinking about having sex. | _____ | _____ |
| 36. My spouse just made me angry. | _____ | _____ |
| 37. My spouse is bugging me about using. | _____ | _____ |
| 38. My parents are bugging me about using. | _____ | _____ |
| 39. I was just told I have a positive urine. | _____ | _____ |
| 40. I didn't use, yet my urine was positive. | _____ | _____ |
| 41. I am watching a drug-related movie. | _____ | _____ |
| 42. I feel anxious. | _____ | _____ |
| 43. Someone just criticized me. | _____ | _____ |
| 44. I haven't used for a long time. | _____ | _____ |
| 45. I feel tense. | _____ | _____ |
| 46. Someone I care for is terminally ill. | _____ | _____ |
| 47. I am in pain. | _____ | _____ |
| 48. I feel a burden on my shoulders. | _____ | _____ |
| 49. I am at a bar having a good time. | _____ | _____ |
| 50. I had a fight with my family. | _____ | _____ |

# 7

# Thinking Your Way Clean: Rational Emotive Behavior Therapy With a Poly-Substance Abuser

*Raymond DiGiuseppe and Jennifer Mascolo*

## I. TREATMENT MODEL

Albert Ellis, the creator of Rational-Emotive Behavior Therapy (REBT), has applied his model to the treatment of addictive behavior (DiGiuseppe & McInerny, 1990; Ellis, McInerny, DiGiuseppe & Yeager, 1988; Ellis & Veltan, 1992). Several videotaped sessions are available that demonstrate the use of this model with addicted clients (DiGiuseppe, 1996; 1997). Some research exists indicating that the irrational beliefs, proposed by this model to mediate psychopathology, differentiate addictive from normal samples (DiGiuseppe, Belser & Primavera, 1992). In addition, REBT has become the basis for a network of self-help groups to rival Alcoholics Anonymous. Although the literature on the REBT model of addictions has been increasing, there are only a few studies that exist demonstrating the efficacy of this model (Brian, 1985; Cox, 1979; Dana, 1985; Foley, 1977; Greven, 1986; Mathews-Larson, J., & Parker, 1987; Ray, Friedlander, & Solomon, 1984; Rosenberg & Brian, 1986).

REBT provides strategies to help clients learn to control dysfunctional *emotions*. REBT's trademark focuses on teaching people the **"ABC's"** of emotional disturbance. Namely, that Activating events elicit their Beliefs about those events which cause emotional Consequences. Clients are taught that disturbed emotional and behavioral Consequences result from the irrational Beliefs that individuals hold rather than from Activating events. The alleviation of emotional and/or behavioral disturbances, in this case, involves Paul's identifying that his emotions and behavior are disturbed, identifying his irrational Beliefs, recognizing that these irrational Beliefs are illogical, antiempirical, and maladaptive, and replacing his dysfunctional cognitions with more adaptive, rational Beliefs.

This model necessitates that clients first describe and acknowledge unhealthy negative feelings and self-defeating behaviors. After the therapist Socratically elicits Paul's acknowledgment that his drug addiction was a self-defeating behavior, Paul would be asked to identify specific activating events that occurred prior to experiencing disturbed feelings. REBT postulates that *demandingness* cognitions are the primary mediators of disturbances. These include "musts," "shoulds," "oughts," and "have to's." Such beliefs are dogmatic, rigid schema that the world must be a certain way because one desires that it be so. Therapists contrast these schema to rational beliefs such as preferences that describe how one wants the world to be but recognize that reality has no obligation to comply with one's desires. REBT postulates that most other disordered cognitions that mediate disturbance are derived from such demanding beliefs. The theory postulates that other cognitions also mediate disturbance including: *Global evaluations of human worth* which involve the belief that oneself or others are totally worthless and condemnable. The rational alternative belief maintains that human worth cannot be calculated and that all people have equal worth. Clients are taught to strive for U.S.A.— unconditional self-acceptance. *Frustration intolerance* involves the belief that one does not have the endurance to suffer frustration and that one should not have to experience frustration. REBT postulates that most humans can tolerate more than they believe they can. In fact, one's level of frustration tolerance is self-defined. *Awfulizing or catastrophizing* involves the exaggeration of harm or danger that can occur from an event. REBT proposes that the therapist teach clients to actively challenge and replace their irrational beliefs with more rational alternatives.

## II. WHAT WOULD YOU CONSIDER TO BE THE CLINICAL SKILLS OR ATTRIBUTES MOST ESSENTIAL TO SUCCESSFUL THERAPY IN YOUR APPROACH?

### Therapists' Skills

Dryden and DiGiuseppe (1992) have identified 13 steps in REBT sessions. They recommend that therapists new to the system follow these steps to avoid common mistakes and to perform all aspects of the model. Table 7.1 presents the 13 steps. The first step is to ask clients what problems they wish to discuss in the session. In the second step, the therapist and client establish agreement on the session goal. Clients often present entirely new issues unrelated to the topics discussed in previous sessions. Therapists may wish to continue with ongoing topics before switching to a new topic. As a result, agreement on the issues to cover in the session needs clarification before continuing. Also, clients often identify the goal as changing the "A" or activating event while therapists desire to change the "C" or emotional consequences. Because REBT recommends working on emotional problems first, the agreement on the goals aspect of the therapeutic alliance may break down.

Steps three, four and five involve assessing the "Cs," assessing the "As," and assessing for secondary emotional disturbance, respectively. At step six, therapists teach clients the "B->C" connection, the idea that emotional disturbance results from disordered ways of thinking.

In the next step (seven) therapists assess clients' irrational beliefs. Irrational beliefs involve tacit, unconscious, schematic cognitions. Clients, therefore, do not experience them in the stream of consciousness, although they are available to our consciousness. Most therapists ask clients, "What were you thinking when you got upset?" Such questions will elicit automatic thoughts, not irrational beliefs. DiGiuseppe (1991a) has suggested two primary strategies to uncover clients' irrational beliefs. **"Inference chaining"** is the most commonly used. Automatic thoughts are inferences that people draw from the perceptions they make, and which they are prepared to make by the irrational beliefs they hold. Follow the logic of the inferences and one uncovers the core irrational belief. Inference chaining involves a series of follow-up questions to the automatic thoughts clients experience in emotionally upsetting situations. Therapists ask clients to hypothesize that their automatic thoughts were true. If a thought were true, what would happen next, or what would it mean to her or him? Clients usually respond with other automatic thoughts. The therapist continues with the same type of question until an irrational belief, a "must," an "awfulizing" statement, an "I can't stand it," or a global evaluation is uncovered.

Not all clients can express their irrational beliefs in language because tacit, schematic cognitions are not stored in verbal memory. DiGiuseppe (1991a) suggested that therapists develop hypotheses about their clients' irrational beliefs. Rather than let clients struggle to become aware of their core irrational beliefs, therapists can offer hypotheses to clients. To do this effectively, and avoid one's own confirmatory bias, DiGiuseppe offers the following suggestions. Therapists will: a) state the hypothesis in suppositional language; b) ask clients for feedback on the correctness of

## TABLE 7.1    The Thirteen Steps of Rational
## Emotive Behavior Therapy

| | |
|---|---|
| Step 1: | Ask client for the problem. |
| Step 2: | Define and agree upon the Goals of Therapy |
| Step 3: | Assess the emotional and behavioral "C". |
| Step 4: | Assess the "A". |
| Step 5: | Assess the existence of any Secondary Emotional Problems. |
| Step 6: | Teach the **B->C** connection. |
| Step 7: | Assess the Irrational Beliefs. |
| Step 8: | Connect the Irrational Beliefs to the Disturbed Emotions and the Rational Beliefs to the Non disturbed Emotion. |
| Step 9: | Dispute Irrational Beliefs: Circle all that you have done: logical, empirical, heuristic, design new rational alternative beliefs, didactic, Socratic, metaphorical, humorous. |
| Step 10: | Prepare your client to deepen his/her conviction in the Rational Belief. |
| Step 11: | Encourage your client to put new learning into practice with homework. |
| Step 12: | Check homework assignments. |
| Step 13: | Facilitate the working through process. |

hypotheses; c) prepare to be wrong; and d) revise the hypotheses based on negative feedback from the client.

The next steps include linking the irrational beliefs with the client's emotional disturbance (eight), and beginning to dispute the irrational beliefs (nine). Disputing irrational beliefs is the most difficult task in REBT. DiGiuseppe (1991b) has presented a detailed explanation of the disputing process by dissecting many hours of Ellis's therapy videotapes. One can dispute an irrational belief by challenging its logic, by testing its empirical accuracy, and by evaluating its functional consequences. Also, therapists will propose alternative rational beliefs (RB) and challenge them with the same arguments to assess if the RB fares any better. DiGiuseppe (1991b) suggested that therapists vary the rhetorical style of their disputing. One can use didactic (direct teaching) strategies, Socratic strategies, metaphors, or humor. Kopec, Beal, and DiGiuseppe (1994) have created a grid with each cell representing a type of argument and a type of rhetorical style. They recommend that therapists identify an irrational belief and generate all of the disputing statements for each cell in the grid before each therapy session. Their data suggest that this activity increases trainees' self-efficacy in disputing. Another important component of disputing is the use of imagery. Therapists and clients can construct scenes of the client approaching the activating event, rehearsing the new rational coping statement, experiencing adaptive emotions, and behaving appropriately.

Step ten involves deepening clients' convictions in their rational beliefs. This is accomplished through continued disputing, by defining how they would behave differently if they actually held the new rational belief (step eleven), and agreeing to actual homework between sessions to achieve their goals (step twelve). Homework could include clients completing REBT self-help homework sheets that guide them through disputing an irrational belief. The rehearsal of imagery or a behavioral activity are often assigned. Homework compliance more often results when client and therapist negotiate the task together. In the final step, thirteen, therapists review other examples of activating events clients have been upset about to promote generalization.

## Therapists' Attributes

Ellis believes that the most important therapist characteristic for effective therapy is the therapist's intelligence (see epilogue in Dryden & DiGiuseppe, 1992). In addition, therapists had better pay close attention to clients' emotions, since clients' emotions lead to the relevant irrational beliefs. Therapists employing REBT had better feel comfortable with a structured, active, directive approach; yet they must flexible enough to work in a less structured manner when necessary. Ellis, McInerny, DiGiuseppe, and Yeager (1988) proposed that therapists working with addictive clients require a high level of frustration tolerance because such clients often leave therapy, progress slowly, and often relapse. Additionally, therapists had better not evaluate their own self-worth by client outcomes. Finally, REBT is a multimodal, integrative form of therapy that uses didactic, Socratic, imaginal, emotive, and behavioral techniques to change dysfunctional thinking, emotions, and behavior. As such, therapists had better feel comfortable employing different treatment modalities (Ellis & Dryden, 1997).

## III. QUESTIONS REGARDING THE CASE MATERIAL

*1. What would be your therapeutic goals for this patient? What are the primary goals and secondary goals?*

The addictions field festers with debate concerning the issues of treatment goals. AA and other 12-step programs require clients to commit to a goal of abstinence. Others propose that controlled abstinence represents a more reachable and acceptable goal. Peele (1989; 1998) has argued that people in treatment rarely if ever maintain abstinence. This goal discourages people from seeking treatment and prevents them from sharing information with their therapists for fear of being rebuked for not abiding to abstinence. Controlled use or harm reduction (Marlatt, Larimer, Baer, & Quigley, 1993) advocates that people will attempt to use less and less of their substance. Advocates of 12-step programs maintain that such a goal colludes with patients to continue their problem. REBT principles can be used to achieve abstinence or controlled use and we are aware of clinicians who successfully employ REBT in both types of programs. However, Ellis and Veltan (1992) have proposed that those who fail with the AA approach can respond to REBT. Also, the present authors are sympathetic to Peele's thinking. However, Ellis, McInerny, DiGiuseppe, and Yeager (1988) recommend that REBT therapists avoid a dogmatic position on this goal issue, a position consistent with the REBT philosophy. Clients will decide which goal to follow, and the therapists may develop a better rapport by following their lead. REBT would propose that forcing an abstinence goal on Paul could create reactance and failure. If we promoted (or demanded or cajoled) abstinence by Paul, he may fail to share his drugging experiences with us. Thus, he would deprive us of important information concerning the stimuli and thoughts that lead to lapses. If Paul chose the goal of controlled use we would monitor his progress. Continued failure with controlled use would lead to us recommending abstinence as a preferable goal.

The secondary goal involves Paul replacing dysfunctional negative emotions that lead to substance abuse with appropriate/adaptive negative emotions. For example, the inappropriate negative emotion of hurt/depression experienced by Paul (i.e., hurt) that stems from loneliness would be replaced with the appropriate emotion of disappointment. Specific episodes of loneliness occurred in Europe, and when Paul had time on his hands, and following his wife's second pregnancy. These led to substance abuse. He experienced depression over his father's criticism and rejection which led to depression and were followed by substance abuse. Paul often coped with depression by substance abuse in other instances as well.

There may be other emotional episodes that Paul experiences when he attempts to deny himself his drug of choice. We would assess his emotional state immediately preceding substance use when he uses and refrains from using to investigate further secondary goals.

*2. What further information would you want to have to assist you in structuring this patient's treatment? Are there specific assessment tools you would use (i.e., data to be collected)? What would be the rationale for using those tools?*

We would collect specific information on the frequency of drug-using episodes and the amount of substance used at each episode. This information would serve as a baseline. We would collect the same data at the beginning of each session to monitor progress. The most important information needed by the REBT model for treatment planning would be the thoughts Paul experiences **just prior** to his emotional episodes and **just prior** to substance use. We would ask him what thoughts he was experiencing at these times and then would employ the inference chaining strategy mentioned above. If this technique failed, we would generate several hypotheses concerning what he was thinking based on the material presented, clinical experience, and the theory.

Due to the fact that REBT theory postulates that drug addiction often involves low frustration tolerance, we might hypothesize that Paul believes that he cannot stand being upset and cannot cope with strong negative emotions. We would also hypothesize that he might think that he cannot stand **not using** his drug of choice. He may experience some emotion concerning deprivation of enjoyment that may be caused by frustration intolerance. To further help identify Paul's irrational beliefs we may have him collect logs of his thoughts in each emotional episode and each substance-using episode.

Additionally, the "payoffs" that Paul experiences when engaging in drug use would require careful assessment, because psychological problems are perpetuated by people focusing on the positive consequences of behavior and ignoring the disadvantages. In this case, Paul's fear of rejection, feelings of loneliness, and feeling criticized may motivate his drinking and drug abuse. However, we would determine if these feelings maintain the drug/alcohol abuse or if the drug/alcohol abuse is maintained by frustration intolerance or both.

The assessment tools reported in the case study are similar to those we would have chosen. We would choose some of them, along with the data on frequency and amount of alcohol and drug use, weekly or monthly, to assess and monitor our progress. Self-report scales that assess irrational beliefs would also be utilized to obtain additional information on which irrational beliefs Paul spontaneously endorses prior to the outset of his therapy. We would also create an idiosyncratic measure of the drug use scenario (Linscott & DiGiuseppe, 1998). Such a measure includes the activating events, irrational thoughts, emotions, and behavior, and the new alternative rational belief and new desired emotions and behaviors. Paul would complete 10 different likert scales on the scenario indicating his commitment to the beliefs. This would also help monitor progress. Table 7.2 presents the scenario-based measure we would collect weekly to monitor Paul's changes in his beliefs.

Enablers often interfere with a substance abuser's treatment. Thus, we would assess Paul's wife's attitude toward his substance use. If she unwittingly supports the problem, we would recommend therapy for her or bring her into family sessions. Additionally, we would identify any dysfunctional emotions that lead to her enabling and identify and challenge the irrational beliefs that may lead to such emotions.

Therapy Evaluation Form

Paul                                                  Session # _____
Date: _____

---

When other people criticize me or indicate in some way that they may not like
me I think to myself: "I need to be approved of by other people. I cannot stand to
have people dislike me. If other people especially my wife or friend dislike me or
disapprove of me, it means I have no worth as a person. I am a no one if others
do not like me. When I think this way, I feel depressed, and upset. I think that it
is easier to cope by having a drink or getting high. So I have a drink or get high
to make myself feel better.

---

1. How often has such a scenario occurred recently?

| 1 | 2 | 3 | 4 | 5 | 6 | 7 |
|---|---|---|---|---|---|---|
| not at all | | | | | | extremely |

2. How concerned have you been about this happening?

| 1 | 2 | 3 | 4 | 5 | 6 | 7 |
|---|---|---|---|---|---|---|
| not at all | | | | | | extremely |

3. How easily can you imagine such a scenario?

| 1 | 2 | 3 | 4 | 5 | 6 | 7 |
|---|---|---|---|---|---|---|
| not at all | | | | | | extremely |

4. How well does the scenario describe you and your relationship with others?

| 1 | 2 | 3 | 4 | 5 | 6 | 7 |
|---|---|---|---|---|---|---|
| not at all | | | | | | extremely |

5. How far back in your life can you recall this scenario occurring?

| 1 | 2 | 3 | 4 | 5 | 6 | 7 |
|---|---|---|---|---|---|---|
| not at all | | | | | | extremely |

6. How much do you think such beliefs help you or hurt you?

| 1 | 2 | 3 | 4 | 5 | 6 | 7 |
|---|---|---|---|---|---|---|
| Helps me | | | | | | Hurts me |

7. How much do you think these beliefs are rational or correct, or are they
irrational or incorrect?

| 1 | 2 | 3 | 4 | 5 | 6 | 7 |
|---|---|---|---|---|---|---|
| Rational & Correct | | | | | | Irrational & Incorrect |

---

An alternative way to think, feel, and act about this situation would be as follows:
"If other people, such as my wife or friends criticize me or disapprove of me for
some reason, I can handle it. I do not need them to approve of me and I can tolerate
other people criticizing me or disapproving of me. Other people's opinion of me
does not affect my worth as a person. I am a worthwhile person regardless of

## TABLE 7.2 (continued)

what others think of me. When I think this way I feel disappointed. I also think to myself that I can stand feeling uncomfortable and I do not need to have a drink or get high to feel better. I can talk myself out of a bad emotional experience. After thinking this way I try to talk to the other person to resolve the conflict.

8. How easily can you imagine the alternatives ways for you to feel and think in this scene?

|   | 1 | 2 | 3 | 4 | 5 | 6 | 7 |
|---|---|---|---|---|---|---|---|
| not at all | | | | | | | extremely |

9. How confident are you about your ability to act on these alternatives ways of thinking, feeling, and behaving?

|   | 1 | 2 | 3 | 4 | 5 | 6 | 7 |
|---|---|---|---|---|---|---|---|
| not at all | | | | | | | extremely |

10. How often have you acted on these alternative ways of thinking, feeling, and behaving in such a scene recently?

|   | 1 | 2 | 3 | 4 | 5 | 6 | 7 |
|---|---|---|---|---|---|---|---|
| not at all | | | | | | | extremely |

**Thank You**

---

*3. What is your conceptualization of this patient's personality, behavior, affective state, and cognitions?*

Paul could be conceptualized as having a dependent personality and possibly, dependent personality disorder. He strongly desires social acceptance and attention. Although many people desire social affiliation, Paul appears to desire it excessively and becomes disturbed or uses alcohol/drugs to cope with not having it. In his relationship with his co-workers, he said that he felt they "really accepted" him for the "first time" when they offered him a beer. Also, he felt upset when his wife had less time for him after the new child. Paul experiences depression and anxiety easily and often. He is emotionally labile and requires only minor hassles to elicit strong emotions. Also, Paul appears to endorse many irrational beliefs. Primarily, Paul believes that he "must not" be alone, he "must" be accepted by others, and he "must not" be criticized by anyone. He appears to condemn himself for lack of approval by others.

Additionally, Paul behaves impulsively with his drug abuse and his interactions with family and co-workers. This impulsivity is reflected in his scores on the NEO Personality Inventory (NEO-PI). This behavior may reflect low frustration tolerance, and or a demand that others do as he wants, when he wants it. He may condemn others for not complying with his wishes. Such beliefs may mediate his anger and aggressive behavior. It is uncertain what role his anger and hostility play in his alcohol/drug use. Clearly an angry/hostile response pattern has been learned in his family of origin. Although he appears to drink to cope with anxiety and depression, it is not apparent that he uses drugs or alcohol to escape his anger. Anger has cost him considerably in his present family. Beck (1976) points out that anger and depression are opposite emotions. Beck proposed that each emotion is elicited by separate cognitions and the cognitions that promote depression/hopelessness/worthlessness are the opposite of those that trigger anger. It appears that Paul has some unstable thoughts. Sometimes he believes his life is hopeless, and at other times he believes that he can control those around him. He believes he is worthless and at other times he believes he is efficacious and powerful and others are worthless. We would work on the problems of depression and anger separately and not assume that they are mediated by the same dynamics. Rather, we would work on his self-deprecation and his other-deprecation, his hopelessness and omnipotent demands that others do as he wants.

Presently, Paul suffers from what REBT calls symptom stress. He appears to become depressed about his poor behavior. This may involve an additional set of beliefs that lead to depression separate from those mentioned above. He may believe he is worthless for acting poorly. Such beliefs exacerbate a cycle of depression and would be targeted first (Walen, DiGiuseppe, & Dryden, 1992).

*4. What potential pitfalls would you envision in this therapy? What would the difficulties be and what would you envision to be the source(s) of the difficulties?*

Potential pitfalls to REBT involve relationship obstacles, therapist obstacles, and client obstacles. The first obstacle, relationship obstacles, primarily stem from a poor match between therapist and client. It would be important for Paul find a therapist who he believes he can work with. There are two types of therapist obstacles encountered: skill-oriented obstacles and disturbance obstacles. Skill-oriented obstacles include such things as: a) failing to clarify one's role with the client; b) spending time dealing with "problems" that clients do not have but were deemed to have due to inaccurate assessment; c) failing to show clients the true roots of their problems (i.e., ideological); d) expecting automatic change once irrational beliefs are identified; e) working at an inappropriate pace; and f) working only on primary problems and ignoring a client's preoccupation with a secondary problem. Disturbance-oriented obstacles include the therapists' irrational beliefs such as, "I have to be successful with my clients all of the time." The third obstacle to client progress involves the client themselves. Client obstacles include such things as: a) failing to dispute irrational beliefs *in vivo*; b) refusing to accept responsibility for unhealthy emotions; c) having low frustration tolerance about working at change; and d) failing to do "homework" assignments. In Paul's case, his difficulty attending therapy may reflect an inadequate commitment to change the target behaviors. In addition, his low level of agreeableness, coupled with his high levels of anger may pose some difficulty for Paul in terms of disputing his irrational beliefs and dealing with the therapist's confrontations. Paul's low levels of openness, as indicated by his NEO-PI scores, may also provide an obstacle.

5. *To what level of coping, adaptation, or function would you see this patient reaching as an immediate result of therapy? What result would be long-term subsequent to the ending of therapy (i.e., prognosis for adaptive change)?*

An immediate outcome of therapy would be Paul's stopping or using drugs and alcohol with less frequency. Attaining this goal would probably result in increased loneliness. This may result in his seeking unsavory company (drinking buddies) or making a poor choice of a mate. Predicting and preparing for these interim states would be an important step in therapy. We would help Paul tolerate being alone long enough to find a good mate and make friends with those who support his sobriety.

The long-term change would be Paul's having learned coping strategies to deal with emotions elicited by being alone, rejected, and criticized. This would allow him to function, in the face of such circumstances, in an adaptive manner and would prevent relapse.

6. *What would be your time line (duration) for therapy? What would be your frequency and duration of the sessions?*

Based on two large samples of over 700 patients each at the Albert Ellis Institute, we have found a mean of 11 sessions and a median of 7 sessions and a 25th quartile of 5 sessions. Given that addiction is a serious problem for Paul, and given the possible diagnosis of personality disorder and the large number of problems to be worked on we would expect at least 25 sessions with Paul before we could attain the goals mentioned above.

7. *Are there specific or special techniques that you would implement in the therapy? What would they be?*

Preferential REBT strategies (philosophical changes) would be the first technique utilized. Ellis and Dryden (1997) identified preferential REBT as interventions focused at the core philosophical beliefs. An elegant solution to the client's problem involves replacing a demanding philosophy with a preferential one. That is, recognizing that the world does not have to give one what one prefers. This strategy entails helping Paul to observe his own psychological disturbances and trace them back to their ideological, emotional, and behavioral roots. In utilizing this strategy, we would stress to Paul that he is not "enslaved" or controlled by his biologically based and learned dysfunctional thinking processes. This strategy employs cognitive, emotive, and behavioral methods. These methods are applied in a forceful and vigorous manner. The forceful nature of REBT may be especially important in Paul's case because of his history of denying that a problem exists. Although Paul's self-referral would work as a strength in this process, his past denial of problems appears to be more reflective of his response pattern than his more recent admission.

Additionally, a technique known as Cognitive-DIBS would also be employed. This technique involves detecting irrational beliefs, debating irrational beliefs by asking for "proof" or "evidence," and discriminating between nonabsolute values and absolutistic values held by the client. Because preferential REBT techniques do not work for every patient, Paul may not achieve a philosophical change. If it appears that a philosophical change will not occur, the techniques of general REBT would be utilized. These techniques would work to challenge Paul's inferential or automatic thoughts.

*8. Are there special cautions to be observed in working with this patient (e.g., danger to self or others, transference, counter-transference)? Are there any particular resistances you would expect and how would you deal with them?*

No danger to self is apparent. However, Paul has a history of aggression, and under the influence of alcohol and other substances, Paul's potential for violence may increase. In addition, his trait anger scores and his style of expressing anger openly (97th percentile and 99th percentile, respectively) indicate that he is highly likely to express his anger through physical violence. This style of coping with anger is evident in two separate incidents he reported involving his wife. The first occasion of violence involved his wife alone, whereas on the second occasion Paul behaved abusively in front of his children. This latter episode suggests Paul may need to be away from his family for some time. A risk of violence may also occur when Paul makes sufficient progress to stops using drugs and alcohol, but has not yet learned to control his reactions to rejection and criticism. At this stage of therapy, we would be sure to include some anger-coping strategies and possibly some environmental supports. These would included reliance on supportive people, spending time away from his family, and more frequent attendance at AA groups or therapy. In addition, Paul's dependent behavior may present some risks when he initially stops drinking. Specifically, he may initiate some romantic or sexual relationships to escape his fear of being alone.

Because Paul reacts negatively to criticism, he may experience the disputing strategies of REBT as disapproval, which could negatively effect the therapeutic alliance. We would carefully challenge Paul's dysfunctional thoughts to avoid any perception on his part that we were critical of him as a person. More reliance on Socratic dialogue would also be helpful.

*9. Are there any areas that you would choose to avoid or not address with this patient? Why?*

People with addiction often provide external reasons for their substance use. Because Paul has a history of alcoholism in his family, was mistreated by his father, was misunderstood by his wife, and so forth, there is the possibility that he will point to these events as partially responsible for his current addiction. Getting stuck on "blaming" others for his addiction would be avoided. Thus, we would be on guard for any possible diversions that Paul might bring up to justify his drug use or avoid talking about it.

*10. Is medication warranted for this patient? What effect would you hope or expect this medication to have?*

No. In the past, Paul attributed medication as the mechanism for change (e.g., he felt Antabuse helped him not take his first drink), not attributing change to his own efforts. Furthermore, due to the fact that Paul has a drug problem, he runs the risk of becoming addicted to the substance. The possibility of a psychological dependency, rather than a physical addiction, warrants a concern. If we found no change in his behavior in 10 to 15 sessions we might reconsider our case formulation. Other possible formulations may include a biological impulsivity disorder or an anger problem. Referral for medication might then be appropriate.

*11. What are the strengths of the patient that can be used in the therapy?*

The fact that Paul is self-referred can be drawn on in therapy. Paul was previously court mandated to attend AA meetings or "pressured" into treatment by family members. The fact that he took the step to come to therapy without a mandate or family pressure suggests that he may be seeking treatment for his own discomfort, rather than to simply reduce the pressure from others. His self-referral suggests that he is in a "contemplative" or readiness stage of change. Many substance abusers are coerced into treatment, and do not wish to change. Paul's perception that change is desirable can be used when progress is slow or resistances occur. At such times we would ask Paul to remember the reasons why he entered therapy.

Paul's recognition of his children's fear of him during his last violent episode provides a further strength that can be utilized in treatments. Again, during periods of resistance we would ask Paul to focus on the consequences of not moving on in treatment and how relapse or regression may effect his relationship with his children. Finally, his dependence on others and his desire to please others may lead Paul to seek approval from, and please, his therapist. The therapist may be able to use this dependency to get Paul to complete his "homework" assignments and follow through on treatment goals.

12. *How would you address limits, boundaries, and limit-setting with this patient?*

We would set the limit of refusing to see Paul if he was high or drunk at a session. Additionally, an agenda and goal would need to be set for each session. If Paul strayed from the goal or agenda, the therapist would point it out to him and attempt to refocus him. We would also monitor compliance with homework and might set limits if Paul lapsed into non-compliance with homework. We would **not** set limits on his substance or drug use outside of therapy. Such a common proscription in the addiction field would lead to a) expecting Paul to improve his problem before treatment; and b) encouraging him to lie to us about this behavior. This would deprive us of important information.

13. *Would you want to involve significant others in the treatment? Would you use out-of-session work (homework) with this patient? What homework would you use?*

Paul's wife may enable him to continue using drugs and alcohol. We may invite her to some sessions to discuss her "enabling" issues. Primarily, her allowing Paul to be immediately gratified (i.e., allowed him to move immediately back into the home after rehabilitation) needs to be addressed. Finally, there may be some indication that the children should be involved in at least one session to allow Paul to hear from them how his substance abuse and violent behavior has impacted on them. Because effective therapy requires an optimal level of arousal for the client, involving his wife and children may provide an awareness of the destructive nature of his addiction and may serve to strengthen his "alleged" awareness of the consequences of his substance abuse on others. This would increase motivation for change.

Out-of-session homework would definitely be used with Paul. First we would assign Paul some bibliotherapy. Self-help books on addiction would be recommended (e.g., Ellis & Veltan, 1992). Next, we would teach Paul to use REBT self-help forms and ask him to complete them after emotionally upsetting events. We would ask Paul to set goals for diminishing his drug and alcohol use and then ask him to reach the goals. Because Paul gets angry at criticism, we would construct imagery assignments. We would first construct rational coping statements. Then we would ask him to imagine anger-provoking events with himself thinking the new rational coping statements, and being annoyed or displeased rather than angry. At a late stage in therapy we would ask Paul to be alone for a weekend or perhaps longer, to not drink or use drugs, and practice the emotional control skills we had worked on to that date so as to not feel upset. Finally, to deal with his issues surrounding criticism, homework may involve having him talk to people who used to criticize him and listen to their criticisms without responding in a verbally or physically aggressive manner.

*14. What would be the issues to be addressed in termination? How would termination and relapse prevention be structured?*

First and foremost, Paul's ability to use relapse prevention skills so that he can cope with any possible lapses to his sobriety would need to be achieved before termination could be considered. Relapse prevention strategies include teaching Paul that everyone has setbacks and that there will be times when he desires to drink or use drugs. However, there are techniques that will have helped him in therapy and these can be used during these setbacks. Paul could remind himself to pinpoint what thoughts, feelings, and behaviors he once changed to bring about his improvement. He could think back to how he previously used REBT to make himself undepressed and not angry. He can rehearse rational beliefs or coping statements, uncovering and challenging irrational beliefs, confront irrational fears by doing and risking things he is normally afraid of (e.g., in Paul's case his fear of being alone).

Termination would approached by fading the frequency of the sessions. Weekly, biweekly, and monthly frequencies would be used. Additionally, the therapist could help Paul anticipate future problems and imagine how he would successfully handle those problems using his newly learned REBT skills. Termination would require that Paul could solve emotional problems he may encounter in the future. His ability to cope with rejection, loneliness, and criticism without getting high would be a required skill. This skill would be assessed by presenting Paul with hypothetical situations similar to ones which had upset him in the past. For each situation, we would ask him how he would dispute the irrational beliefs, what new rational beliefs he could construct to cope with the situation, and how he would behave.

Within the last few sessions, the therapist would focus on reiterating major points that had been discussed throughout the therapy. Finally, the therapist would schedule follow-up sessions to monitor Paul's progress.

*15. What do you see as the hoped-for mechanisms of change for this patient, in order of importance?*

Specifically, Paul would develop consequential thinking skills to assess the negative consequences of his substance use and generate and utilize such skills whenever in the presence of stimuli that previously elicited drinking and/or drug use. Additionally, Paul would learn to generate alternative solutions that would enable him to cope with emotionally upsetting situations in a manner different from drinking and drug using. Finally, Paul would learn to control upsetting situations by identifying his beliefs, challenging his beliefs, and replacing them with more adaptive beliefs, especially when he is faced with social rejection, disapproval, and criticism. It is hoped that Paul's new skills would help him to internalize a broad range of rational beliefs so that they become a part of a general philosophy of rational living.

## REFERENCES

Beck, A. T. (1976). *Cognitive therapy and the emotional disorders*. New York: International Universities Press.

Brian, T. J. (1985). Ego stage and psychologically-oriented treatments of incipient alcohol abuse. *Dissertation Abstracts International, 45*, 2302–2303.

Cox, S. G. (1979). Rational behavior training as a rehabilitative program for alcoholic offenders. *Offender Rehabilitation, 3*, 245–256.

Dana, R. O. (1985). Pretreatment assertion levels as they relate to treatment outcome in an alcohol abusing sample. *Dissertation Abstracts International, 46*, 956.

DiGiuseppe, R. (1991a). A rational-emotive model of assessment. In M. E. Bernard (Ed.), *Using rational emotive therapy effectively* (151–172). New York: Plenum.

DiGiuseppe, R. (1991b). Comprehensive disputing in rational-emotive therapy. In M. E. Bernard (Ed.), *Using rational emotive therapy effectively* (pp. 173–195). New York: Plenum.

DiGiuseppe, R. (Ed.) (1996). *Coping with addiction*. Therapist: Albert Ellis. New York: Institute for Rational Emotive Therapy.

DiGiuseppe, R. (Ed.) (1997). *Anger management with a recovering female addict*. Video demonstration of a psychotherapy session, Dr. Janet Wolfe therapist. New York: The Albert Ellis Institute.

DiGiuseppe, R., & McInerny, J. (1990). Rational emotive models of addiction. *Journal of Cognitive Psychotherapies: An International Quarterly, 4*(2), 121–134.

DiGiuseppe, R., Belser, D., & Primavera, L. (1992, Aug.). Rational emotive models of addiction: Which beliefs to target in intervention. Paper presented as part of the symposium "Addiction interventions: Alternatives to the 12 step model." Presented at the 100th annual convention of the American Psychological Association, Washington, D.C.

Dryden, W., & DiGiuseppe, R. (1990). *A rational emotive therapy primer*. Champaign, IL: Research Press.

Ellis, A., & Dryden, W. (1997). *The practice of rational emotive behavior therapy* (2nd ed.). New York: Springer.

Ellis, A., McInerny, J., DiGiuseppe, R., & Yeager, R. (1988). *Rational emotive therapy with alcoholics and substance abusers*. New York: Pergamon.

Ellis, A., & Veltan, E. (1992). *When AA does not work for you: Rational steps to quitting alcohol.* New York: Barricade Books.

Foley, J. D. (1977). Rational-emotive therapy compared with a representative institutional treatment program on the self-concept of male alcoholics. *Dissertation Abstracts International, 37*(9-A), 5607.

Greven, G. L. (1986). Effects of a rational emotive therapy program on the irrational beliefs of inpatient alcoholics. *Dissertation Abstracts International, 47,* 2166.

Linscott, J., & DiGiuseppe, R. (1998). Cognitive assessment. In A. S. Bellack & M. Hersen (Eds.), *Behavioral assessment: A practical handbook* (pp. 104–125). Boston: Allyn and Bacon.

Marlatt, A., Larimer, M., Baer, J., & Quigley, L. (1993). Harm reduction for alcohol problems: Moving beyond the controlled drinking controversy. *Behavior Therapy, 24*(4), 461–503.

Mathews-Larson, J., & Parker, R. A. (1987). Alcoholism treatment with bio-chemical restoration as a major component. *International Journal of Biosocial Research, 2,* 92–104.

Peele, S. (1989). Ain't misbehavin: Addiction has become an all-purpose excuse, *The Sciences, 29,* 14–21.

Peele, S. (1998). All wet: The gospel of abstinence and twelve-step, studies show, is leading American alcoholics astray. *The Sciences, 38,* 17–21.

Ray, J. B., Friedlander, R. B., & Solomon, G. S. (1984). Changes in rational beliefs among treated alcoholics. *Psychological Reports, 55,* 883–886.

Rosenberg, H., & Brian, T. (1986). Cognitive behavioral group therapy for multiple-DUI offenders. Special Issue: Drink Driving in America: Strategies and Approaches to Treatment. *Alcoholism Treatment Quarterly, 3,* 47–65.

Walen, S., DiGiuseppe, R., & Dryden, W. (1992). *Practitioner's guide to rational-emotive therapy* (2nd ed.). New York: Oxford.

# 8

## Client-Centered and Holistic Approach for Older Persons With Addiction Problems

### Kathryn Graham and Jane Baron

### I. THE TREATMENT MODEL

This approach to treatment was developed in two cities in Ontario, Canada in the early 1980s almost simultaneously and mostly independently. It was designed to meet the special needs of older persons who had problems related to their use of alcohol and psychoactive medications. There were a number of reasons why traditional approaches were not considered adequate or appropriate for older persons, including special needs of some older persons that precluded participation in many treatment programs (e.g., mobility problems, hearing problems), cultural and generational differences between older persons and their younger counterparts in treatment in terms of types of problems and drugs of abuse (Graham, Brett, & Baron, 1997), an unwillingness to enter treatment despite potentially life-threatening consequences of substance use, and a need to control the pace of change (see Bergin & Baron, 1992 and Graham et al., 1995 for a more detailed description of the justification and development of these programs).

Although the approach was *developed* for older persons, there is no necessity for it to be *restricted* to older persons. Nonelderly persons who abuse substances often have multiple problems, a reluctance to engage in treatment, and a need to control the pace and focus of treatment. The need and effectiveness of responding to "where the client is at" has been recognized more recently in motivational counselling (Miller & Rollnick, 1991).

The approach is defined by two main principles that clearly differentiate it from most traditional treatment: (1) the person receiving treatment controls the treatment, including the goals of treatment; and (2) substance abuse problems are addressed in the context of the person's overall need to improve his or her life. The implications of these principles are that each person receives a different treatment program, that the focus of treatment may only indirectly involve use of alcohol or other drugs, and that some level of treatment is provided for as long as the person feels it is needed.

## Brief Description of the Treatment Model

As described in the preceding section, the main tenets of the approach are that it is client-centered (individualized and controlled by the client) and holistic. The overall goal of one program is described as follows:

"to improve the physical, psychosocial, spiritual, and environmental health of seniors who are living independently in the community and who are experiencing problems associated with the use of alcohol and other psychoactive drugs" (p. 3, Bergin & Baron, 1992)

Thus, the goal addresses *problems* associated with substance use, while goals relating to actual use are considered subsidiary to this goal. This orientation reflects the reality that people typically enter treatment because of the *negative consequences of their use of alcohol or drugs,* not because of their use, per se. The practical implication of viewing substance *use* as a secondary goal is that some persons can be helped without any *explicit* focus on substance use. More often, however, working with clients to address life problems identifies the role of alcohol or drug use in causing these problems and the need for them to address their use directly. Nevertheless, the goal is always to improve the person's life, while reducing or stopping alcohol/drug use is a merely a means to this goal. This is more than just a semantic difference. For one thing, it means that the counselor is prepared to help the person resolve problems that may not be related to substance use in any obvious way. This does not mean that the counselor personally provides help in all areas. Rather, it means that the counselor undertakes clinical case management in its broadest sense, linking the client to community resources and other help and support as needed. This linking could involve anything from referral for a psychiatric assessment to helping the client obtain vocational or marital counselling to exploring with the client various community options for use of leisure time. The interconnectedness of use of alcohol and other drugs with other aspects of the person's life (both past and present) that under-lies this approach to treatment is demonstrated in Figure 8.1 (taken from Bergin & Baron).

## Stages of Treatment

### Assessment/Engagement/Treatment Planning

The first stage of treatment involves assessment, goal setting, and rela-tionship building. Several critical things happen at this stage. First, the counselor begins to work with the client to identify ways in which the client would like to see his or her life improved—that is, setting short- and long-term goals for change. As has been described elsewhere (Graham et al., 1995), the client does not have to agree to quit or reduce drinking or drug use or even acknowledge that alcohol/drug use is a problem; however, for treatment to proceed, the client must be willing to change his or her life at least to some extent. If a need for change is not recog-nized by the client (e.g., in some instances when the program has initiated contact with a potential client on the basis of a referral from a social or health care worker or a family member who is concerned about the per-son's drinking or drug use), treatment would not be initiated, although the person would be free to reactivate the relationship with the counselor at any time.

A second important aspect of this initial phase is responding to the client's *immediate* problems by assisting him or her to set realistic, achiev-able short-term goals. Often clients are feeling hopeless and overwhelmed. An important first stage of treatment is to demonstrate that change can occur in small achievable steps.

The third critical element of the early stage of treatment is the building of trust between the client and the counselor. By working with the client to identify the client's goals and by responding to the most pressing immediate concerns *as defined by the client,* the counselor demonstrates to the client that his or her wants and needs will be addressed. It is critical that the client comes to trust the counselor because the client often has little or no confidence that he or she can achieve change and relies on the confidence, knowledge and experience of the counselor that change can and will occur. From the other side, the counselor must also trust the client. Client-centered treatment as defined by the present approach means that the client knows best about the goals and directions of his or her own treatment, *not* the counselor.

### Treatment

Treatment involves helping the person develop a vision for how they would like their life to be and helping them to achieve that vision. This

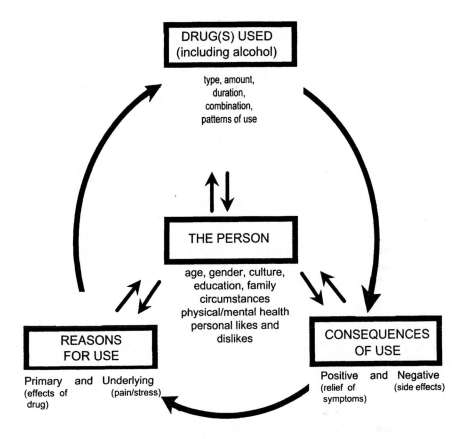

**FIGURE 8.1**    The LESA drug use model.

includes the work done in the initial phase of treatment as well as services provided as part of ongoing support (described in the next section). During the main part of treatment, the counselors assist clients to: "explore their beliefs, attitudes and feelings about themselves, significant others, contemporary society, and about change;" "identify, clarify and decide upon areas for personal change;" "recognize and solve problems associated with their use of [alcohol and other] drugs;" and "consider options for change, make decisions, and develop plans for activities which will support a healthy lifestyle". The counselors also "reinforce clients' desires to make changes and support them while they do so, and facilitate clients' use of appropriate community support services" Bergin & Baron, 1992, p. 4). (For more concrete details of the approach as used with older persons see Bergin & Baron (pp. 34–42); Graham et al., 1995 (pp. 30–35); Saunders, Graham, Flower, & White-Campbell, 1992.) The two programs that developed this approach for older persons also use support groups both as part of treatment and for ongoing support. These are facilitated by a counselor but involve primarily mutual support.

### Ongoing Support

Some clients are able to change their lives and reduce or stop drinking quickly and with minimal help. For others, however, their alcohol or drug-related problems are well-entrenched in life problems that fostered the development of substance abuse as well as a life style that contains few alternatives to substance abuse. The availability of long-term support is part of the current approach, since the client-centered focus of treatment implies providing treatment for as long as the client deems necessary. Moreover, long-term support also allows the client to reactivate more intensive treatment during times of crisis, relapse, or other times of need. Although the commitment to long-term support might involve extensive services to clients, generally such support involves minimal services delivered at fairly low cost, often provided mainly in the form of mutual support groups (Bergin & Baron, 1992; Nurco, Stephenson, & Hanlon, 1990–1991).


## II. ESSENTIAL CLINICAL SKILLS AND ATTRIBUTES

Being successful at using this approach involves certain personal attributes, as well as specific skills and knowledge. As a prerequisite, the counselor should have training in one of the helping professions which he or she can draw from, but be able to function as a generalist. The counselor should also have training in addictions and addictions counselling.

### Personal Attributes

The type of person who is be best suited to using this approach to counselling has the following personal characteristics: warm, nurturing, empathic, supportive, realistically optimistic, nonconfrontational, comfortable with small changes, process-oriented, flexible, imaginative, and creative. This person sees setbacks as a challenge to learn from rather than as failure. The person should also have a certain pragmatism often developed from having dealt with some issues in his or her own life and be fairly well adjusted, especially in terms of not having unresolved issues around addiction.

## Skills

The counselor should have knowledge and skills in various counselling techniques and be able to apply them appropriately. The counselor using this approach needs to be able to: break things down into small steps but at the same time see the whole picture; recognize that changes in one area often lead to changes in other areas; recognize the client's strengths; and respond to the client's priorities. In addition, the counselor should be able to develop a trusting relationship with the client, build up the client's confidence and self-esteem, keep the focus on the client's goals and wishes, facilitate the clients doing things for themselves if possible, and portray a sense of hopefulness. Finally, the counselor needs to have good listening and problem-solving skills, the ability to access community resources for the benefit of the client, and the ability to respond to a variety of needs, either directly or by helping the client connect with appropriate services.

## Knowledge

The counselor needs to have a good working knowledge of community resources. This includes knowing which physicians have an understanding of addictions issues, the kinds of resources that are acceptable to different types of clients, and other aspects that will facilitate the client obtaining the needed services or support. The counselor needs to have this knowledge *and* be able to share it with the client.

As much as possible, the counselor should have knowledge of the client's cultural context. For example, when the approach is used with older people, the counselor needs to be familiar with issues of aging and with elder-specific needs and resources. If the approach is used in the context of a large program in which admissions are not restricted by age, gender, ethnicity, or other factors that help define the client's cultural context, it is useful to have counselors specialize in specific groups so that they can be as familiar as possible with the context and resources relating to their clients.

Finally, another aspect of treatment relevant to the characteristics of the counselor is matching the counselor to particular known needs of a client. While this is not always possible or necessary, there may be certain clients who can benefit most from a counselor of a certain gender, age, or other characteristics. In developing a treatment approach for a particular client, this may be one factor to consider.

## III. THE CASE OF "PAUL;" 15 CLINICAL QUESTIONS

*1. What would be your therapeutic goals for this patient? What are the primary and secondary goals? Please be as specific as possible.*

The counselor's initial goal is to build a therapeutic relationship, a partnership with the client, that forms the basis for treatment. The focus is on getting to know the person, the person's aspirations, strengths, and interests as well as the problem areas. As part of this holistic approach, the counselor tries to get to know these aspects of the person's life from the client's perspective. The main question driving this process is: How would the client like things to be different?

As described in the description of the approach, the first part of treatment involves helping the client to develop his own personal goals. Paul's case history provides a great deal of information about him which suggests a number of areas that *might* become the focus of change. These areas will be identified as *potential* goals that he might choose to address.

*Short-term goals:*
1. Maintain job.
2. Mend relationship with children regarding recent aggressive behavior.
3. Reduce/eliminate alcohol/drug use to the extent necessary to achieve goals 1 and 2.
4. Develop long-term goals.

*Long-term goals:*
1. Develop strategies/support system to achieve long-term non-hazardous use of alcohol/drugs; likely to strive for abstinence as a long-term goal.
2. Manage depression.
3. Explore and develop management techniques for anger and impulsivity; reduce these aspects of his behavior, if possible.
4. Explore and development healthy satisfying relationships with peers outside of the drinking milieu.
5. Acknowledge and understand personal history, including the possible explanation of learning disabilities or Attention Deficit Disorder (ADD) for some of his problems in childhood and adolescence; develop acceptance and sensitivity to his own personal history (e.g., learned behaviors that form part of his stress reactions).
6. Develop healthy life style, including satisfying relationships and activities as well as good physical and health maintenance programs.

As mentioned these are *potential* goals that would be likely from the history but would only be adopted if Paul makes these goals his own. The counselor has the responsibility to help him identify potential areas for change, but the final decision as to whether any particular goal will be pursued rests with him.

2. *What further information would you want to have to assist you in structuring this patient's treatment? Are there specific assessment tools you would use (i.e, data to be collected)? What would be the rationale for using these tools?*

Paul and the counselor need to explore more fully what Paul gets out of using substances. Knowledge of the role of alcohol in his life, the effects of alcohol on him, his reasons for use, and the social milieu for using would be part of goal setting and relapse prevention (see Figure 8.1). Some standardized measures that could be used to help address this issue include the Inventory of Drinking Situations (IDS), the Inventory of Drug-Taking Situations (IDTS), the Situational Confidence Questionnaire (SCQ), and the Drug-Taking Confidence Questionnaire (DTCQ). In a different area, it would be useful to have more information about the nature of his relationship with his wife and her role in his life.

3. *What is your conceptualization of this patient's personality, behavior, affective state, and cognitions?*

The case history indicates that Paul is impulsive, angry, and depressed. The scores on the MMPI and the NEO-PI are consistent with this history. While it is not usual to use standardized personality measures such as the MMPI and the NEO-PI as part of this approach to treatment, if the scores were available and the client gave permission to use them, they might be discussed and used for treatment planning with the client.

Although Paul has considerable psychological problems, he also appears to have longstanding caring relationships with his wife, children, father, AA sponsor, and others, suggesting a capacity for good relationships and a sensitivity to others (e.g., feeling guilty about leaving his siblings behind when he left home).

His success at work and his continuing relationship with his wife suggest considerable strength and resilience considering the extent of his problems from childhood and his long-term history of substance abuse.

In terms of his current cognitive/affective state, he appears to be depressed, hopeless, scared, and anxious. He also appears to be hurting, emotionally labile, aggressive, and somewhat unpredictable in his behavior. It is interesting that he appears to provide no excuses for his substance abuse or blame others in any way (according to the information provided in the case history). His emotional state reflects the severity of the crisis in his life where he appears to be at risk of losing the two main stabilizing features of his life—his wife and children and his job.

*4. What potential pitfalls would you envision in this therapy? What would the difficulties be and what would you envision to be the source(s) of the difficulties?*

One difficulty that would apply to any therapy for Paul is catching the motivators (wife, family, job) in time. It is expected that he will need long-term treatment, but he will also need some short-term success to build on. Immediate focus and response to these areas would facilitate support for more long-term progress. Losing these aspects of his life, on the other hand, could cause him to give up.

Another potential pitfall is not being able to keep Paul in treatment for the time that is needed for him to make lasting changes. He has shown considerable success in making short-term change but has a history of not being able to sustain this change. An important aspect of treatment will be preparing him for the long-term effort and possible setbacks. Thus, there is a balancing act of sufficient short-term success to build hope and confidence, but not letting resolution of the immediate crisis be interpreted as resolution of the problem that precipitated the crisis.

Finally, the model of treatment recommended for Paul involves individual counselling with the counselor functioning as a case manager and accessing resources in the community. One potential pitfall is a possible lack of needed resources, especially physicians and psychiatrists who understand alcohol and drug problems and will treat the person holistically.

*5. To what level of coping, adaptation, or function would you see this patient reaching as an immediate result of therapy? What result would be long-term subsequent to the ending of therapy (i.e., prognosis for adaptive change)?*

The immediate result of therapy would be that Paul would be able to manage his substance use well enough to maintain family relationships and job. This should be attainable since he has done it before. The long-term focus of therapy would be on addressing other issues in his life to help him sustain long-term change.

As will be described later in section II, Paul seems to have considerable strengths, such as a strong work history, long-term relationships with wife and others, and no apparent physical health problems. If he can stay with the process long enough, he can likely achieve good adaptation.

*6. What would be your time line (duration) for therapy? What would be your frequency and duration of sessions?*

The time line for case management/counselling for Paul would be 2 years of intensive treatment followed by 3 to 5 years of supportive counselling. During the first couple of months, the counselor would meet with him every week or 10 days for counselling sessions of about one hour in length; after that probably every 2 weeks. Depending upon the extent of other therapy in which he was involved, he would probably be seen less frequently during the second year (probably every month). During the period of ongoing support, the counselor would see Paul or speak to him on the telephone every 6 weeks or so, seeing him more frequently if issues come up such as relapse. The support period actually extends indefinitely as Paul would be able to return for more intensive treatment at any time he finds this necessary.

*7. Are there specific or special techniques that you would implement in the therapy? What would they be?*

During the intensive phase of treatment, Paul would address issues of immediate concern such as family, job, and sobriety and start to manage other problems such as depression, impulsivity, and anger. In addition to those activities described as part of the general process (i.e., relationship building, goal setting, building on small successes, clinical case management), the following specific techniques might be used: taking antabuse for the short-term if this is helpful for him; cognitive-behavioral relapse prevention training; helping him plan ways not to drink in places that are important to him (e.g., seeing kids); exploring learned behavior from childhood, such as how to cope with stress and anger without running away or exploding; helping him find an exercise program that he might enjoy, since he appears to be a physical person and this would help him reduce stress.

Ongoing support would involve: maintaining supportive contact to show interest in how things are going; being available for more intensive counselling, if necessary; referring him to other services, if necessary; helping him develop peer support activities and hobbies; maybe involving Paul in men's anger group; and helping Paul to feel good about himself and value his strengths. This phase also involves replacing substance-using behavior with something else.

The approach generally is eclectic and practically oriented. In Paul's case, he is going to have to engage in some behavior modification initially in order to get his life in order, but for the long term he is going to have to figure out why he does what he does and work on changing this pattern. He needs to develop a life plan including goals, as well as patterns of behavior to achieve these goals. Much of his early life seems to have been influenced by substance use; therefore, some of the developmental activities of adolescence and early adulthood will likely become tasks of this period of his life.

*8. Are there special cautions to be observed in working with this patient (e.g., danger to self or others, transference, counter-transference)? Are there any particular resistances you would expect and how would you deal with them?*

Paul does not appear to be an immediate danger to himself or others. Right now, he is pretty vulnerable and needs support. Long-term stability will be difficult to achieve because he has never experienced this—one form of resistance may be an unwillingness to stick with the process.

He also seems to be involved in a fairly "macho" culture with his workmates related to his drinking. This might be addressed by matching him with a gentle older male counselor (if possible) who can serve as a role model to help him develop his more sensitive side. This matching with an older man may risk some transference relating to unresolved issues with his father. This transference, if it occurred, would need to be dealt with as part of therapy.

Another caution relates to peer support groups. The information regarding his drinking and drug use indicates that it is primarily associated with his interactions with male peers. While he might ultimately benefit from peer support, he needs first to use individual counselling to clarify the type of male/peer relationships that would be supportive to his short- and long-term life goals.

*9. Are there any areas that you would choose to avoid or not address with this patient? Why?*

No, although there are some issues that might best be addressed before others; however, even the order depends on what he brings to the table. In addition, some problems are probably better addressed in other contexts (e.g., anger management, marital counselling). Nevertheless, with the holistic client-centered approach, whatever the client identifies as areas for change should be addressed, either directly by the counselor or indirectly through referral.

*10. Is medication warranted for this patient? What effect would you hope or expect the medication to have?*

If Antabuse works to help stabilize him, this could be used. After his drug use decreases, use of antidepressants could be explored,

*11. What are the strengths of the patient that can be used in the therapy?*

The case history indicates a number of strengths. He has had positive relationships with his wife and children and these relationships are important to him. He has also demonstrated the ability to form positive relationships and derive benefits from mentors such as his high school teacher, his AA sponsor, his boss, and even his father. He also seems to have cared about and had positive experiences with his mother and brothers and sisters. Given his alcohol and drug use history, his ability to maintain successful employment is impressive. This would seem to be an area that has been an important strength for him in the past. He has also succeeded in short periods of sobriety, showing both motivation and the capability of quitting. He also showed some control in being able to switch from IV cocaine to smoking and in stopping abuse of opiates once he left the army. There is also some evidence of his sensitivity toward others (reflected by his attitude to his siblings when young and to his children now). Finally, he seems to be in good general health.

*12. How would you address limits, boundaries, and limit-setting with this patient?*

Because it is the client's therapy, the counselors only set boundaries relating to themselves and what they will do, especially in making clear what they can and cannot do. Building a trusting relationship in the beginning helps to set limits by establishing a respectful and constructive process. The major limit set by the counselors is that they will not provide counselling while the client is intoxicated. The client is asked to refrain from alcohol or drug use prior to a counselling session, as intoxication will impair the process. If the client has been drinking or using drugs, he is asked to call the counselor ahead of time, if possible, so that the session can be rescheduled. This limit is not intended to be punitive, and if the client slips and needs to reschedule, this is not seen as a problem.

No other limits other than this seem needed for Paul. He does not appear to show a history of being dependent or using people, and it does not appear that he is likely to be aggressive toward the counselor.

*13. Would you want to involve significant others in the treatment? Would you use out-of-session work (homework) with this patient? What homework would you use?*

Although this would probably not be addressed initially, sometime in treatment, Paul and his wife would need to work out a successful arrangement if they are planning on reuniting. As part of Paul's treatment, the counselor might see the two together a few times, but those sessions would likely focus on obtaining his wife's support for relapse prevention, rather than on their relationship. If marital counselling was wanted, the counselor would probably refer the couple to another counselor for this aspect of recovery. It may also be that the wife would want or need to be referred for individual counselling for herself.

In terms of out-of-session work, the counselor would want Paul to be doing something between counselling sessions, but the nature of this work would depend on the content of the session. It might involve keeping a drinking log to identify how he felt before and after drinking and considering alternatives to drinking. Alternatively, he might be asked to think about some of the issues discussed in the session. For example, he might be asked to think about specific questions such as "What would you like life to look like? What are a few things you would like to achieve? What's working, what's not working? What are your likes/dislikes?" The counselor would also help the client try to identify and build in rewards for himself between sessions.

*14. What would be the issues to be addressed in termination? How would termination and relapse prevention be structured?*

Relapse prevention would be part of treatment. Because supportive counselling is available indefinitely, termination is not a major issue. On leaving treatment, Paul should have developed ongoing support in the community and know how to use resources to help him maintain his gains.

*15. What do you see as the hoped-for mechanisms of change for this patient, in order of importance?*

The main mechanisms for change involve having a life plan, having strategies to cope with deficits (anger, impulsiveness), identifying reasons for change and ensuring that some enjoyable aspects (e.g., internal interests, life satisfaction) rather than feelings of deprivation are associated with change.

## IV. DISCUSSION

As demonstrated by the preceding discussion of Paul's case, the approach is adaptable for nonelderly clients, although it was developed to meet the special needs of older persons who have alcohol and drug problems. It seems especially suitable in the present case, where the person has multiple problems, a long history of substance abuse, and a history of relapse.

The approach differs from traditional treatment in several ways, most obviously the holistic focus on life problems rather than use, per se and the open-ended client-centered treatment program. While both deviations from traditional approaches may be controversial, the issue of the costs of a treatment approach that involves indefinite duration of services needs some justification. First, although the costs of long-term support may be perceived to be high, these costs need to be weighed against the costs of nonsupport (e.g., social and correctional services used by alcohol/drug abusers). Second, this approach addresses the reality that relapse is common. As the addictions field has recognized the extreme likelihood of relapse following treatment, greater attention is being paid to the provision of longer term support and case management. Hawkins and Catalano (1985) described the following factors associated with relapse to drug abuse: absence of a strong prosocial interpersonal network, conflict and lack of support associated with family, involvement with drug-using friends, isolation, lack of involvement in productive roles, lack of involvement in active leisure/recreational activities, negative emotional states, and physical symptoms (pp. 918–920). Accordingly, case management models that have been developed for drug abusers involve fairly intensive programs focused on helping clients to restructure their lives, addressing such issues as employment and involvement in nondrug leisure activities, as well as counselling focused directly on relapse prevention (Catalano, Hawkins, Wells, Miller, & Brewer, 1990–1991; Martin, Isenberg, & Inciardi, 1993). The need for restructuring of life style also applies to persons who have alcohol problems. As described by Allsop:

> "It is highly probable that if intervention simply focuses on inoculation of the client, with a soupçon of coping skills, with little regard for the environment to which she or he returns, the probability for 'resolution breakdown' is high." (p. 149, 1990).

Thus, what appears to be excessive costs of the approach in terms of the duration of treatment may actually be a more rationale and ultimately cost-effective solution than the alternative of post treatment crisis-driven use of services.

## REFERENCES

Allsop, S. (1990). Relapse prevention and management. *Drug and Alcohol Review, 9*, 143–153.

Bergin, B., & Baron, J. (1992). *LESA: A program of lifestyle enrichment for senior adults with alcohol and other psychoactive drug problems.* Ottawa: Centretown Community Health Centre.

Catalano, R. F., Hawkins, J. D., Wells, E. A., Miller, J., & Brewer, D. (1990–91). Evaluation of the effectiveness of adolescent drug abuse treatments, assessment of risks for relapse, and promising approaches for relapse prevention. *The International Journal of the Addictions, 25*(9A & 10A), 1085–1140.

Graham, K., Brett, P. J., & Baron, J. (1997). A harm-reduction approach to treating older adults: The clients speak. In P. G. Erikson, D. M. Riley, Y. W. Cheung, & P. A. O'Hare (Eds.), *Harm reduction: A new direction for drug policies and programs* (pp. 429–452). Toronto, Ontario: University of Toronto Press.

Graham, K., Saunders, S. J., Flower, M. C., Birchmore Timney, C., White-Campbell, M., & Zeidman Pietropaolo, A. (1995). *Addictions treatment for older adults: Evaluation of an innovative client-centered approach.* Binghamton, NY: Haworth Press.

Hawkins, J. D., & Catalano, R. F. J. (1985). Aftercare in drug abuse treatment. *International Journal of the Addictions, 20*, 917–945.

Martin, S. S., Isenberg, H., & Inciardi, J. A. (1993). Assertive community treatment: Integrating intensive drug treatment with aggressive case management for hard-to-reach populations. In J. A. Inciardi, F. M. Tims, & B. W. Fletcher (Eds.), *Innovative approaches in the treatment of drug abuse* (pp. 97–108). Westport, CT: Greenwood Press.

Miller, W. R., & Rollnick, S. (1991). *Motivational interviewing. Preparing people to change addictive behavior.* New York: Guilford Press.

Nurco, D. N., Stephenson, P. E., & Hanlon, T. E. (1990–1991). Aftercare/relapse prevention and the self-help movement. *International Journal of the Addictions, 25,* 1179–1200.

Saunders, S. J., Graham, K., Flower, M., & White-Campbell, M. (1992). The COPA project as a model for the management of early dementia in the community. In G. M. M. Jones & B. M. L. Miesen (Eds.), *Care-giving in dementia: Research and applications* (pp. 324–356). New York: Tavistock/Routledge.

# 9

# Client-Driven, Research-Guided Treatment for Substance Users: Bringing Harm Reduction to Clinical Practice

*Frederick Rotgers*

## I. THE TREATMENT MODEL

The central tenets of Client-driven, Research-guided Treatment (CRT) for substance users derive from a variety of sources. As its name implies, therapists using the CRT approach rely heavily on both client goals and commitments, and on research validated intervention strategies in working with substance users. Drawing from cognitive-behavioral treatments (cf. Hester & Miller, 1995; Meyers & Smith, 1995; Monti, Abrams, Kadden & Cooney, 1989; Morgan, 1996; Rotgers, 1996), motivational interviewing (Miller & Rollnick, 1991), the stages of change model of Prochaska and his colleagues (Prochaska, DiClemente & Norcross, 1992), and harm reduction philosophies (Marlatt, 1996), CRT places a strong emphasis on adopting a pragmatic approach to helping clients change substance use.

CRT represents a conceptual and philosophical shift, rather than a technical innovation. It replaces the traditional, medical-model approach to working with substance use disorders in which the therapist is in charge of treatment and makes prescriptions (i.e., attend 90 meetings in 90 days; abstain totally from all psychoactive substances), which the client is obliged to follow if treatment is to be considered successful.

Instead, CRT is driven by client factors. The client is recognized as a decision-maker who can and will make his or her own choices. The therapist's role becomes that of a coach or a guide, rather than a dictator or a guru, whose primary goal is to assist the client in mobilizing his or her strengths and finding viable paths to behavior change.

The main process of CRT consists in developing, with strong client input, an individualized menu of behavior change options aimed at goals to which the client is committed. The therapist works with the client to: 1) develop a strong commitment to specific, achievable, client-chosen goals (both short- and long-term); 2) implement behavior change strategies that are chosen by the client in consultation with the therapist who recommends various strategies based on clinical research findings; 3) develop and implement long-term maintenance strategies for the behavior changes achieved.

Central to CRT is the philosophy of harm reduction. Harm reduction approaches are based on the assumption that there is a continuum of harm associated with substance use, and that not all substance use is, in and of itself, harmful. Therapeutic goals from the perspective of the therapist focus on helping the client to move from substance use that is associated with greater harm to levels of use associated with lesser harm. While abstinence is considered to be the anchoring point of minimal risk and harm associated with substance use in most cases, the therapist actively supports any changes in substance use behaviors that reduce harm and risk, no matter how small the changes may be. Among users who are not yet committed to abstinence, continued use is accepted as a reality, but becomes a strong focus for intervention, often in the form of efforts to help the client change use patterns rather than eliminating use altogether or to make a commitment to reducing use to less harmful levels.

This, of course, raises the issue of therapist goals vs. client goals, and who decides which goals are to become the focus of treatment. In CRT, while the therapist may have goals that he or she hopes the client will adopt, it is the client's choices that govern the direction of treatment. Some clinicians may be thinking that "allowing" clients this range of freedom of choice will inevitably lead to clients choosing some form of continued use, with possible attendant lessened, though continuing, negative consequences. Research is clear, however, that most clients not only prefer to select their own treatment goals (in consultation with the therapist, to be sure), but that when given a choice between continued, but reduced, use and abstinence, clients seeking help with substance use problems overwhelmingly choose abstinence as their use goal, contrary to clinical lore.

Harm reduction is consistent with the Stages of Change model developed and validated by Prochaska and colleagues (Prochaska et al., 1992).

Under this model, behavior change is conceived of as a process that often takes place incrementally and over time. From this perspective the therapist's role becomes not unlike that of a coach who attempts to enhance motivation and commitment to change, provides possible options for implementing changes, teaches skills the client may not have, and reinforces the client's successive approximations to a harm-free relationship with drugs. Harm reduction philosophies also suggest that therapists can be most helpful by instituting a "low threshold" policy for treatment entry and engagement. From this perspective, it is not necessary for a client who is ambivalent about abstinence to completely stop using in order to obtain help changing substance use behavior. Rather, services are designed to meet the client where he or she is at with respect to possible treatment goals and stage of change.

Having roots in harm reduction also means that CRT is highly pragmatic with respect to expectations of the rapidity, degree, and extent of changes clients can be expected to make, and with respect to the role that treatment can effectively play in a client's life. From this perspective, more is not always better, particularly if increasing treatment intensity and time commitment leads to increased difficulties for clients in other life areas. Thus, if entering a long-term inpatient rehabilitation program is likely to result in job loss, or family disintegration, thus further increasing stresses on an already stressed client, the CRT therapist, though perhaps recommending this option, will also attempt to help the client fully evaluate the pros and cons of such a course of action and to develop less difficult options. In the end, it is the client's decision that prevails, as it is the client who must both commit to and implement the behavior change methods agreed upon.

Pragmatism in CRT has other implications. Engagement and retention are nearly as important as client behavior change within CRT. It is a truism that if the client does not come to treatment, does not become involved in efforts at change, and finds treatment to be highly intrusive or inconsistent with personal beliefs and values, then treatment cannot be successful. Thus, consistent with the adoption of "low threshold" requirements for treatment entry, CRT also focuses on helping clients stay engaged in some level of contact with the therapist until behavior change is well established. Once formal, regular treatment is ended, the therapist still maintains periodic contact with the client to insure ready availability of treatment should "booster" sessions be needed. This focus is also supported by research findings suggesting that longer contact with treatment providers results in better outcomes.

CRT is not wedded to any one particular approach or set of approaches to helping clients change substance use. Rather, CRT adopts a multimodal approach to treatment, attempting to help clients discover behavior change methods that work best for them. Nevertheless, knowledge of effective methods derived from clinical research is used by the therapist to develop suggested strategies for a particular client based on an assessment of that client's particular problems and life circumstances. This is in contrast to the prescriptive "one size fits all" approach, usually based on 12-step philosophy, that has characterized most substance abuse treatment in the United States. While 12-step-based approaches may work well for some clients, research indicates that they do not work for all. While abstinence may be the safest goal for all clients, not all clients choose abstinence, or if they have chosen abstinence, not all clients are not fully ready to implement it. Thus, CRT relies heavily on having available multiple options for clients to use in assisting the process of behavior change. This means that often the therapist must become proactive in assisting members of the client's community in developing alternatives to traditional 12-step support groups and treatment methods. Having a variety of options readily available to clients greatly enhances the likelihood that the client will be able to develop, implement, and maintain effective change strategies. Adopting such a multimodal approach also means that the therapist must be aware of and willing to use the entire range of treatment options currently available, including psychoactive medications.

Finally, but perhaps most importantly, CRT depends on comprehensive assessment to enable the therapist to understand where the client is with respect to his or her substance use and possible changes in it, the factors that appear to drive substance use, and to assist the client in designing a change plan with a reasonable likelihood of success. Assessment continues throughout CRT as clients change, or as difficulties in changing surface during the course of treatment.

In sum, CRT is a holistic approach that puts the client at the center of treatment, attempts to empower clients with respect to their own decision making and behavior changes, and makes use of whatever resources are available to assist clients in the process of reshaping their own lives. It is in many ways antithetical to the prescriptive, therapist-driven model current in the most common approaches to helping substance users in the United States. It is based on respect for the client as a human being, and solidly grounded in research findings on the components of effective therapeutic change.

## II.  ESSENTIAL CLINICAL SKILLS AND ATTRIBUTES

Therapists working within a CRT framework need a variety of skills to be successful. These skills can be divided into personal therapist characteristics and depth of knowledge of substance use and substance use disorders.

Effective CRT therapists must be able to be respectful, empathetic, objective, and patient with clients. Clients may often take longer to commit to a course of action, be slower to implement that course of action, and apparently unwilling or unable to endure even minor levels of discomfort than the therapist would like. The ability to continue working with such a client in a respectful, empathetic, and nonjudgmental fashion, even though that client may not be fulfilling the therapist's expectations for change, is essential to CRT. Nonetheless, the therapist does not sit by and merely observe. He or she is always working with the client to consider the pros and cons of various courses of action, and to encourage the client to commit to a safer, healthier course than the current one.

Therapists working within a CRT framework need to be aware of their own feelings, attitudes, and beliefs about clients who continue to behave in what, to the therapist, may appear to be self-defeating ways. CRT therapists on a regular basis must confront what in psychodynamic approaches are called "counter-transference" issues. Being clear about one's own personal biases and beliefs about substance users is critical to being an effective clinician within a CRT framework. Beliefs, such as those rudely encapsulated in the old joke about knowing an addict is lying because his or her lips are moving, need to be recognized and dealt with by the therapist if he or she is not to subtly communicate negative expectations to clients.

CRT therapists must be broadly knowledgeable about clinical research on the efficacy of various intervention approaches, the natural history of substance use disorders, current and emerging intervention methods such as new pharmacotherapies, and the availability of a variety of support and other services in the therapist's (and client's) community. Because family involvement is often essential to successful behavior change, the CRT therapist must have a working knowledge of how to use family members to assist the client in making changes. The CRT therapist needs to have a wide variety of options available to present to his or her clients for consideration in developing a plan of action. In order to target intervention suggestions as precisely as possible to client needs, the therapist must also be skilled at conducting thorough assessments of client substance use, factors associated with substance use, comorbid psychopathology, family support, motivation, and a variety of other factors that may have an impact on a particular client's ability to meet his or her treatment goals.

## III. THE CASE OF "PAUL:" 15 CLINICAL QUESTIONS

*1. What would be your therapeutic goals for this client? What are primary and secondary goals?*

As with all clients, the initial goal with Paul would be to discover, through a thorough assessment, the environmental, intrapersonal, and interpersonal factors that appear to be associated with this particular client's substance use. Once these factors have been delineated with reasonable initial clarity, the primary therapeutic goal would be one of helping Paul to make a strong commitment to implementing a course of action leading to change in substance use or other behaviors over which the client has direct control. This would be accomplished by reviewing the results of the assessment with Paul, obtaining Paul's views on the validity of the assessment results, and soliciting his thoughts as to what treatment goals might be most appropriate to aim for at this time. In CRT the specific goals are always selected by Paul, albeit with recommendations and suggestions from the therapist based on the therapist's clinical experience and knowledge of effective interventions and safer vs. less safe levels of substance use.

Once the initial assessment has been done, the therapist engages in a decisional balance exercise with Paul with respect to various behavior change options. Based on Paul's perceptions and degree of commitment to specific changes as a result of this exercise, the therapist and client would then pursue the second therapeutic goal—that of developing together a plan of action to which Paul is willing to strongly commit himself.

In Paul's case, the therapist might want to explore further with him the perceived costs and benefits of continued use of alcohol, and its relationship to his cocaine use. The initial focus might be on deriving a more precise picture of this relationship and helping Paul develop a strong commitment to change his drinking as a first step toward perhaps reducing or eliminating his use of cocaine. Should Paul be willing to commit to an abstinence goal, and given his prior success with Antabuse, the therapist might want to raise for discussion the possibility of a pharmacological aid to abstinence such as resumption of Antabuse or a trial on ReVia (naltrexone). Other abstinence focused options and their pros and cons would also be reviewed, with the goal of helping Paul commit to a specifically detailed plan of action with measurable outcomes that can be assessed over the course of treatment.

If Paul is reluctant to abstain from alcohol, even for a short time, the therapist might discuss the possibility of moderate drinking training with a goal of helping Paul keep his drinking below levels at which he is likely to use cocaine as well.

Throughout, the therapist's stance is to help Paul objectively examine options, and to make a commitment to pursuing a particular course of action which he, Paul, has chosen for himself. The therapist acts as a resource for change strategies that might be helpful to Paul in achieving his goals.

*2. What further information would you want to have to assist you in structuring this client's treatment? Are there specific assessment tools you would use? What would be the rationale for using these tools?*

As mentioned above, a comprehensive assessment, data from which is fed back to Paul as part of the goal setting and commitment process, is critical. There are a number of simple instruments that are available to assist the therapist in assessing these critical motivational aspects of a client. Simply having the client select his or her substance use or other goals from among a list of possible goals, and rate on a 10-point Likert scale how committed he/she is to achieving those goals can be an effective way of tapping motivation. Prochaska, Norcross, and DiClemente (1994) also discuss several easy, brief ways of assessing stage of change.

Using assessment instruments that enable clients such as Paul to compare his substance-use-related problems with those of others is often helpful in motivating clients to make changes. A comprehensive structured interview, such as the Comprehensive Drinker Profile (Miller & Marlatt, 1984) coupled with normed questionnaires that provide standard score equivalents that can be used to help clients understand the nature and severity of their substance-related problems, compared with those of others, can be a used as part of a motivational feedback interview. The volume published by the National Institute on Alcohol Abuse and Alcoholism, *Assessing Alcohol Problems: A Guide for Clinicians and Researchers* (Allen & Columbus, 1995), contains a variety of instruments suitable for assessing problem drinkers. Comparable, though less comprehensive, volumes, the *Diagnostic Sourcebook on Drug Abuse Research and Treatment* (Rounseville, Tims, Horton & Sowder, 1993), and the *Directory of Client Outcome Measures for Addictions Treatment Programs* (Addiction Research Foundation, 1994) have been published by the National Institute on Drug Abuse and Addiction Research Foundation, respectively.

Notably absent from the case description is any indication that Paul's use of cigarettes or other nicotine delivery systems was assessed. Given that cigarette smoking is often strongly associated with alcohol, and sometimes other drug, use and can serve as a "trigger" for slips or relapse in those patients, it is important to assess Paul's use of this legal, but potentially very harmful, drug. Whether or not Paul had ever been successful at limiting or stopping use of cigarettes, and if so how he accomplished this, could provide a clue as to possible effective strategies he might try with the other drugs he uses.

It is also important to continually reassess such client characteristics as self-efficacy with respect to achievement of possible treatment goals, both at the beginning of treatment and as treatment progresses. Again, simple "home grown" assessments such as having Paul rate on a 10-point scale how confident he is that a particular goal is attainable can be helpful both in selecting appropriate goals, and avoiding selection goals that may be too difficult. This latter is important to help Paul avoid a sense of failure as a result of being unable to achieve goals that are set too high.

I would want to obtain more information, most likely through specific interview questions, about how Paul saw his previous treatments and the results he achieved with them, as well as about successful or partly successful efforts to change his own behavior that he had made in the past. This information can point the therapist toward interventions that have been at least modestly successful for Paul in the past, and which with fine-tuning might be successful for him again.

Finally, I would assess Paul's environment and potential supports further than appears to have been done, focusing on how these supports might be extended. Aside from people in AA and his father, what social network supporting abstinence or a reduction in drinking and drug use does Paul have, and what steps might be taken to help him develop a more effective support network. To the extent that Paul was willing, members of this support network might be directly enlisted in his therapy.

*3. What is your conceptualization of this client's personality, behavior, affective state, and cognitions?*

Paul impresses me, based on the case description, as being a discouraged young man whose self-efficacy with respect to reducing or stopping problematic substance use is quite low. Although he appears to be a young man who may have difficulty relating to others in a steady, appropriate fashion, it is difficult to determine from the case history alone the extent to which this difficulty is "characterological" or related mostly to substance use.

It is clear, for example, that Paul has been able to establish some close relationships, to rekindle relationships that had been lost, and to make use of social support to change his behavior. He also appears to have a reasonable capacity for self-examination and self-assessment (for example, he realizes that he needs more than just a support group to effect lasting behavior changes), but may require assistance in translating this ability into concrete action plans.

Affectively, Paul appears to be mildly to moderately depressed, although this is not surprising given the many difficulties he is experiencing at the time of this initial interview. The relationship between depression and his substance use is, of course, difficult to determine precisely as long as the substance use continues at present high levels.

Finally, Paul's apparent tendencies toward impulsive decision making and susceptibility to social pressure to drink (a very high-risk situation for him with respect to cocaine use) suggest that some work will need to be done to help him become more skilled at considering a variety of alternative behaviors and their likely consequences for himself and others in both the short and long-terms. This will likely require, if he is willing, some efforts to teach him to delay or defer deciding on actions, even if doing so means having to tolerate short-term negative affect.

A word is also indicated here about the role of standardized personality assessment instruments in treatment planning with CRT. Standardized personality assessment instruments have little specific predictive validity with respect to substance use or other behavioral variables of importance in this case. At best they can suggest hypotheses to the therapist about how Paul might respond to specific interventions or situations, but they provide little specific information about these issues. Because behavior is controlled as much by situational factors as by internal, stable personality characteristics, it is important in the CRT approach to examine the client's behavior in context, rather than relying on global personality measures to guide treatment.

In addition, because CRT is largely client-driven rather than therapist-driven, and much of the work of behavior change revolves around helping the client weigh pros and cons of various behavioral options in specific contexts, global personality factors become much less important than they may be in other approaches. Rather, the focus is on the here and now and on assisting the client to develop and practice sound decision-making skills. The goal of treatment is *not* to remake the individual's personality, but rather to assist the individual in making use of his strengths in approaching specific situations he encounters in his daily life.

Thus, rather than relying on standardized personality tests for a picture of how the client will respond to particular situations or interventions, the therapist makes use of direct observation and client self-report in the form of self-monitoring.

*4. What potential pitfalls would you envision in this therapy? What would the difficulties be and what would you envision to be the source(s) of the difficulties?*

I would envision several possible difficulties in this therapy. First, and related to Paul's tendency toward impulsive decision making and his discouraged present emotional state, would be a high likelihood of dropping out of treatment if the therapist is not successful in increasing Paul's hopefulness for change, and expectation that change will occur. For this reason, an early focus on small, achievable goals, closely negotiated with Paul, would seem to be essential in helping to avoid treatment dropout. Paul seems likely to want rapid, major changes, when pragmatically, slower, smaller ones may be the most possible.

A second potential source of difficulty stems from Paul's social environment, and the apparent close association between his work, social life, and the factors that contribute most significantly to drinking and drug use. Because it may be necessary for Paul to shift his social network away, for example, from work buddies who are heavy drinkers, to other people who are not, it will be important to work with him to develop a reasonable new network, as well as reasonable expectations for how quickly he will be able to integrate this network into his overall life style.

To counter this potential difficulty, though, is Paul's favorable view of 12-step support groups, as well as his improving relationship with a sober father. Both of these factors suggest avenues along which Paul might proceed to restructure his social environment to be more supportive of his goals for reduction or cessation of substance use.

*5. To what level of coping, adaptation, or function would you see this client reaching as an immediate result of therapy? What result would be long-term subsequent to the ending of therapy (i.e., prognosis for adaptive change)?*

Because he comes to treatment so discouraged, it may be some time before Paul will be able to return to the level of functioning he exhibited following his initial inpatient treatment. However, it is clear from the case history that Paul has the capacity to function at a reasonably high level of coping given appropriate environmental supports. The immediate expectation I would have for treatment would be to help Paul develop a game plan for change in reasonable, achievable increments that would serve to enhance his flagging sense of self-efficacy, and help him move toward restructuring his behavior and environment to be more supportive of his goals. Initially, clarification of those goals would be an important therapeutic outcome, as would a plan for Paul to learn skills he might need to be able to work effectively toward those goals.

In the long-term, it is always difficult to predict the level at which clients will continue to function. Life circumstances can change dramatically and unexpectedly, presenting clients with situations with which they are ill prepared to cope. In fact, it seems clear that long-term treatment outcome is much more dependent on the extent to which these unexpected life circumstances occur and the ready availability of "back-up" resources for clients to draw upon in these times of crisis. Providing this "back-up is one of the primary reasons for keeping in touch with Paul even after "formal" treatment ends, to both monitor his continued progress and to keep the working relationship salient enough that Paul will return for help before his life again becomes as chaotic as it is at the time of treatment entry.

*6. What would be your time line (duration) for therapy? What would be your frequency and duration of sessions?*

Therapy would last as long as was necessary for Paul to begin to experience increased self-efficacy and have demonstrated to himself and the therapist that he was able to effectively analyze problem situations on his own and develop reasonable strategies for coping with them. Given that Paul has demonstrated some ability to develop and use coping strategies, at least temporarily, the process may, in fact, be a fairly rapid one. Because CRT attempts to assist clients in building upon their strengths, a number of which Paul has already demonstrated, therapy could very well be short-term. The actual duration of treatment will be determined by Paul's own self-assessment in conjunction with feedback from the therapist and significant others who may be involved in Paul's treatment. However, the therapist would continue, with Paul's agreement, to keep in touch with him for some time after regular meetings had ended. This serves to keep the working relationship active, and to lower the threshold for Paul to reenter treatment if he encounters unforeseen difficulties.

As far as duration and frequency of sessions during active treatment, this would be determined by Paul in consultation with the therapist, and based on assessment of rapidity of progress. As with other aspects of CRT, duration and frequency of sessions are determined primarily by Paul, although the therapist also participates in the process by informing Paul of the therapist's availability to meet for longer sessions or at increased frequency.

CRT therapists make every effort to accommodate to both the client's perceived needs and the therapist's assessment of the client's needs. This often results in a process of continuous negotiation with the client aimed at keeping the barriers the client might perceive to change as minimal as possible. By accommodating to the client, rather than forcing the client to accommodate to the therapist, the therapist lowers the barriers to continued engagement with the client in the change process.

*7. Are there specific techniques you would implement in the therapy? What might they be?*

A CRT therapist will choose from among a variety of therapeutic techniques to suggest to and use to work with a client. The process here is one of helping Paul discover, initially starting with empirically validated treatment methods, which methods will work best for him. Given the case history, and Paul's difficulty in following through with homework assignments in a previous treatment experience, the therapist should be very careful with respect to the design of homework, and how demanding the homework assignments would be.

The exact nature of the techniques to be suggested by the therapist would depend upon a thorough functional analysis of Paul's substance use. Such an assessment is essential in defining the exact nature of the difficulties that Paul experiences in achieving and maintaining reduced use. Because Paul has already had some treatment, he may already be

able to provide a useful picture of triggers, situations, and his own difficulties in coping with them. The results of this analysis would be discussed with Paul, specific techniques for helping him cope with high risk
situations and triggers would be presented, and then Paul, in consultation with the therapist, would decide which techniques might make most
sense given his particular circumstances.

Although it is difficult to be precise as to which techniques would be
suggested in the absence of a functional analysis, ones which take advantage of previous successes (i.e., perhaps a use of medication from within
a community reinforcement approach [Meyers & Smith, 1995]), suggestions
to reaffiliate with a 12-step or other support group, and implementation of
a variety of cognitive restructuring techniques to assist Paul in coping
with negative emotional states, might be suggested by the therapist.

Finally, given Paul's increasing problems with anger, the therapist
might suggest anger-management training (i.e., Novaco, 1975), aimed at
helping Paul learn non-substance-related methods for controlling anger
and inhibiting aggression. Whether this would be necessary would
depend on the relationship between Paul's escalating aggressiveness and
his substance use as determined by the functional analysis.

   *8. Are there special cautions to be observed in working with this client (i.e.,
danger to self or others, transference, counter-transference)? Are there any
particular resistances you would expect and how would you deal with them?*

There are several possible areas of difficulty that the therapist must be
alert to in working with this client. First is the distinct possibility of suicidal behaviors should Paul become discouraged with the ease and pace of
change. The therapist will need to be alert to signs of discouragement
and be prepared to step back from action-oriented techniques at times to
work on motivational enhancement.

With respect to possible danger to others, the most likely target of
Paul's anger appears to be his ex-wife whose patience with him may be
at an end, but who may be unwilling to engage in a dialogue with Paul
and the therapist about how to improve communication between them.
The therapist needs to carefully monitor Paul's anger toward his ex-wife,
as well as his perception of her willingness to allow him contact with his
children, and to be ready to raise these as issues in treatment with Paul.

With respect to resistances, CRT conceptualizes these as being of three
sorts: those created by the therapist-client interaction (and thus controllable to a large extent by the therapist); those that result from a faulty
functional analysis of Paul's difficulties (these are also controllable to a
large extent by the therapist through asking appropriate questions of
Paul); and those that are due to an absence of perceived, or genuine,
options on the part of Paul. All of these sources of resistance are, to some

extent, under the therapist's control, and can be reduced by careful thought, planning, and intervention by the therapist.

Finally, as with any client-driven, harm-reduction-based treatment process, the therapist needs to be alert to his or her own feelings about the client and the rate and extent of client changes. Harm reduction requires therapists to be able to both help and get out of the way when client resistance surfaces. Because clients are in charge of the process, therapists who have difficulty accepting that clients may not always agree to do what the therapist thinks necessary may find that the CRT approach produces significant levels of frustration. However, by recognizing that within a CRT framework the therapist's role is one of persuasion and helping clients make incremental movement, rather than entirely one of effecting rapid permanent changes in clients (only *clients* do this!), therapists can minimize the frustration they may experience with the pace of client change.

*9. Are there any areas that you would choose to avoid or not address with this client? Why?*

No. However, if Paul reacts negatively to the therapist broaching particular issues the therapist would be well advised to table those issues for the moment. One of the goals of CRT is to keep Paul engaged in the process of change. Pushing Paul faster or farther than he/she is ready to move is often a recipe for client dropout. Therefore, the therapist, true to the client-driven aspect of CRT, allows the client to set the agenda, albeit with input and coaching from the therapist. If particular issues are ones that the client is not yet prepared to address, the therapist has two options: table the issue or discuss with the client the pros and cons of addressing the issue at that time, and then allowing the client to decide which based on his or her readiness to confront a particular issue.

*10. Is medication warranted for this client? What effect would you hope or expect the medication to have?*

A medication consultation is definitely indicated for Paul. Two issues in the case history suggest this course. First, is the possibility of a clinical depression, although a clear differential diagnosis of a major depressive disorder from a more situationally determined depression will be difficult unless Paul elects to become abstinent and is able to maintain that abstinence for several weeks. However, this possibility is one that should be raised with Paul.

The second possible pharmacologic intervention to be considered and raised with this client is that of either a resumption of Antabuse, or perhaps more productively, introduction of ReVia (naltrexone), a new medication that is effective at reducing urges to drink and curtailing excessive drinking. Given Paul's report of a strong association between his drinking and cocaine use, exploration of this possibility with him should be a priority with the therapist.

Again, the process of implementing a medication regimen is one of negotiation and presentation of pros and cons of such an approach to the client. The client then makes the choice. Given Paul's previous positive response to a pharmacological intervention, it is likely that he would be receptive to such interventions at this time.

Clearly, the hoped for effect of pharmacological interventions with Paul would be to facilitate the work of behavior change. Antidepressant treatment might do this by helping Paul to have more energy to engage in the process of change, and to feel less discouraged about the prospects for change. A secondary effect might be to help at a neurochemical level to assist his body in recouping the neurotransmitters depleted by his use of cocaine.

ReVia or Antabuse would clearly serve as supports early in treatment to help reduce some of the "pressures" Paul feels to drink, and buy time in which he can begin to learn effective techniques for resisting temptations to drink.

*11. What are the strengths of the client that can be used in the therapy?*

Paul appears to have three primary strengths—an ability to find employment, an ability to establish and maintain cordial relationships (particularly with his ex-wife and children), and an ability to achieve abstinence for relatively long periods. These strengths are ones that provide a foundation for helping Paul continue to maintain motivation for change, and establish new relationships and systems that can support changes that Paul is able to make.

In addition, it can be considered a strength that Paul has, in the past, responded appropriately, at least at first, to learning of negative consequences associated with aspects of his substance use. Thus, he discontinued IV drug use upon learning he suffered from hepatitis.

*12. How would you address limits, boundaries, and limit setting with this client?*

As with any client, the CRT therapist must make clear the limits of his or her availability, confidentiality, and so forth at the onset of treatment. However, within those limits, the CRT therapist is willing to negotiate the parameters of therapy with Paul. Because CRT is client-focused and driven, much of the decision making about limits and boundaries must be Paul's responsibility. He is always responsible for the implementation of agreed upon strategies for behavior change.

Of most concern with Paul is his history of increasing anger and violent behavior. The therapist needs to be very clear with Paul as to the limits of confidentiality with respect to potential threats Paul might make. In addition, the therapist may want to do a decisional balance exercise with Paul (Miller & Rollnick, 1991) with respect to the pros and cons of responding to conflicts with anger and/or aggression.

*13. Would you want to involve significant others in the treatment? Would you use out-of-session homework with this client? What homework would you use?*

To the extent that Paul and important people in his life were willing, their involvement in his treatment could be critical to both immediate behavior changes and to maintaining those changes over time. Particularly with respect to the administration of any medications such as Antabuse or ReVia, involvement of significant others using a Community Reinforcement model (Meyers & Smith, 1995) can be very helpful in insuring that Paul will continue to both take the medications and continue to recognize the benefits of so doing.

The question of out-of-session homework is more problematic. Given Paul's history of noncompliance with homework assignments, the therapist may want to spend some time doing a functional analysis of that noncompliance, and reinforcing for Paul the benefits of completing homework assignments. One tack the therapist might want to take is to avoid calling out-of-session behavioral exercises "homework". This is based purely on a hunch that Paul's negative experiences in school may very well have revolved around "homework." A simple reframing of the out-of-session behavioral exercises may facilitate Paul's compliance with them. Further, negotiating small, manageable exercises at the start rather than imposing "standard" assignments, then increasing the difficulty and extent of the exercises as Paul begins to see the utility of them, may be helpful in encouraging Paul to follow through with them.

The specific exercises to be suggested would be determined by the results of the functional analytic assessment and input from Paul. Based on the case history, some possible exercises might be self-monitoring of urges to use, practicing refusal skills, and challenging irrational beliefs and cognitions. However, the exact nature and extent of such exercises would be determined in consultation with Paul as noted.

*14. What would be the issues to be addressed in termination? How would termination and relapse prevention be structured?*

Paul would largely determine termination. Because the CRT therapist aims at establishing a comfortable working relationship with Paul, it is hoped that Paul will wish to maintain some contact with the therapist over the long-term. As clients become more skilled and confident at implementing and maintaining the behavior changes toward which they aim, the therapist begins to suggest that perhaps the frequency of sessions might be tapered, or that Paul begin to examine possible alternative supports to meeting with the therapist. If the client is suggesting the possibility of termination before the therapist feels goals have been fully achieved, then this becomes a topic for discussion and review of the parameters of treatment. However, Paul will decide the exact nature and timing of termination.

Relapse-prevention training is an essential part of treatment and involves working closely with Paul to structure a plan that appears most workable from his perspective. This plan might involve participation in support groups, contractual relationships with significant others, and a plan for periodic "check-up" sessions with the therapist in the future.

*15. What do you see as the hoped-for mechanisms of change for this client, in order of importance?*

Because of its pragmatic emphasis, CRT relies for behavior change on the basic strengths and skills of the client, either those brought to the treatment or learned by the client through treatment. The process of change relies on what has long been hypothesized to be an innate human drive toward effective coping, a drive that nonetheless can be misdirected by virtue of faulty learning, inappropriate environmental contingencies, irrational thinking, poor problem-solving skills, or a combination of these factors. Virtually all human beings are capable, given the appropriate settings, opportunities, and motivation, of learning effective ways of coping with stresses in their lives. CRT focuses on attempting to enhance all of these factors and to help the client construct his life in such a way as to reinforce and promote the most effective coping possible.

Change in CRT is not due to supernatural or other intangible or unmeasurable factors, although environmental contingencies or cognitive restructuring associated with such factors (i.e., a decision to revise one's spiritual life) may contribute to change. Rather, change comes about through the process of assisting clients to restructure their own thinking and behavior, and where possible their environments, in the service of a healthier life style than the client had prior to entering treatment.

CRT recognizes that not all clients can achieve the ideal state of being (whatever that might be), but that virtually all can make positive, healthy changes in their lives. The focus of CRT therefore is on helping the client maximize the changes the client is willing to make and helping the client learn and implement the skills to do so.

# REFERENCES

Addiction Research Foundation. (1994) *Directory of client outcome measures for addictions treatment programs.* Toronto: Addiction Research Foundation.

Allen, J. P., & Columbus, M. (Eds.). (1995). *Assessing alcohol problems: A guide for clinicians and researchers.* National Institute on Alcohol Abuse and Alcoholism Treatment Handbook Series 4. NIH Publication No. 95-3745. Washington, DC: Government Printing Office.

Hester, R. K, & Miller, W. R. (Eds.). (1995). *Handbook of alcoholism treatment approaches: Effective alternatives, 2nd Edition.* Boston: Allyn & Bacon.

Marlatt, G. A. (1996). Harm reduction: Come as you are. *Addictive Behaviors, 21,* 779–788.

Meyers, R. J., & Smith, J. E. (1995). *Clinical guide to alcohol treatment: The community reinforcement approach.* New York: Guilford Press.

Miller, W. R., & Marlatt, G. A. (1984). *Manual for the comprehensive drinker profile.* Odessa, FL: Psychological Assessment Resources.

Miller, W. R., & Rollnick, S. A. (1991). *Motivational interviewing: Preparing people to change addictive behavior.* New York: Guilford Press.

Monti, P. M., Abrams, D. B., Kadden, R. M., & Cooney, N. L. (1989). *Treating alcohol dependence.* New York: Guilford Press.

Morgan, T. J. (1996). Behavioral treatment techniques for psychoactive substance use disorders. In F. Rotgers, D. S. Keller, & J. Morgenstern (Eds.), *Treating substance abuse: Theory and technique.* New York: Guilford Press.

Novaco, R. W. (1975). *Anger control: The development and evaluation of an experimental treatment.* Lexington, MA: Heath.

Prochaska, J. O., DiClemente, C. C., & Norcross, J. C. (1992). In search of how people change: Applications to addictive behaviors. *American Psychologist, 47,* 1102–1114.

Prochaska, J. O., Norcross, J. C., & DiClemente, C. C. (1994). *Changing for good.* New York: William Morrow.

Rotgers, F. (1996). Behavioral theory of substance abuse treatment: Bringing science to bear on practice. In F. Rotgers, D. S. Keller, & J. Morgenstern (Eds.), *Treating substance abuse: Theory and technique.* New York: Guilford Press.

Rounseville, B. J., Tims, F. M., Horton, A. M., & Sowder, B. J. (1993). *Diagnostic source book on drug abuse research and treatment.* NIH Publication No96-3508, Washington, DC: Government Printing Office.

# 10

# Relapse Prevention and Harm Reduction in the Treatment of Co-Occurring Addiction and Mental Health Problems

## *Kimberly Barrett and G. Alan Marlatt*

### I. THE CASE OF PAUL:
### DESCRIPTION OF TREATMENT MODEL

The model used to address Paul's multiple problems—substance abuse, depression, marital/family conflict, and violent behavior—involves the use of a Harm Reduction Philosophy in the application of Relapse Prevention, and Cognitive-Behavior Therapy treatment models. Family therapy will also be used to address many of the interpersonal and inter-generational aspects of the client's problems.

Harm Reduction provides a pragmatic and humanistic alternative to the moral/criminal/disease model of addiction (Marlatt & Roberts, 1998). The therapeutic focus shifts away from the actual occurrence of drug or alcohol use, to the consequences of addictive behaviors. The black and white dynamics of abstinence and relapse, which traditionally have meant treatment failure and possible rejection from treatment for the client, are replaced with a model that accepts the client where he or she is in the change process, reducing barriers and stigmas in treatment for clients who are yet unable or unwilling achieve abstinence (Marlatt, 1996). Harm reduction approaches incorporate motivational enhancement methods for promoting change, and help to engage the client in an active partnership with the therapist in developing treatment goals and strategies for change. Change is process oriented and gradual, and success is not defined as a final outcome but movement in the direction of less risk and harmful consequences to the client.

A harm reduction model also addresses a broader range of problems with the client, treating the client as a whole person, seeing addictive and other harmful behaviors as interacting with other psychological, interpersonal, and social/environmental problems that the client may be experiencing. The client will thus learn to understand the relationship between the functions of their substance abuse and other problems as they occur in multiple contexts.

Relapse Prevention (RP) is a cognitive-behavioral treatment that combines behavioral skill training procedures with cognitive intervention techniques to assist individuals in maintaining desired behavioral changes (Kendall & Hollon, 1979). Based in part on the principles of health psychology (e.g., Stone et al., 1979) and social-cognitive theory (Bandura, 1986), RP uses a psychoeducational self-management approach to substance abuse and other harmful behaviors (such as Paul's anger problems). The client is taught to see relapse as a process, and learns to identify and understand high-risk situations that may trigger the occurrence of a relapse. Developing new social and cognitive coping responses as alternatives to addictive/problem behaviors involves skills training and the application of newly acquired skills to the client's high-risk situations. Modification of maladaptive beliefs and expectancies concerning substance use, and developing strategies for changing personal habits and life style are also components of the RP model. Involving family members and significant others in RP treatment can be an integral part of the learning and change process (Marlatt & Barrett, 1994; McCrady, 1989; O'Farrell, 1991; O'Farrell, Choquette, Cutter, & Brown, 1996).

RP procedures can be applied in treatment designed to prevent relapse, reduce relapse risk, or to manage ongoing relapse problems. In the RP approach, relapse is viewed as a transitional process, rather than an outcome failure. One of the primary goals of the approach is to provide the client with skills and cognitive strategies to prevent a lapse from escalating into a total relapse. A lapse can be viewed as an opportunity for learning, and can potentially increase clients' motivation to change and to cope differently with their substance abuse. For example, if Paul experienced a lapse in his alcohol and cocaine use following a fight with his wife, he could identify conflict with his wife as a high-risk situation, thus a trigger for relapse. He then may view his substance use as a method of coping with anger. In order to cope more effectively with marital conflict and its resulting emotions Paul could apply a number of coping strategies—for example, learning communication and problem solving skills, learning to express his emotions and needs to his wife before they build to the point of anger; remembering to take a break during disagreements if he felt his anger building; and perhaps learning to utilize exercise or relaxation exercises as a way to cool off if the marital conflict ended with his feeling angry.

In the RP model, three categories of high risk situations are associated with the highest relapse rates—negative emotional states, interpersonal conflict, and social pressure to return to substance use. If the individual is able to execute an effective coping response in a high risk situation, the probability of relapse decreases. As individuals make progress in identifying and coping effectively with more high-risk situations, their feelings of confidence and self-efficacy increase. As their perception of control over problems and risks increases, the likelihood of relapse decreases. If the client fails to utilize previously learned coping responses, it is important to determine what has inhibited the appropriate response, such as a lack of assertiveness, failure to appraise the risk of the situation, or perhaps a decline in motivation. Again, this information will become part of the treatment process in a way that provides the client and therapist with further information for change. It is an ongoing part of treatment to help the client to reduce guilt and self blame for relapse, in that such emotions and cognitions demoralize clients and erode their motivation to change.

Family involvement in substance abuse treatment has solid empirical support (Steinglass, 1994) and serves to enhance client motivation and engagement in treatment. Family Therapy models of alcoholism and drug abuse treatment (Jacob, Dunn, & Leonard 1985; Kaufman, 1994; McCrady 1989, Moos, Finney, & Cronkite, 1990; O'Farrell 1991; O'Farrell et al., 1996; Steinglass, 1994; Steinglass, Bennett, & Wolin, 1987) offer a range of systemic, social learning, and behavioral techniques designed to identify and change interactional and behavioral sequences that lead to substance use; and to pinpoint the functions of addictive behaviors in the family system. The family is guided through processes which facilitate more adaptive coping and problem-solving methods, and the development of healthier avenues for emotional expression. O'Farrell (1996 ) has developed a couples' approach which includes Behavioral Marital Therapy in combination with Relapse Prevention.

Family therapy would be useful in the treatment of this case in order to help Paul and his wife to create a substance-free life style, to develop the ability to communicate and express emotion in a constructive manner, and to learn to understand the behavioral sequences and symptom functionality of substance abuse in their family. Treatment of this nature involves assessing the degree to which substance abuse has permeated and impeded overall family functioning and development—especially in respect to the disruption of regular routines, rituals and holidays, the ability to resolve conflict, solve problems, and negotiate normal developmental tasks. Normal developmental hurdles that have been missed or detoured due to the family's intensive involvement in the cycles of addiction are to be addressed, as well as intergenerational patterns of family interaction that have been created or distorted by substance abuse (Steinglass, Bennett, & Wolin, 1987).

Examining the impact of substance abuse and domestic violence on children's emotional development and the ability for parents to monitor, show affection for, and discipline their children appropriately and consistently is also pertinent to this case.

## II. WHAT WOULD BE THE CLINICAL SKILLS OR ATTRIBUTES MOST ESSENTIAL TO SUCCESSFUL THERAPY IN YOUR APPROACH?

The clinical skills necessary in the treatment of Paul are multiple. They involve establishing and maintaining an atmosphere of trust, patience, and acceptance; increasing Paul's motivation for change; and developing a working process of collaboration in goal setting and developing change strategies between the client and therapist. The therapist should be trained in using motivational interviewing techniques (Miller & Rollnick, 1991), harm reduction, relapse prevention, and cognitive-behavior therapy. Additionally, an understanding of the family dynamics of addiction, and the ability to utilize systemically based interventions in both psychological treatment and relapse prevention are also important skills required in this case.

First, in the utilization of a treatment model that espouses a harm reduction philosophy, it is essential that the therapist be readily able to meet the client where he or she is, in a manner that projects a nonjudgmental, nonmoralistic, and nonpunitive stance. Rather than focus on the black and white states of substance use vs. abstinence, the therapist can educate and guide the client toward the use of a process-oriented model that aims for abstinence without demanding perfectionism. Relapse is considered normative behavior in the treatment of cocaine addiction (James & Johnson, 1996, Wallace, 1991).

A harm reduction model examines the patterns and consequences of addictive and other destructive behaviors (i.e., violence) in the context of other psychological problems and the interpersonal milieu. The acceptance of the client at his current stage in the addiction/change process eliminates the barrier of abstinence as a precondition for treatment. Abstinence creates a high threshold for entering treatment, while harm reduction presents a low one. The client feels accepted by the therapist in a way that reduces stigma and diminishes the anxiety that may accompany fear of relapse and subsequent rejection by the treatment provider.

The therapist seeks information to gain understanding about the client's previous struggles with substance abuse, sobriety, and relapse, as part of creating a therapeutic alliance. In gathering such information, the therapist can both convey empathy and normalize the abstinence-relapse cycles as part of the process of change. Such efforts on the part of the therapist build a foundation of trust and provide the client with reassurance of continued acceptance should any aspect of previous relapse patterns return in the current treatment.

Secondly, the clinician possesses skills that will build and enhance client motivation. Eliciting goals that resonate with the client's values and life style, building on strengths and past successes at abstinence are important motivational components elicited by the therapist. Motivational interviewing (Miller & Rollnick, 1991) techniques also deemphasize diagnostic labels and personal pathology that may reduce personal choice and responsibility. The clinician skilled at motivational interviewing emphasizes personal responsibility, and helps the client to identify his own concerns and goals for change. The client is actively engaged in developing strategies for facilitating change and problem solving. Goals and strategies for change are negotiated between the client and therapist. Change strategies may also be sought from significant others. Resistance is seen as an interactive, interpersonal behavior pattern that takes place between the client and therapist. Resistance is not seen as a pattern of denial or refusal to change, and is handled by the use of reflection with the client, and by the self-examination of communication style and strategy used on the part of the clinician.

Key clinical skills involved in motivational interviewing as outlined by Miller offer many similarities to a Rogerian, client centered approach, and include: 1) the expression of empathy; 2) the creation of cognitive dissonance about current maladaptive behaviors, or increasing the awareness of the discrepancy between where the client is, and where the client wants to be. The client will become more aware of the costs of his present behavior and how it conflicts with important personal goals; 3) the therapist avoids arguments and head-on confrontations with the client, and use a softer, more persuasive style; 4) the therapist rolls with client resistance; and 5) the therapist helps the client to believe that change is possible, and supports the client's efforts and responsibility for change.

Therapists trained in behavior therapy, family therapy, and relapse prevention can assist their clients to understand the functional relationship between their addictive behaviors, emotional difficulties, and interpersonal relationships. For example, Paul was angry at his wife for being less available to him and for not working after the birth of their second child. He felt stressed due to financial pressure, and his wife was not there to assist him. Paul also had reported that his mother had had little energy for the children after the birth of his youngest sibling, and at that time was less able to protect the family from his father's drinking, temper, and abuse. Paul may have experienced feelings of abandonment and helplessness when his mother became less available to hold the family together. After his second child was born, Paul may have experienced similar feelings of anger and abandonment in his marriage, along with abdicating control and responsibility for his own substance abuse and emotional behavior. Hidden expectations that were not met by his wife, and his lack of ability to communicate those expectations to her were likely to be precipitants of relapse that Paul and his family could learn to understand and remediate through the development of improved skills in emotional expression and conflict resolution.

## III. FIFTEEN CLINICAL QUESTIONS

*1. What would be your therapeutic goals for this patient? What are the primary goals and the secondary goals? Please be as specific as possible.*

### Primary Goals

The proximal goal in the treatment of Paul is the reduction of harmful consequences to himself and others, and hopefully, the achievement of abstinence as a distal goal. Other primary goals include reducing Paul's depression, and eliminating his violent behavior while developing means for appropriate emotional expression and interpersonal problem solving.

The first goal for Paul is learning to understand the emotional and situational events that lead to relapse, and to increase his sense of self-efficacy in regard to achieving prolonged periods of abstinence. Paul has reported very little success with prolonged periods of abstinence. The use of RP within the framework of Harm Reduction can provide Paul with hope in what has been a chronically hopeless situation. Within this framework, relapses will be utilized as an educational part of the treatment process, providing both Paul and the clinician with information that is useful in working toward an eventual goal of abstinence.

Reducing Paul's depression will likely involve the use of antidepressant medication, and collaborating with Paul to gain greater understanding of the historical and cognitive roots of his depression. Hopefully, helping Paul to stabilize both his substance abuse and his depressed/ agitated moods will help the client and therapy process as we begins to address his violent behavior at work and with his wife.

## Secondary Goals

Secondary goals involve working toward a deeper understanding of his problems in the context of his family of origin and marital relationship. Both of Paul's parents have requested his forgiveness without facilitated discussion of some of the traumas experienced by their children during the course of family development. Exploration of intergenerational patterns of addiction in both Paul's and his wife's family would be useful in helping to prevent cycles of relapse in the present adult generations, and could provide valuable information for building healthier family rituals and interactions for Paul's children. Developing more positive family relationships and traditions may prove useful for breaking the intergenerational cycle of substance abuse.

   2. *What further information would you want to have to assist you in structuring this patient's treatment?*
   We know little about Paul's personal motivations for change. Why does he want to quit drinking and using drugs? What are his doubts and fears about quitting and achievement of abstinence? What will he be losing or sacrificing by quitting? What are the rewards he associates with abstinence? We need to assess both his intrinsic motives and sense of efficacy toward change, as well as his extrinsic motives, which relate to his wife and children. We would ask Paul to complete a decision matrix (Marlatt & Gordon, 1985) which would allow him to examine both the immediate and delayed effects of substance use, expanding his thinking from the pleasurable short-term effects to that of the longer-term, more negative consequences.
   Paul would be asked to utilize self-monitoring procedures, such as keeping a journal or daily record of his urges and cravings, substance use; and antecedent or situational events, cognitions, and affective states associated with cravings or use. This would help Paul and the therapist to identify high-risk interpersonal, emotional, and or situational influences that underlie his addictive behavior pattern, as well as to illuminate skill or coping deficits that may contribute to relapse. A functional analysis of Paul's addictive behaviors would be conducted, utilizing self-monitoring and interview data, as well as gathering similar collateral information from his wife.
   Other assessment instruments used would be the Addiction Severity Index, a structured interview, and a repeat of the Beck Depression

Inventory. The Situational Confidence Questionnaire (Annis & Davis, 1988) would be given to Paul in order to assess Paul's perceptions of self-efficacy in handling potential relapse situations.

We would also like information about the kinds of activities that Paul enjoys that do not involve substance use, and whether or not he has friends who are supportive of his sobriety.

Paul's wife can provide useful information regarding Paul's problems, both in terms of her conceptualization of his problems, and with respect to their cycles of marital conflict and Paul's substance abuse. How has his wife tried to set limits and boundaries on his drinking, drug use, and violence? Has she ever called the police and reported his physical abuse of her? How would she describe high-risk situations for Paul? Does she drink or use drugs? Why and how often does she use valium? Why does she give it to Paul? What have been her reasons for staying in the marriage? What strategies has Paul utilized in the past that she views as helpful in his recovery process?

In order to assess other family dynamics, and to assure the safety of Paul's children, the following questions would be asked: Is Paul ever physically abusive to his children? If so, has this ever been reported? Does Paul's substance abuse prevent or interrupt regular family activities, such as dinnertime, holidays and family celebrations, recreational outings and weekends? How does Paul's wife handle his substance use and emotional outbursts around the children? How does Paul explain his behavior to his children? How would Paul and his wife describe their typical marital conflicts and stresses in their relationship? What are the strengths of their marriage? Does Paul spend any positive time with his children? How do Paul and his wife demonstrate affection and establish discipline with their children? Do the children see their grandparents? What is the current status of Paul's relationship with his parents? Would they be willing to participate in family therapy with Paul?

*3. What is your conceptualization of this patient's personality, behavior, affective state, and cognitions?*

Paul presents as a person who is often preoccupied with himself, irritable, explosive, and prone toward interpersonal violence. He is depressed, lacks self-confidence, and exhibits an attitude of hopelessness and defeat. He takes little responsibility for his negative and destructive behaviors. He is able to work well at his job when sober, and seems to make friends easily at his place of employment.

Paul grew up in a chaotic, inconsistent, and abusive family environment. There were few rules, limits, or protective boundaries in his family relationships. He experienced a conflictual and abusive relationship with his father, and similarly destructive interactions between himself and his siblings. Although his mother was a loving person, she became less and less available to Paul as she became exhausted from managing numerous family stresses. Paul saw his mother attempt to cope with marital conflict, his father's alcoholism and abusiveness, taking care of six children, and working nights outside of the home. In trying to buffer the children from their father's temper, she accepted her husband's abuse, and modeled a manner of conflict resolution that involved acquiescing and smoothing things over in order to calm him down. Paul observed his father's anger being reinforced by his mother, in her attempts to maintain peace in the family. Paul probably learned that the role of a wife and mother is to keep her husband happy at any price to herself and children. His mother ultimately failed, however, in that she was not able to protect the children from their father's abusiveness. She was also unable to draw the line where his alcoholism was concerned.

Paul is uncertain of his place and value in relationships with others. He longs for belonging, and seeks interpersonal contact through hanging out and drinking with the guys. One of his first powerful feelings of being accepted by his peers is associated with being given a can of beer. He gathers most of his self-esteem from his capabilities at work. He repeatedly gains the friendship and respect of his employers and co-workers, and probably is both talented and personable while at work. Unfortunately, his fellow employees often become his drinking partners, creating situations where he blurs his boundaries and position of respect as a supervisor, eroding his job security and his fragile sense of self-esteem. This creates feelings of failure, leads to irresponsible and explosive behavior, and is part of his cycle of substance abuse.

Paul's upbringing presented him with few models or tools for building positive intimate or social relationships. It is likely Paul views his wife's role as similar to that of his mother. He has expectations that his wife should monitor his behavior and affective states, and help him to manage his anger and substance abuse. He has difficulty with compromise and the give and take processes required in marriage. Paul wants more closeness with his wife, but does not know how to be open in order to develop an intimate relationship. Their early courtship was organized around their mutual suffering as children of alcoholic families, and their marriage was precipitated by pregnancy. It seems as though they had few deliberate plans as to how to create a more positive family life for themselves.

Paul and his wife thus began to replicate many negative dynamics found in their families of origin—poor communication and problem-solving skills, the intrusion of alcohol and drugs into family life, explosive and abusive anger, and the use of valium too "calm down" the anger, stress, and conflict. Paul's wife may be giving him valium to smooth out the rough spots, just as Paul's mother did with his father. Paul is also angry at his wife for becoming less available after their second child was born, and again may experience her withdrawal as being similar to that of his mother.

Paul most likely uses drugs and alcohol to help manage his negative affective states and the pain of interpersonal conflict. He is often angry at others, but he is also lonely. He most likely has frequent thoughts about his own worthlessness, and lack of meaningful connection to friends and his family. Paul may admonish himself for his abusiveness to his wife and children, yet he also attributes responsibility for his bad behavior to others, particularly to his father, mother, and his wife. It is difficult for him to allow his father to help him in his recovery, in that his father has demanded forgiveness for his past behavior at the same time that he has demanded that Paul stop using drugs and alcohol. Paul was not ever allowed to make this demand of his father, and as a child he was helpless in seeking protection from his father's addiction and abuse. Paul is likely to be angry at his father, as he was the model for many of Paul's current problems. This anger is connected to Paul's lack of ability to take responsibility for his own behavior.

*4. What potential pitfalls would you envision in this therapy? What would the difficulties be and what would you envision to be the sources of the difficulties?*

Paul's impulsivity has most likely been closely related to previous relapses, decisions to stop aftercare, Antabuse, etc. The biggest risk to treatment is that Paul will drop out as the crisis passes and he gains false confidence regarding his sobriety.

Establishing trust and creating an atmosphere of hope would be initial barriers to overcome in that Paul is depressed, discouraged, and perhaps distrustful in regard to clinicians and the treatment process. He also has had trouble being open in therapy before. Additionally, Paul's past perceptions of success—at maintaining sobriety, being busy at work, and having little conflict with his wife—have led him to stop treatment in the past. Another source of potential difficulties involves Paul's potential for incarceration due to drunk driving, violent behavior at work, or for domestic violence.

Paul has always been able to get another job after being fired or taking time off for treatment. It is possible that his luck may run out in this respect, and that he would become unemployed for a long period of time. Financial stress and this loss to his self-esteem would present major obstacles in maintaining sobriety and overcoming depression.

Paul will need to find friends who do little or no drinking. Having a male peer group, and feeling a sense of belonging and acceptance in that group, is important to Paul. If he does not find such a group to connect with, he risks a loss of social support and friendship. This could lead to a return to companionship with his drinking buddies, and a likely relapse.

*5. To what level of coping, adaptation, or function would you see this patient reaching as an immediate result of therapy?*

As an immediate result of therapy, Paul would be likely to feel less depressed, more hopeful, and experience an increase in his sense of efficacy regarding his ability make an active contribution to the treatment process and in his own recovery. The prospect of family therapy and developing anger-management skills may provide Paul with further motivation to maintain abstinence in order to stabilize and improve relationships with his wife and children.

Long-term results would consist in Paul feeling less depressed, more optimistic, and more balanced in his daily moods. Paul would feel a greater sense of mastery in respect to understanding his addictive behaviors, and would be able to utilize behavioral and affective coping skills that would help him to reduce and manage lapses, and prevent serious relapse in respect to drugs and alcohol, and violent behavior. Paul would have developed a more consistent relationship with his children, and may engage in social and recreational outlets that do not involve getting high. He would have an increased ability to resolve communication problems and dependency issues with his wife and parents.

*6. What would be you time line (duration) for therapy? What would be your frequency and duration of the sessions?*

Therapy sessions, of 60–90 minutes each, would be held twice weekly for the first two to three months of therapy, in order to accommodate both the individual and family sessions, and for the purpose of providing Paul with intensive support as he attempts to achieve sobriety. Thereafter, sessions would be held weekly for 60–90 minutes, unless Paul and the therapist felt the need for additional weekly sessions. Weekly therapy sessions would continue for the next 12 months, reducing in frequency to biweekly as Paul's progress permitted. The probable duration of therapy would be 2 years.

*7. Are there specific or special techniques that you would implement in the therapy? What would they be?*

The techniques used in the therapy are contained and outlined within the Relapse Prevention, Harm Reduction, Motivational Interviewing models, Behavioral Marital Therapy, and Family Therapy models, as discussed elsewhere in this chapter.

*8. Are there special cautions to be observed in working with this patient (e.g., danger to self or others, transference, counter-transference)? Are there any resistances you would expect and how would you deal with them?*

It would be important to set guidelines with Paul about substance use during scheduled appointments. Paul would not be seen for a therapy session if the therapist felt that he was high at the time of their meeting. Reports of relapse between sessions would be used to help Paul in the process of identifying triggers for relapse, and how to better apply preventative coping skills.

The therapist should be aware of developing false confidence in Paul's ability to be sober and responsible, both during initial meetings (Paul is very good at creating a good impression initially, demonstrated by his ability to get jobs, maintaining a positive relationship with his bosses), as well as after Paul has demonstrated several months of sobriety (a time when he gains false confidence).

It would be important to monitor Paul's violent behavior toward his wife, children, employer, and co-workers, encouraging his employer and significant others to set boundaries and clear consequences with Paul regarding his violent behavior. The therapist should monitor his or her own feelings of fear when working with Paul, as they may represent real danger in the treatment of clients with violent or antisocial tendencies (Meloy, 1995).

The combination of Paul's depression, conduct disturbances, substance abuse, and impulsivity increase his risk for suicidality. It would be important to monitor any suicidal ideations that Paul may have.

It would be expected that Paul's major resistances will occur in respect to maintaining ongoing involvement and commitment to the therapy process, especially if his initial progress is significant. This resistance would be addressed by discussing and predicting resistance with Paul early in therapy as a part of the relapse prevention process, as well as pacing and monitoring Paul's urges to leave therapy during the duration of the therapy process. Paul would be asked to collaborate with the therapist in the development of strategies to prevent premature termination.

Additionally, in that Paul has had a difficult time revealing and understanding his own emotional pain in the past, it is likely that this resistance will occur again, both in individual and family sessions. The therapist can address this issue in therapy through the creation of a supportive and trusting environment, and by recognizing and commenting on nonverbal indications of emotional distress communicated by Paul in therapy sessions. Helping Paul to acknowledge his own sadness and distress, in combination with empathic validation for the development of these feelings in his historical family context, may help Paul to learn to recognize and be more open with his emotions.

*9. Are there any areas that you would choose to avoid or not address with this patient? Why?*
None.

*10. Is medication warranted for this patient? What effect would you hope or expect the medication to have?*
Antidepressant medication would be helpful to reduce depression, impulsivity, and mood swings. Naltrexone to reduce craving relapse magnitude.

*11. What are the strengths of the patient that can be used in therapy?*
Paul has overcome a heroin addiction, a significant factor in his favor. This evidence of past success in overcoming heroin can be used to increase his sense of motivation and efficacy at overcoming alcohol and cocaine addiction.

Although Paul has experienced many failures—with overcoming his addictions, with his family relationships, and with his employment, he has continued to persevere in his attempts to get sober, keep working, and stay married. When sober, Paul takes pride in his work abilities, and works to maintain a good relationship with his crew. Paul is skilled at his job, and develops a positive relationship with his employers. He is easily hired and maintains the support of his employers even after he has behaved irresponsibly on the job.

Paul has many positive childhood memories of his family in addition to memories of conflict, physical violence, and substance abuse. Paul still holds feelings of fondness for his parents, and demonstrated caring and empathy for his siblings while growing up. He expresses a desire for friendships and close family relationships. His wife has also remained committed to him, despite his relapses, violence, and continual marital conflict. It is possible that there is love and strength remaining in their marital bond.

*12. How would you address limits, boundaries, and limit setting with this patient?*
Paul would be informed of our need to report child abuse, actual or threats of physical violence toward his wife or co-workers.

No therapy sessions will be held if he was under the influence of drugs or alcohol.

Paul's wife would be encouraged to set limits on his violence. She must first develop a plan to assure her own safety and the safety of the children. She must report any physical abuse to the proper authorities. A community reinforcement approach would be used to set contingencies on Paul's violent behavior. Access to his job and family would be dependent on his ability to stop his physical assaults on his wife and co-workers.

Paul's wife must agree to help establish a drug- and alcohol-free home environment, and not to assist Paul with obtaining valium or other drugs. Paul's wife must set limits in terms of her willingness to stay married to Paul. If she participates in the therapy process, she may set a contingency of eventual abstinence on Paul's part in order to remain together.

Paul does not wish to attend an inpatient treatment program. If outpatient therapy was not producing significant progress, an inpatient program would be required in order for therapy to continue.

*13. Would you want to involve significant others in the treatment? Would you use out-of-session homework with this patient? What homework would you use?*

Paul's wife would be involved during many, (but not all) of the initial sessions in the early phases of his treatment. We would utilize a couple's approach to relapse prevention as outlined by McCrady and O'Farrell. Family therapy would include Paul's wife and children, and at times meetings would be scheduled between Paul and his parents. Paul would be given the opportunity to resolve past grievances with his parents, and to learn to separate his history from current family dynamics. Family therapy would address family organization through the establishment of more appropriate roles, rules, routines, and boundaries. Developing improved problem solving and parenting skills would help to prevent Paul's children from suffering further abuse, and provide them with more appropriate modeling experiences. Establishing healthier family rituals and traditions would address life style issues and diminish the likelihood of the intergenerational transmission of Paul's family dynamics.

Homework would be used regularly as part of therapy. Self and couples monitoring procedures, the identification of high-risk situations, and the utilization of new affective and behavioral coping strategies would be assigned, (as outlined in the RP model, and the RP couples' model). The RP homework would focus both on substance abuse and anger management. Paul would also be encouraged to experiment with new social and recreational activities, both alone and with his family. Paul and his wife would also be given assignments that related to daily family life and parenting—assigning chores, developing clear rules, rewards, and consequences for positive and negative behavior in the children. Marital therapy assignments might address developing more positive and caring ways of interacting, and learning to spend time together as a couple, without drugs, alcohol, or children.

Paul would be asked to attend AA, Rational Recovery, or SMART meetings at least once weekly. Support group meetings would not take the place of regular therapy sessions.

*14. What would be the issues to be addressed in termination? How would termination and relapse prevention be structured?*

Paul's therapy is likely to be quite intensive for the first year. If progress is made, the intervals between sessions would be increased. Paul would be encouraged to test his own self-management techniques, without the structure and contingencies provided in therapy. Paul would be encouraged to continue to attend his addiction-focused support group. As Paul demonstrated successful self-management for several weeks at a time, individual/family sessions would be terminated. In their final sessions, Paul and his wife would identify behaviors, emotions, and situations that were indicators that one or both of them may need to return to therapy for a few refresher or problem solving sessions.

*15. What do you see as the hoped-for mechanisms for change in this patient, in order of importance?*

The primary mechanism for change in this case is the identification of the causal and interactional mechanisms that influence Paul's behavior. A functional analysis of behavior, and the utilization of cognitive-behavioral procedures will assist the client and therapist in exploring and identifying the cognitive, affective, situational, and interpersonal components of Paul's substance abuse, depression, and violent behavior.

Secondly, reducing the harmful consequences of Paul's behavior, and increasing Paul's motivation for change, will provide reinforcement for Paul and his family in their attempts to change, and reduce the likelihood that Paul will injure his wife or children. The consequences of drunk driving and violent behavior will be stressed as behaviors with a high priority for elimination, as they pose the potential for greatest harm to others, as well as to Paul himself. Reducing the harmful consequences of substance abuse provides Paul with a new vehicle in which to return to the road of sobriety, with abstinence as the destination or goal. However, a harm reduction approach will reduce feelings of failure if relapse occurs. The combination of harm reduction and RP provide the therapy process with valuable tools for helping the client toward steady, long-term sobriety.

The use of antidepressant medication is equal to the above mechanisms in its importance in order to help reduce Paul's depression and hopelessness. The possibility of stabilizing Paul's mood and depression increases his capacity to profit from psychotherapy, and may help to facilitate some improvement in family and work relationships as treatment begins.

Family therapy is a process that will help Paul to understand his behavior in an intergenerational and interpersonal context. His childhood was highly traumatic and stressful, and his marriage to another child of an alcoholic is likely fraught with many dysfunctional tendencies.

Working through and resolving his anger about the past, and developing a more appropriate sense of marital roles, and how to effectively meet personal dependency needs should help stabilize Paul's relationships with significant others, and help him to stop blaming his family for his mistakes and irresponsible behavior. Learning how to be an effective parent would decrease Paul's sense of helplessness in a family context, and would also reduce family stress and the potential for abuse.

Lastly, the development of a balanced life style, through the discovery of new ways of relaxing, having fun, and building drug-free friendships, will increase Paul's sense of satisfaction in life, and reduce his need to be "one of the guys." Paul also would need to become more consistent in his work habits, developing a daily rhythm that is not stressful, and not becoming overly concerned about being liked by the men he supervises. He would need to avoid working long hours, or long weeks. Reinforcement of Paul's abilities with his hands, and helping him to build an internal system for using positive self-appraisal and reinforcement would help him utilize his vocational talents as a means of maintaining self-confidence and self-esteem.

## REFERENCES

Annis, H. M., & Davis, C. S. (1988). Assessment of expectancies in alcohol dependent clients. In D. M. Donovan & G. A. Marlatt (Eds.), *Assessment of addictive behaviors: Behavioral, cognitive, and physiological processes.* New York: Guilford Press.

Bandura, A. (1986). *Social foundations of thought and action: A social cognitive theory.* Englewood Cliffs, NJ: Prentice-Hall.

Jacob, T., Dunn, N. J., & Leonard, K. (1985). Patterns of alcohol use and family stability. *Alcohol Clinical Expectancy Research, 7,* 382–385.

James, W. H., & Johnson, S. L. (1996). *Doin drugs: Patterns of African American addiction.* Austin, TX: University of Texas Press.

Kaufman, E. (1994). Family therapy: Other drugs. In M. D. Galanter & M. D. Kleber (Eds.), *American psychiatric press textbook of substance abuse treatment* (pp. 331–348). Washington, D.C.: American Psychiatric Press.

Kendall, P. C., & Hollon, S. D. (1979). (Eds.). *Cognitive-behavioral interventions: Theory, research, and procedures.* New York: Academic Press.

Marlatt, G. A. (1996). Harm reduction: Come as you are. *Addictive Behaviors, 21,* 779–788.

Marlatt, G. A., & Roberts, L. J. (1998). Introduction to a special issue: Harm reduction as an alternative to abstinence in treatment of comorbidity. *In Session, 4-1,* 1–8.

Marlatt, G. A., & Barrett, K. S. (1994). Relapse prevention. In M. D. Galanter & M. D. Kleber (Eds.), *American Psychiatric Press textbook of substance abuse treatment* (pp. 285–299). Washington, D.C.: American Psychiatric Press.

Marlatt, G. A., & Gordon, J. (1985). (Eds.). *Relapse prevention: Maintenance strategies in the treatment of addictive behaviors.* New York: Guilford Press.

McCrady, B. (1989). Extending relapse models to couples. *Addictive Behaviors, 14,* 69–74

Meloy, J. R. (1995). Antisocial personality disorder. In G. O. Gabbard (Ed.), *Treatments of psychiatric disorders* (pp. 2273–2290). Washington, D.C.: American Psychiatric Press.

Miller, W. R., & Rollnick, S. (1991). *Motivational interviewing.* New York: Guilford Press.

Moos, R. H., Finney, J. W., & Cronkite, R. C. (1990). *Alcoholism treatment: Process and outcome.* New York: Oxford University Press.

O'Farrell, T. J., Choquette, K. A., Cutter, H. S. G., & Brown, E. (1996). Cost benefit and cost effectiveness analyses of behavioral marital therapy with and without relapse prevention session for alcoholics and their spouses. *Behavior Therapy, 27*(1), 7–24.

O'Farrell, T. J. (1991). Using couples therapy in the treatment of alcoholism. *Family Dynamics of Addiction Quarterly, 1,* 39–45.

Steinglass, P., Bennett, L., & Wolin, S. (1987). *The alcoholic family.* New York: Basic Books.

Steinglass, P. (1994). Family therapy: Alcohol. In M. D. Galanter & M. D. Kleber (Eds.), *The American psychiatric press textbook of substance abuse treatment.* Washington, D.C.: American Psychiatric Press.

Wallace, B. C. (1991). *Crack cocaine: A practical treatment approach for the chemically dependent.* New York: Brunner/Mazel.

# 11

## Family Therapy

*Helen S. Raytek*

### I. THE TREATMENT MODEL

Current family therapy treatment approaches for substance abuse problems are generally one of the following three models: family disease models, family systems models, and behavioral models (McCrady & Epstein, 1996). The family therapy model described in this chapter is a behavioral approach. Behavioral family therapy uses a social learning framework to conceptualize substance abuse and family functioning. This model emphasizes the reciprocal interactions between the substance abuser and other family members in determining repetitive and dysfunctional interaction patterns (McCrady & Epstein, 1995). Behavioral family therapy focuses on current factors that maintain substance abuse, not on historical factors. Factors that maintain substance use can be based in the individual (physiological or psychological factors) or in dyadic or broader family interactional patterns. Antecedents more related to the individual may be features of the physical environment, certain times of the day, and withdrawal symptoms. Family antecedents include stressful interpersonal situations such as arguments. External antecedents to substance use are assumed to be related to that use because of repeated pairings with positive or negative consequences of use or through anticipation of those consequences. Cognitions, emotions, and expectancies are assumed to mediate the relationship between external antecedents and substance use.

Specific behaviors of family members may serve as antecedent stimuli for substance use and as reinforcement for substance use. The substance abuser's episodes of substance use may in turn be antecedent stimuli for behaviors of family members intended to cope with the substance use.

These reciprocal influences operate in complex stimulus-response chains which are often circular in their functioning. Over time, behavioral models would predict a complex set of interactions among family members in which the behaviors of each family member serve, sometimes simultaneously, as an antecedent to the other family members' behaviors, as a response to the other family members' behaviors, and as reinforcing or punishing consequences of the other family members' behavior. It is important to note that even though the non-substance-using family members may be seen as being involved in a trigger for the substance abuser's substance use, the substance abuser is always viewed as responsible for making the decision to use substances or not to use substances.

The non-substance-using family members have a number of important influences on the substance abuser. These include behaviors intended to control the substance abuser's substance use such as criticizing the substance abuser for neglecting family responsibilities, and inadvertently reinforcing substance use behavior by providing increased attention to the substance abuser while using substances or by shielding the substance abuser from experiencing the negative consequences of substance use. The non-substance-using family members' functioning is affected by the level of stress caused by the substance abuser's substance use and general problems related to substance use.

Interactions in couples with an alcoholic spouse have more dysfunctional aspects even when he or she is not ingesting alcohol than do the interactions of nonalcoholic couples. The dysfunctional processes include hostile and coercive verbal interaction, a paucity of effective communication skills, a lack of intimate, positive exchanges, and a low frequency of spending free time together. When the alcoholic ingests alcohol, the interactions between the spouses may become even more negative. Spouse-involved treatment of alcohol dependence allows for a specific focus on relationship issues and is associated with better treatment compliance, more positive management of relapse episodes, improved marital stability, and increased marital satisfaction (McCrady, Stout, Noel, Abrams, & Nelson, 1991).

The primary focus early in behavioral family treatment is to help the substance user attain and maintain abstinence by modification of antecedents to substance use and by reinforcing the negative consequences of substance use and the positive consequences of abstinence. The initial sessions utilize behavioral techniques to help the client gain abstinence from substances. These techniques include self-monitoring of substance use and urges to use, functional analysis of substance use in terms of triggers and consequences, rate reduction procedures, stimulus control, self-management, and reinforcement of abstinence. This phase of treatment includes exploration of the ways in which the behavior of other family members may serve as antecedents and reinforce consequences of substance use. The positive consequences of substance use also have to be addressed so that the client can find alternative ways of fulfilling needs that the substance use previously fulfilled.

Relapse-prevention interventions are also important since the initiation of abstinence is often not as difficult for clients as the maintenance of abstinence. Marlatt and Gordon (1985) have proposed a relapse-prevention model for addictions treatment. Treatment in a relapse-prevention framework addresses the identification of high-risk situations for drinking, the development of coping skills to deal with these situations, the enhancement of self-efficacy, the continuous rehearsal of these skills, relabeling of outcome expectancies for substance use and for abstinence, and the relabeling of substance use episodes as "slips" which require the use of coping strategies rather than as signs of absolute failure.

McCrady (1987) has extended the relapse-prevention model to include spouses. She proposes that (a) the nondrinking spouse engages in coping responses related to high-risk situations; (b) these coping responses may influence the probability of the alcoholic's engaging in a coping response; (c) nondrinking spouses have efficacy beliefs about their own ability to cope with high-risk situations and these efficacy beliefs will affect the probability of engaging in a coping response; (d) nondrinking spouses make attributions about the reasons for positive changes in the drinking behavior of their partner which will affect their behavior; (e) nondrinking spouses' expectancies about the negative effects of alcohol on their partners will increase the probability of engaging in a coping response that may help prevent drinking or attenuate drinking episodes; and (f) drinking episodes will affect nondrinking spouses' expectancies, self-efficacy, and attributions.

Behavioral family therapy assesses the coping skills that the substance user and other family members have for dealing with antecedents of substance use. The substance user may lack skills such as drink/drug refusal, assertiveness, cognitive restructuring, and problem-solving. Family members may lack communication and problem-solving skills. Family members may also provide positive consequences for substance use such as taking care of the substance user when he or she is intoxicated or protecting him or her from the consequences of use in other ways.

After the substance user attains abstinence, family therapy then addresses the modification of patterns of family interaction, communication, and problem-solving skills. Family themes, rules, and roles that interfere with effective family functioning may also be explored (McCrady & Epstein, 1996).

Empirical research in the behavior family therapy treatment model for substance abuse has focused on spouse-involved cognitive-behavioral treatment for alcohol dependence (McCrady & Epstein, 1995); no study has evaluated broader family models, even though the role of other family members is a clear part of the model. This treatment model includes behavioral marital therapy interventions to help improve the relationship functioning of the couple. A number of studies have found moderately better outcomes for spouse-involved treatment for alcohol and drug dependence as compared to individually focused approaches (Fals-Stewart, Birchler, & O'Farrell, 1996; McCrady, Stout, Noel, Abrams, & Nelson, 1991; O'Farrell, Cutter, Choquette, Floyd, & Bayog, 1992). Spouse-involved treatment has led to more days abstinent during and after treatment, fewer relapses, longer time to relapse, fewer days of drug use, fewer drinks on days when drinking, fewer negative consequences from substance use, better marital adjustment, and fewer days separated.

Thus, the general treatment strategy in family-involved cognitive-behavioral treatment for substance abuse addresses three areas. One focuses on the client's use of cognitive and behavioral methods to deal with his or her substance use. This includes self-monitoring of substance use and urges to use, developing functional analyses of substance use, and developing and implementing alternate plans to cope with the needs he or she formerly satisfied by substance use. The second set of interventions focuses on the role of other family members, particularly the non-substance-using spouse, in the substance abuser's substance use. This includes having the spouse or other family members reinforce abstinence through verbal and concrete rewards, ignoring ongoing substance use, supporting the substance user when he or she copes with urges without using a substance, and helping the former substance user to be alert to signs of possible relapse. Behavioral contracting (Ossip-Klein & Rychtarik, 1993) may be helpful for specifying the behaviors expected from the substance user (such as attending treatment sessions) and identifying rewards other family members will give when the substance abuser fulfills his or her responsibilities in the contract. The third set of interventions focuses on improving marital functioning through communication and problem-solving training.

## II.  ESSENTIAL CLINICAL SKILLS AND ATTRIBUTES

A behavioral family therapy approach to the treatment of substance abuse is a complicated form of treatment. A therapist using this approach would have to have training and experience in several areas, as well as familiarity with the empirical findings on substance abuse problems and family treatment. The therapist should be knowledgeable about the effects, dosages, withdrawal symptoms, and behavioral treatments for various substances of abuse. The therapist should also have skills needed to conduct family therapy sessions, including the ability to attend to the complexities of several family members interacting. Being able to be empathic and build a treatment alliance with all of the family members involved in the treatment is a central clinical skill involved in conducting family therapy.

Assessment and diagnostic skills in several areas are also important. Areas for assessment and diagnosis include the substance abuse itself, coping skills of the substance abuser, and family interactional patterns. The therapist should also have a good referral network and know when to make use of outside professionals for adjunct services.

## III. THE CASE OF "PAUL;" 15 CLINICAL QUESTIONS

*1. What would be your therapeutic goals for this patient? What are the primary and secondary goals? Please be as specific as possible.*

A constructive method for actively determining Paul's treatment goals would be to involve him in a discussion of his goals for treatment, giving him feedback on how I see his goals (for example, if he wants to continue controlled drinking and I see that as risky), and coming to mutually agreed upon treatment goals.

A primary goal for Paul would be becoming engaged in treatment and fulfilling the responsibilities involved with weekly treatment sessions. Another primary goal for Paul would be abstinence from all substances and the development of positive reinforcers for abstinence. He has been using substances for 20 years and appears to have developed few coping skills for dealing with his needs without resorting to the use of substances. Continued substance use would inhibit his developing more constructive coping skills to deal with situations in which he may experience urges to use. It is also likely that use of a certain substance by Paul can trigger the use of other substances. For example, he reports that his cocaine use usually follows heavy drinking. The use of one substance may increase his urges for other substances and lessen his ability to handle those urges. Another reason that abstinence would be the preferred primary treatment goal for Paul is that after periods in which he had controlled use (for example, occasionally drinking a few beers), he would go on to heavier use of several substances.

Secondary goals for Paul include the development of strategies to maintain therapeutic gains and prevent relapses. In the periods during which Paul has been abstinent from all substances, he seems to have been able to function well at work and with his family. However, in the past, he has not been able to maintain abstinence. When he has returned to substance use, he has begun to experience conflict at work and with family members. Paul's substance use is probably triggered by several factors including socializing with other construction workers who drink regularly and using substances as a means to experience relief from angry and sad feelings. During treatment, Paul would have to develop new ways to deal with these situations. For example, he would benefit from developing a social network of people who do not use substances. Paul would also have to find ways of expressing and managing angry and sad feelings without using substances. Paul would also benefit from improving his communication and problem-solving skills.

*2. What further information would you want to have to assist you in structuring this patient's treatment? Are there specific assessment tools you would use (i.e., data to be collected)? What would be the rationale for using those tools?*

The first decision to be made about Paul's treatment is the level of care that is appropriate. He currently reports drinking two six-packs of beer a day and smoking $500 of cocaine per week. He has also been smoking marijuana 4 to 5 days per week and occasionally taking Valium for sleep disturbances (approximately once a week). During the past year, he has not been able to maintain more than 2 days of sobriety at a time. I would want more information on Paul's environmental supports for abstinence. There may not be enough support for Paul to become abstinent on an outpatient basis. He also has a history of withdrawal symptoms and may experience such symptoms again. These withdrawal symptoms may be managed better on an inpatient basis. Though Paul is hesitant to enter a residential program since he does not think his employer would continue his employment if he missed additional work, it may be that an inpatient stay or at least inpatient detoxification is necessary in order to remove himself from the contexts in which he uses substances.

It is always important to consider involving family members in a person's treatment since they can serve as a support for abstinence. In Paul's case, I would have to assess which family members it would be appropriate to involve. Paul is still living with his ex-wife and their two children. I would need to clarify the status of Paul's relationship with his ex-wife. Their marriage had been good during times in which Paul was abstinent. Conflict, including domestic violence, arose when Paul used substances. It could be that Paul's ex-wife would be willing to provide support in treatment for Paul to attain abstinence. That possibility would have to be assessed as well as the risk of Paul committing further acts of violence toward his ex-wife. Other family members that could be involved in Paul's treatment include his father, mother, and the sister and brother who live in the area. His father is a recovering alcoholic and is involved in AA. Paul describes his mother as a gentle, loving person. I would want to know if either or both of Paul's parents would be willing to be involved in his treatment. I would also want information on skills deficits of other family members that may be related to Paul's substance use, the role of substance use in the family, patterns of communication, problem-solving, and family roles, rules, and boundaries.

I would also want further information directly related to Paul's substance use including determining antecedent stimuli for use (Annis' Inventory of Drinking Situations or another drinking patterns questionnaire could be used) and consequences of alcohol and other drug use (the Rutgers Consequences of Use, DrInc from Project Match, or the Michigan Alcoholism Screening Test could be used). I would also want to assess Paul's motivation for abstinence, his perceptions of positive and negative consequences of using substances and of abstinence, the stage of change that he is in, and his goals for treatment. The primary factors contributing to the maintenance of substance use need to be assessed including skills deficits and the relative importance of individual, familial, and other interpersonal systems. A physical exam and lab tests would be useful for indicating possible physical harm that Paul's twenty years of substance use may have caused.

Finally, I would want to assess Paul for concomitant emotional disorders such as a depressive disorder. The Symptom Checklist-90-R could be a helpful tool for a broad screening for a range of symptoms. I would then use relevant sections of the SCID for diagnosing specific emotional disorders. I would also want to determine if a comorbid condition was primary (independent of substance use) or secondary to substance use. Finally, I would ask for a neurological consultation to assess for possible minimal brain damage secondary to the head injury he received at age sixteen.

*3. What is your conceptualization of this patient's personality, behavior, affective state, and cognitions?*

The case report provides information about historical factors contributing to Paul's substance use and general functioning. He appears to have been the target of angry and abusive treatment both from his father (who was an alcoholic when Paul was young) and from his older brother who was left in charge when their mother would work at night and their father would go out drinking. Paul also recalls that the home was often chaotic when he young. After his older brother left home (when Paul was thirteen), Paul felt that he received much more of his father's anger and abuse. Paul ran away frequently during that period, often staying with friends for weeks at a time. The abusive treatment Paul received and the general chaos could have led to Paul's becoming an angry, impulsive, and undisciplined person and may have increased his vulnerability to substance use. Paul's father's drinking heavily when Paul was young would have modeled substance use as a coping style.

Results of psychological assessments that Paul received 6 years ago (during his residential treatment?) are included in the case report and are suggestive of a personality style vulnerable to substance abuse. On the MMPI, Paul had elevations in scores for hypochondriasis, depression, hysteria, and psychopathic deviate. These elevations indicate Paul's feeling depressed and hostile, being impulsive and rebellious, and using denial to deal with stress. NEO-PI factor scores show similar results with Paul scoring very high on Neuroticism, low on Openness, and very low on Agreeableness and Conscientiousness. Testing results showed Paul to be high on impulsivity when compared to both normals and substance-abusing comparison groups. His trait anger scores were at the 97th percentile and his style of expressing anger openly rather than controlling or bottling up anger was at the 99th percentile. Other testing showed a moderate-severe level of depression and a moderate level of hopelessness. Those test results, though they are six years old, provide useful information and are consistent with Paul's history. We get a picture of Paul experiencing a great deal of anger and sadness but trying to deny these problems. It makes sense that he would have been drawn to the use of substances to escape painful feelings.

Currently, Paul appears to continue to have problems with anger, impulsivity, and depression. He appears to have positive expectations about the effects of substances in alleviating his feelings of anger and sadness. He may believe that he is capable of using substances in a controlled manner without experiencing loss of control. He seems to have low self-efficacy for coping with stress without substances. His view of himself as a substance user may be a central part of his self-image and he may have little ability to conceive of himself living a life without using substances.

Paul appears to function on two different levels depending on whether he is abstinent or not. In periods of abstinence, he appears to function well in work and family environments. In periods of substance use, he seems to be more impulsive, argumentative, and has more difficulty managing his anger. Paul currently appears to be remorseful about recently striking his ex-wife in front of his children. He also is quite concerned about his occupational outlook in that problems at work related to substance use have created a very bad reputation for him in the construction field. Paul seems to be realizing that he needs more help than AA can provide. He also seems to be experiencing more fully some of the negative consequences of his substance use.

4. *What potential pitfalls would you envision in this therapy? What would the difficulties be and what would you envision to be the source(s) of the difficulties?*
Paul has used alcohol and other drugs for most of the last twenty years and they have been an integral part of his life. In addition, family members

(his father and brother) and co-workers also have a history of heavy substance use. Paul has little familiarity with approaching life without substances. To be abstinent from all substances, Paul would have to find new ways to handle many situations and develop a social network of other people who are also abstinent. Change is always difficult and Paul will most likely experience ambivalence about becoming abstinent. He will miss the positive consequences he experienced from substance use. And even though Paul currently seems to be quite upset about the negative consequences of his substance use (hitting his ex-wife in front of his children and their being afraid of him), he has a long history of minimizing the seriousness of his substance use. For example, he went back to drinking even after having received six DWIs. Paul also seems to dislike the structure and discipline which attaining and maintaining abstinence will require. (He dropped out of high school; he did not like the discipline of the army; and he has always dropped out of aftercare and AA after a period of participation.) It also appears that when Paul has been abstinent from substance use for a period of time, he begins to forget the negative consequences he had experienced from the substance use and drops out of treatment or AA. He then has always had a brief period of limited substance use, followed by a return to high levels of use.

Paul's polysubstance use presents another difficulty. It may be difficult to link negative consequences specifically to each of the substances that Paul uses. He may be ambivalent about becoming abstinent from all of the substances. It also may be that different interventions will be necessary in order to help Paul attain abstinence from alcohol, cocaine, marijuana, and Valium. Paul's use of one substance may also create a high-risk situation for use of another (for example, cocaine use following heavy drinking).

*5. What level of coping, adaptation, or function would you see this patient reaching as an immediate result of therapy? What result would be long-term subsequent to the ending of therapy (i.e., prognosis for adaptive change)?*

Paul has had a 20-year history of substance abuse along with several episodes of treatment and periodic involvement with AA. The chronic, relapsing nature of his substance abuse points to the need for a long-term treatment plan which would ideally involve other family members. The level of functioning that Paul could attain as an immediate result of therapy is directly related to his motivation and ability to attain and maintain abstinence. If Paul continues even occasional substance use during therapy or is not prepared to prevent relapses, he is likely to return to high levels of substance use. When Paul uses substances heavily, he functions poorly at work and with his family. Long-term functioning would also be directly related to Paul's ability to remain abstinent. If Paul could maintain abstinence, he would have the opportunity to work on more general problems such as managing his anger and improving his inter-personal and occupational functioning.

*6. What would be your time line (duration) for therapy? What would be your frequency and duration of the sessions?*

As I mentioned above, an initial decision would have to be made about whether Paul should begin treatment in a residential facility. He has been using several substances heavily for a long period of time and may not have enough social support to attain abstinence on an outpatient basis. It may be beneficial to Paul to spend three to four weeks in a residential facility in order to remove himself from the daily contexts in which he experiences urges and uses substances. If Paul started the current treat-ment with a residential stay, I would try to involve family members in a few sessions while Paul was still in inpatient care. The focus of these ses-sions would be on helping to build Paul's motivation to be abstinent and doing some basic problem-solving around how he could handle his first days out of residential care without using substances.

Continuing care on an outpatient basis would be a very important part of Paul's treatment. In a family therapy approach to aftercare, I would initially assess which family members could be a support to Paul and would be willing to participate in therapy with him. As I mentioned previously, possible family members to be involved in treatment include his ex-wife, mother, father, brother, and sister. I would have weekly family therapy sessions of 60 to 90 minutes in duration. These are longer sessions than therapists usually do for individual therapy. The longer session length for family therapy allows for the various family members involved to discuss their views and reactions to issues and also allows the thera-pist to monitor and intervene with ongoing interactional patterns. The initial period of weekly therapy would ideally last for 4 to 5 months. This would allow for Paul and other family members to identify triggers to his substance use, develop ways to manage those triggers, adjust to an abstinent life style, develop relapse-prevention skills, and improve family communication and problem-solving. Since Paul has had many experi-ences of relapsing to substance use, it would be good for him and involved family members to have ongoing booster sessions, perhaps on a monthly basis, for at least a year following the weekly therapy sessions.

*7. Are there specific or special techniques that you would implement in the therapy? What would they be?*

As mentioned above, the initial focus of behavioral family therapy for substance abuse is on helping the substance user attain abstinence. Early in the therapy, I would assess Paul's motivation for abstinence. I would help him with a decisional balance sheet in which he would think about the positive and negative consequences of continued substance use and of abstinence. As part of this process, I would ask other family members to give feedback to Paul on the negative consequences they have seen arise from his substance use. This motivational framework would be used throughout the therapy to help Paul maintain abstinence and prevent relapses.

I would ask Paul to keep a separate daily self-monitoring card to record urges, triggers, and use for each of the substances he has been using (alcohol, cocaine, marijuana, and Valium). The monitoring and recording of urges would be one way of helping Paul deal with urges. We would also develop functional analyses for each of the substances and possibly identify the substance to be targeted first in treatment (possibly alcohol). Family members involved in the treatment would be asked to give input to help identify triggers and ways in which family members play a role in various parts of the process of Paul's substance use (such as cueing or punishing substance use). I would then help Paul develop ways to manage the situations in which his urges occur. This would include stimulus control and drink refusal skills. For example, Paul appears to have relapsed before after beginning to have a few drinks with co-workers after work. I would help Paul and other family members look at ways he can handle his time after work in order to avoid situations that would lead to urges to drink. Each week we would look at upcoming high risk situations for substance use to help Paul develop behavioral and cognitive plans for coping with those specific situations. I would also help Paul develop more general coping skills such as assertiveness training, anger management, challenging irrational thoughts, relaxation techniques, recreational outlets, and attaining a balanced life style.

I would recommend some kind of behavioral contract for Paul, perhaps with his ex-wife, to increase treatment compliance. Behavioral contracting may be helpful for specifying the behaviors expected from Paul (such as attending treatment sessions) and identifying rewards other family members will provide him when he fulfills his responsibilities specified in the contract. I would also address the coping behaviors of other family members as they relate to Paul's substance use. I would explore their motivation for entering and continuing in treatment, their perceptions of the positive and negative consequences of Paul's (hopefully) achieving abstinence, learning new ways to discuss Paul's substance use, learning new responses to Paul's substance-related behavior, and individual skills to enhance each of their own individual functioning when appropriate. Potential social situations and people who would be supportive of Paul's abstinence (such as his children, his parents, and AA) could be identified and Paul could plan how to spend more of his time in those contexts. General family patterns of poor communication or problem-solving could be identified and addressed in the later weeks of treatment.

*8. Are there special cautions to be observed in working with this patient (e.g., danger to self or other, transference, counter-transference)? Are there any particular resistances you would expect and how would you deal with them?*

Even though Paul has a history of depression, he does not appear to have experienced suicidal ideation in the past. However, he is upset and remorseful about having hit his ex-wife in front of his children and being in danger of losing his current job. Therefore, his level of depression and possible suicidal ideation should be monitored. He has acted violently towards his ex-wife. If she is involved in the current therapy, her safety would have to be monitored and insured.

Paul could show resistance to the treatment process in several ways. Paul appears to have previously minimized the costs to himself and others of his substance use. Even though he currently appears remorseful about how he recently acted while intoxicated, he may again minimize the negative consequences of substance use, lose motivation to attain or maintain abstinence, and refuse to stop his use of substances. The loss of the positive consequences to his substance use could also increase Paul's ambivalence about being abstinent. Paul could show this ambivalence by not complying with the components of treatment (for example, by missing sessions or not doing homework).

I would try to handle these resistances by being aware of Paul's ambivalence and conveying understanding to him of the difficulty involved in attaining and maintaining abstinence. I would acknowledge the loss he experiences as he tries to live his life without substances and also emphasize the negative consequences he has experienced because of his substance use and the positive consequences of abstinence for him. I would recommend some kind of behavioral contract for Paul, perhaps with his ex-wife, to increase treatment compliance. Behavioral contracting may be helpful for specifying the behaviors expected from the Paul (such as attending treatment sessions) and identifying rewards other family members will provide him when he fulfills his responsibilities specified in the contract.

Based on Paul's case history, possible transference reactions he could have during family therapy would be anger at the therapist for encouraging abstinence, and feeling that the other family members and the therapist are ganging up against him by emphasizing the negative consequences of substance use. Possible counter-transference reactions from the therapist include feeling overwhelmed with the long-standing, serious nature of Paul's polysubstance abuse and the many negative consequences he has experienced, anger at Paul that he continued substance use even after experiencing serious negative consequences, and feeling hopeless about Paul's being able to change.

*9. Are there any areas that you would choose to avoid or not address with this patient? Why?*

There are many historical factors that can be identified as possibly having contributed to Paul's developing a substance abuse problem: the abuse and chaos he experienced as a child, having a father who was an alcoholic, and having experienced difficulties in school. These distal causes to his substance abuse would not be focused on in the current treatment. The current treatment would focus on current triggers to urges and substance use and ways to develop skills to cope with those situations.

As mentioned above, it would have to be assessed whether it would be constructive to involve Paul's ex-wife in family treatment. If she were not involved in the current treatment, I would not address with Paul the marital issues he had experienced with her except as a way to help him build his motivation for abstinence. I would, however, address his feelings of loss about the divorce because those feelings may be part of his current triggers for urges and substance use.

*10. Is medication warranted for this patient? What effect would you hope or expect the medication to have?*

As part of Paul's 6 weeks of aftercare to residential treatment several years ago, he did take Antabuse and felt it was helping him avoid a first drink. However, he stopped taking the Antabuse shortly after discontinuing the aftercare. He soon began drinking with co-workers again. I would talk with Paul about whether Antabuse could be a tool currently for him to avoid drinking. He might be more compliant with taking Antabuse if he did it daily in front of one of his family members. I would hope that if Paul did decide to use Antabuse, it would help him not impulsively give in to an urge to drink.

Another medication that could be considered for Paul is naltrexone. We do no know how much Paul experiences urges and craving when sober, but high urge people seem to respond well to naltrexone, experiencing a reduction in the number and intensity of their urges to drink.

*11. What are the strengths of the patient that can be used in the therapy?*

Paul appears to love his children and he was shocked and remorseful when they became fearful of him after he struck his wife. He says he realizes he needs more help than AA could provide and was able to recontact his former therapist in order to get the help he needs. His desire to be a good parent and role model for his children could be a central motivation for him to comply with treatment and maintain abstinence.

Even though Paul's wife did divorce him, they had maintained a friendly relationship. Although Paul had been physically violent toward her on several occasions, the physical abuse came after episodes of heavy drinking. Paul does appear to have some capacity to relate intimately in a caring fashion and that ability could be developed further and could help him achieve his goals in the current treatment. Paul's ex-wife has participated in Alanon and she may be willing to participate to some extent in Paul's current therapy. Additionally, even though Paul's attendance at AA meetings was sporadic, he did maintain regular contact with his sponsor and, therefore, appears to be somewhat willing and able to participate in a therapeutic relationship. The case report also shows that he had enjoyed AA meetings in the past and reported "getting a lot out of them." It also seems that Paul benefited from the residential treatment six years ago. He was able to become more expressive in group therapy and was able to talk about being concerned about the impact on his children of his violent behavior. The case history reports that his affect became less angry and depressed during the remainder of the residential treatment after Paul's expression of his feelings. Hopefully, he could experience these gains again in the current treatment.

Another strength Paul has is his ability to be a good worker. His performance at work used to make him feel good about himself. Though he has had difficulty at work in recent years, such as interpersonal conflicts and absences from work, these difficulties were directly related to ongoing substance abuse. Before Paul's substance use had become such a problem, Paul had been promoted to foreman and he took pride in his reputation as a hard, conscientious worker and in the fact that he was tough but reasonable and fair with his crew.

*12. How would you address limits, boundaries, and limit-setting with this patient?*

I would emphasize to Paul the importance of his complying with treatment requirements such as coming to sessions on time, being open and honest to members of his family during family sessions, doing homework between sessions, and working to attain and maintain abstinence. If Paul had difficulty in any of these areas, I would address it in an empathic manner. I would reflect to Paul how difficult it is to make changes in his life, but also reinforce how negatively substance use has affected his life. I would also acknowledge how much effort it takes to try to change long-standing patterns and encourage him to make the effort. In sessions, I would ask Paul's family members to verbalize support and encouragement. I would hope that these kinds of interventions would help Paul fulfill the treatment requirements. However, if he became even less compliant with treatment requirements, I would have to set firmer limits. If Paul attended sessions sporadically, even after looking at that issue in sessions, I would have to consider terminating the treatment.

The major boundary I would point out in treatment is that Paul is the person who is responsible for whether or not he uses any substances. Some of the focus in sessions would be on how family member may contribute to triggers to his use or protect him from consequences of use, but the family members are not *responsible* for whether or not he uses substances.

*13. Would you want to involve significant others in the treatment? Would you use out-of-session work (homework) with this patient? What homework would you use?*

In doing family therapy, I would obviously want to involve other family members in Paul's treatment in order to increase his motivation for abstinence, give input on situations that trigger his substance use, support him as he deals with urges, and praise him for progress. As I mentioned previously, his ex-wife, mother, father, brother, and sister are the main family members to ask to join Paul in sessions. I might also ask his son and daughter to come to a few sessions to discuss the situation in which Paul struck his ex-wife. Involving his children could increase his motivation for abstinence and help Paul and his children discuss their feelings about the violence they witnessed. Paul's AA sponsor appears to be an important person to him. I probably would not ask to involve Paul's sponsor directly in treatment, but I would encourage Paul to continue to attend AA and have contact with his sponsor.

Homework between sessions would be helpful to reinforce what Paul learned in the sessions, help him maintain new behaviors, and help him generalize coping skills to other situations. Part of Paul's homework would be to record on a daily basis urges to use or use of each of the substances and what situations triggered urges and use. I would also ask him to review interventions we did each week in sessions and then do more examples of those approaches for homework. This would include making and reviewing lists of positive and negative consequences of substance use and abstinence, developing and implementing self-management plans for triggers, practicing drink refusal, assertiveness, communication, and problem-solving skills, and planning constructive activities with friends and members of his family. Homework for other family members could include rewarding Paul for abstinence and practicing communication and problem-solving skills.

*14. What would be the issues to be addressed in termination? How would termination and relapse prevention be structured?*

Paul and his family would probably benefit from weekly sessions going on for 4 or 5 months that would help Paul be abstinent long enough to feel comfortable with changes he has made, to be able to manage urges, and to develop new pleasurable activities which substitute for the positive consequences of substance use. However, for many clients, substance abuse is a relapsing disorder that requires "chronic" treatment (continuing periodic contact with a treatment provider). Therefore, it may be better for Paul not to terminate treatment but to move from weekly sessions to less frequent contact with his therapist for a period of months, if not years. Family members could be involved in these periodic "booster" sessions. These "booster" sessions would focus on Paul and family members continuing to exercise skills learned in treatment and monitoring signs of possible relapse.

In addition, relapse-prevention techniques should be reviewed thoroughly in several of the final weekly sessions Paul and his family attend. I would help Paul and his family identify signs of impending relapse, learn to guard against signs of relapse and handle them if they occur, develop a relapse contract that involves Paul and other family members, help them learn to challenge seemingly irrelevant decisions (minor decisions that bring someone closer to a drink), help them guard against the abstinence violation effect (seeing a slip as a mistake that Paul could learn from and continue to move forward), and draw a relapse roadmap. As part of learning the relapse-prevention approach, I would help Paul and his family look at how he has relapsed to substance use in the past. He seems to have relapsed after he minimized the negative consequences of use, gradually stopped applying coping skills, stopped using Antabuse, and dropped out of aftercare sessions or attended AA only sporadically. We would talk in sessions about these being possible warning signs for relapse and have Paul and other family members agree on how to discuss and handle these signs. I would suggest that Paul consider returning to regular weekly sessions after even one drink or one episode of using another substance.

*15. What do you see as the hoped-for mechanisms of change for this patient, in order of importance?*

The intensive assessment of substance use and its consequences, feedback from family members, and increased knowledge about substance abuse problems would all be central in motivating Paul to become abstinent and engage in new behaviors that facilitate change. The step-by-step progression of the treatment should help enhance feelings of self-efficacy for Paul and other family members. After feeling success at addressing smaller areas for change, Paul and his family would feel more able to address more difficult behavior change. This treatment approach also tries to increase positive reinforcers for abstinence including the quality of family relationships as a way to provide a strong incentive to maintain abstinence. Finally, learning new cognitive and behavioral coping skills would provide Paul and his family with a broader behavioral repertoire for coping with high-risk situations.

## REFERENCES

Fals-Stewart, W., Birchler, G. R., & O'Farrell, T. J. (1996). Behavioral couples therapy for male substance-abusing patients: Effects on relationship adjustment and drug-using behavior. *Journal of Consulting and Clinical Psychology, 64,* 959–972.

Marlatt, G. A., & Gordon, J. R. (Eds.). (1985). *Relapse prevention.* New York: Guilford Press.

McCrady, B. S. (1987). Extending relapse prevention models to couples. *Addictive Behaviors, 12,* 329–339.

McCrady, B. S., & Epstein, E. E. (1995). Marital therapy in the treatment of alcohol problems. In N. S. Jacobson & A. S. Gurman (Eds.), *Clinical handbook of couple therapy* (pp. 369–393). New York: Guilford Press.

McCrady, B. S., & Epstein, E. E. (1996). Theoretical bases of family approaches to substance abuse treatment. In F. Rotgers, D. S. Keller, & J. Morgenstern (Eds.), *Treating substance abuse: Theory and technique* (pp. 117–142). New York: Guilford Press.

McCrady, B. S., Stout, R., Noel, N., Abrams, D., & Nelson, H. (1991). Comparative effectiveness of three types of spouse involved alcohol treatment: Outcomes 18 months after treatment. *British Journal of Addiction, 86,* 1415–1424.

O'Farrell, T. J., Cutter, H. S. G., Choquette, K. A., Floyd, F. J., & Bayog, R. D. (1992). Behavioral marital therapy for male alcoholics: Marital and drinking adjustment during the two years after treatment. *Behavior Therapy, 23,* 529–549.

Ossip-Klein, D. J., & Rychtarik, R. G. (1993). Behavioral contracts between alcoholics and family members. In T. J. O'Farrell (Ed.), *Treating alcohol problems: Marital and family interventions* (pp. 281–304). New York: Guilford Press.

# 12

# Application of the Community Reinforcement Approach

*Robert J. Meyers, Jane Ellen Smith, and V. Ann Waldorf*

## I. TREATMENT MODEL

### Overview

The Community Reinforcement Approach (CRA) is a broad spectrum behavioral program for treating substance abuse problems that has been empirically supported with inpatients (Azrin, 1976; Hunt & Azrin, 1973), outpatients (Azrin, Sisson, Meyers, & Godley, 1982; Mallams, Godley, Hall, & Meyers, 1982), and homeless individuals (Smith, Meyers, & Delaney, 1998). Three recent meta-analytic reviews cited it as one of the most cost-effective alcohol treatment programs (Finney & Monahan, 1996; Holder, Longabaugh, Miller, & Rubonis, 1991; Miller et al., 1995).

CRA is based on the belief that environmental contingencies can play a powerful role in encouraging or discouraging drinking or drug-using behavior. Consequently, it utilizes social, recreational, familial, and vocational reinforcers to assist clients in the recovery process. Its goal is to rearrange various aspects of an individual's "community" such that a sober life style is more rewarding than one involving alcohol and drugs.

### CRA Functional Analyses

Many alcohol programs continue to be based on the belief that problem drinkers are in "denial," and that confrontation is the best way to address this. So the typical message received by clients upon entering treatment is, "You're alcoholic and you can never drink again." CRA therapists believe that this attitude overlooks the fact that drinking serves an important role in the individual's life. Knowledge of the context in which the drinking occurs is vital for the CRA program, and consequently a functional analysis is utilized in order to identify the antecedents and consequences of that behavior (see question III. 2). Once the antecedents are outlined, the client can be taught the skills needed to respond to them differently. The consequences for the drinking are explored to determine both the factors that maintain the behavior, and the negative ways in which the client's life has been affected.

## Sobriety Sampling

At least a limited period of abstinence at the start of treatment is deemed essential for all, regardless of whether this is the client's long-term goal. This "time-out" allows the client to experience the sensation of being sober on a daily basis. After a short time this tends automatically to focus attention on positive changes in cognitive, emotional, and physical symptoms. Furthermore, it disrupts old drinking habits, elicits family members' support, and affords some practice in setting and achieving manageable goals.

Sobriety Sampling operates on the assumption that one can more successfully hook individuals into treatment by not overwhelming them with rigid rules and frightening expectations. Consequently, the length of the period of sobriety is negotiated. Typically the therapist first suggests 90 days, knowing fully that this will leave plenty of room for bargaining downward. The suggestion should be backed with the rationale that the first 90 days appears to be the time during which most relapses occur (Marlatt, 1980). However, since the majority of clients report that they are unwilling or unable to make a 90-day commitment, the CRA therapist works with a client to select a shorter time period that appears challenging yet obtainable. Whether the negotiated period for sobriety is 3 or 30 days, the therapist will need to help the client devise a plan for accomplishing this at least until the necessary skills can be taught. Assuming that a client reaches the negotiated sobriety goal, the therapist typically discusses the advantages of sampling sobriety for an additional limited period. The many reinforcers already received by the client for being abstinent are reviewed with the intent of making further abstinence appealing.

## Monitored Disulfiram

Some clients appear unable to achieve a period of abstinence early in treatment, despite their desire to do so. For these individuals, the addition of disulfiram (Antabuse) to their treatment program may be indicated. Disulfiram is a medication that acts as a deterrent to drinking, since the ingestion of any alcohol while taking it causes an individual to become ill. If a client makes the decision to try disulfiram, it must first be cleared by a physician, and then a monitor must be identified. The monitor, who is a concerned family member or friend, is invited to a therapy session so that he or she can be trained to communicate with the client in a supportive manner during the daily disulfiram administration.

## CRA Treatment Plan

Two instruments form the basis of CRA's behavioral treatment plan: The Happiness Scale and the Goals of Counseling form. The former is a questionnaire that inquires about an individual's current level of happiness in 10 life categories. Once problem areas are identified, the next step entails devising behavioral goals. The Goals of Counseling form provides a useful framework for this exercise, as it includes the same 10 categories listed on the Happiness Scale (see question III. 1).

## Behavioral Skills Training

An essential component of the CRA program involves identifying behavioral skill deficits, and then providing training to enhance those skills. In terms of *communication skills training,* the CRA program offers seven guidelines for precise communication in a manner that minimizes a defensive reaction from the listener. The steps are: be brief, be positive, use specific (quantifiable) terms, label your feelings, give an understanding statement, accept partial responsibility, and offer to help. Behavioral rehearsal and modeling are relied upon to train these skills.

The second area of focus within CRA's behavioral skills program is *problem-solving training.* A modified version of D'Zurilla and Goldfried's (1971) approach is utilized. The purpose of the procedure is to teach clients a structured format for addressing problems in any area. The steps are: define the problem, brainstorm possible solutions, eliminate undesired solutions, select one potential solution, generate possible obstacles, devise a plan for each obstacle, and evaluate the effectiveness of the solution.

The third part of CRA's behavioral skills training is *drink (or drug) refusal.* There are several components to this program, including enlisting social support, reviewing high-risk drinking situations, and assertively refusing alcohol. The latter incorporates both problem-solving and communication skills (Monti, Abrams, Kadden, & Cooney, 1989).

## Job Skills

A major aspect of most people's "community" is their job environment, and consequently it is an important potential source of reinforcement. This may come in the form of pleasant social interactions with co-workers, stimulating challenges, praise from supervisors, enhanced self-esteem, and financial incentives. A steady job also competes with drinking and serves as a deterrent because of the structure it introduces into a day.

CRA's job counseling program consists of three parts: getting a job, keeping a job, and enhancing job satisfaction. For unemployed clients, initial training is based largely on Azrin and Besalel's *Job Club Counselor's Manual* (1980). Time should then be devoted to analyzing the sequence of events that typically has resulted in the client being fired or quitting in the past. Finally, the Happiness Scale asks specifically about job satisfaction, and consequently provides an avenue for determining whether the client finds his or her job reinforcing. Again, CRA works to enhance the level of satisfaction in all nondrinking areas of a person's life, so that they can work together to compete with drinking.

### Social/Recreational Counseling
Since CRA's goal is to make an individual's nondrinking activities as reinforcing as his or her drinking activities, considerable attention must be paid to the client's social life. Most clients need some assistance in identifying new nondrinking activities, and so client and therapist work together to generate lists of options, complete new functional analyses for nondrinking behaviors, or use problem-solving to overcome obstacles to participating.

### CRA's Relationship Therapy
It is common to discover that a problem drinker's relationship with his or her loved one is stressed. CRA works with couples to enhance their relationship, primarily by teaching effective communication and goal-setting (see question III. 13).

### CRA's Relapse Prevention
Relapse prevention actually begins with the first CRA session, since a functional analysis outlines the triggers for drinking and identifies high-risk situations. Immediately, plans are set in motion to develop behaviors that compete with drinking. In the event that a lapse occurs, a separate CRA Functional Analysis for Drinking Behavior (Relapse Version) is available. CRA therapists also discuss relapse prevention in terms of an Early Warning System. Essentially, the behavioral chain of events that leads up to a drinking episode are diagrammed, and the client is coached to detect behavioral warning signals early in the process.

## II. WHAT WOULD YOU CONSIDER TO BE THE CLINICAL SKILLS OR ATTRIBUTES MOST ESSENTIAL TO SUCCESSFUL THERAPY IN YOUR APPROACH?

A successful CRA therapist must have sound, fundamental counseling skills. Supportiveness, empathy, and a genuinely caring attitude are key to establishing the client-therapist relationship. However, CRA also requires that the therapist be directive, energetic, and engaging. Indeed, CRA-therapist trainees are often encouraged to consider themselves cheerleaders as well as therapists! It is their enthusiasm and motivation that facilitates the same in the client. As a behavioral program, CRA makes extensive use of modeling, role-playing, and shaping. Such an action-oriented approach implies that the CRA therapist does not submissively wait for the therapy session to move on its own. Rather, the therapist engages the client and works with him or her to solve problems. In line with this, problems are always defined as the property of both the client and the therapist. For instance, whereas another therapist might point out to the client, "Communication skills training could really benefit you," the CRA therapist says, "It looks like we really need to do more work in the area of communication skills. Where do you think we should start?"

Firmly based in operant principles, CRA uses positive reinforcement for each and every step, no matter how small. Consequently, a CRA therapist must be willing to look continually for opportunities to reinforce clients. For example, if a client arrives 20 minutes late for a session, the CRA therapist would say something along the lines of, "I'm glad you made it today. I'm sorry we don't have the whole 60 minutes to work together, but I'm just glad you're here and we have 40 minutes together. Thanks for coming." In addition to reinforcing a client's attempts at change, a CRA therapist must be committed to helping a client identify potential positive reinforcements in the community. By helping the client find "payoffs" for learning new skills and trying new behaviors, the client creates his or her own motivation for change. Common examples are found in the willingness of clients to modify their communication styles to minimize interpersonal conflict with significant others in their lives. Other examples include situations in which individuals learn assertiveness to bolster their self-esteem, or practice job interviewing skills in order to eventually enjoy the pleasures of a paycheck.

Finally, substance abuse is not viewed as an isolated behavior independent of the rest of the individual's life. Instead it is seen as complexly intertwined with all of the individual's other problems, and thus attention must be given to the context in which the substance abuse occurs. Thus, the CRA therapist must also possess the skills to work with couples, or in some cases, act as a case manager. Knowing community resources and being willing to actively help a client directly solve problems other than substance abuse is essential.

## III. IT IS IMPORTANT TO THE GOALS AND MISSION OF THIS VOLUME THAT YOU ANSWER EACH OF THE FOLLOWING QUESTIONS REGARDING THE CASE MATERIAL

*1. What would be your therapeutic goals for this patient? What are the primary goals and the secondary goals? Please be as specific as possible.*

Prior to identifying goals, the CRA therapist would ask Paul to complete a 1-page Happiness Scale. This questionnaire lists 10 life categories and instructs clients to indicate their current degree of satisfaction on a scale of 1 (completely unhappy) to 10 (completely happy) in each area: drinking/drugs, job/education, money management, social life, personal habits, marriage/family relationships, legal issues, emotional life, communication, and general happiness. This provides information about problem areas at the start of counseling, as well as progress updates as therapy continues. The therapist would ask Paul to select several areas in which he wants to start working immediately. Assume Paul decides upon drinking/drugs, job progress, and marriage/family relationships. The therapist might suggest adding a category, such as social life, if he or she believes that it should be addressed right away.

The therapist would then assist Paul in identifying some short-term goals and the strategies for obtaining them. The Goals of Counseling form is useful for this exercise as it contains the same 10 categories listed on the Happiness Scale. In formulating these goals, three basic rules are taught: keep them brief, specific (measurable), and use positive terms (stating what you *will* do, as opposed to what you will *not* do anymore). In the process of identifying strategies for achieving the goals, it often becomes clear that the client does not yet possess some of the necessary skills. These interventions are typically marked with an asterisk (*) to serve as a reminder to the therapist that the skills need to be taught. Sample items from a Goals of Counseling form are presented in Table 12.1. These represent the goals that Paul would begin working on immediately.

In terms of the strategies selected to obtain the various goals, several interventions that had been somewhat successful in the past; namely, disulfiram and AA meetings, were incorporated along with the behavioral CRA procedures. As noted, the actual short-term goals would be established in the first session, and progress toward them continually monitored. Modified or new goals would be introduced as needed. For example, within the marriage/family relationships category, Paul's interactions with his children would be examined, and specific goals would be established if necessary. Also, if Paul and his ex-wife decided to renew their relationship, additional goals would be set both in terms of improving communication and increasing their pleasurable time together

## TABLE 12.1    Goals of Counseling

| Goals | Strategies | Time Frame |
|---|---|---|
| 1. *In the area of drinking or drugs I would like:* | | |
| a. To stay clean and sober. | a. take disulfiram daily with a monitor. | Next 30 days |
| | b. attend therapy 1x/wk. | |
| | c. attend AA daily. | |
| | d. use functional analysis to identify drinking/drug triggers.* | Next week |
| | e. practice problem-solving to control urges.* | |
| | f. practice drink-refusal.* | |
| 2. *In the area of job progress I would like:* | | |
| a. To attend work sober every scheduled day. | a. (see above strategies) | Next 30 days |
| | b. attend even if I have a hangover. | |
| b. To remain calm and in control of my anger at work. | a. practice problem-solving and communication skills to control anger.* | |
| 3. *In the area of marriage/family relationships I would like:* | | |
| a. To remain calm and in control of anger when speaking with ex-wife (no violence). | a. practice problem-solving to control anger.* | Next 2 weeks |
| | b. invite ex-wife to a session to work on communication with each other. | |
| 4. *In the area of social life I would like:* | | |
| a. To add 1 new alcohol-free social activity. | a. make a list of possible social activities. | Next week |
| | b. select 1 and try it 1x. | |

(e.g., resume church or morning meditations). As for the emotion category, if depression resurfaced as a problem, relevant goals would be set. Within the drinking/drug category, long-term goals would focus on aftercare, since Paul repeatedly experienced difficulties whenever he determined that aftercare services were no longer needed.

*2. What further information would you want to have to assist you in structuring this patient's treatment? Are there specific assessment tools you would use (i.e., data to be collected)? What would be the rationale for using those tools?*

The main assessment instruments for the CRA program are the two functional analyses. The first one examines drinking behavior, so that the antecedents and consequences for the alcohol use can be outlined (Table 12.2). The CRA therapist would begin this discussion by asking the client to describe a fairly common drinking scenario. Questions would be posed until both the external and internal triggers for drinking are clearly outlined. The former are environmental factors, such as people, places, and times frequently associated with alcohol use. The therapist would label this environmental context as a high-risk situation for the client, and would move on to an exploration of internal triggers: the thoughts, physical sensations, and emotions that set the stage for the drinking episode. Eventually, the therapist would teach the client to view these triggers as cues for responding with a healthy, nondrinking behavior.

The middle segment of the CRA functional analysis entails gathering basic quantity and frequency information about the drinking behavior. The severity of the alcohol problem often can be gleaned from this, and progress can be monitored by referring back to this data throughout treatment. The final part of the functional analysis examines the consequences of the drinking behavior. The short-term positive experiences would be explored first, since these are the factors that maintain the behavior. The goal is to acknowledge the function of the drinking, and to work toward either finding alternate routes to those same outcomes, or modifying a series of behaviors so that the outcomes are no longer needed. The long-term negative consequences column on the CRA chart serves as a reminder to the therapist to inquire about several basic areas in which drinking is likely to have had a negative impact: interpersonal, physical, emotional, legal, job, and financial. These signify the valuable reinforcers that have been lost or otherwise affected as a result of the substance use.

The CRA functional analysis for pleasurable nondrinking behaviors (Table 12.3) demonstrates that the client already is engaging in enjoyable activities that do not involve alcohol. The therapist would encourage the client to increase the frequency of participation in these or other pleasurable, alcohol-free activities. However, the functional analysis would first be used to outline both the common precursors for this behavior as well as some of the unfavorable consequences. The therapist would teach the client to recognize these triggers and to respond more regularly to them with a healthy behavior. Later, the therapist would teach problem-solving skills in an effort to reduce any negative consequences associated with these activities.

**TABLE 12.2 CRA Functional Analysis for Drinking Behavior (Initial Assessment)**

| External Triggers | Internal Triggers | Drinking Behavior | Short-Term Positive Consequences | Long-Term Negative Consequences |
|---|---|---|---|---|
| 1. *Who* are you usually with when you drink? | 1. What are you usually *thinking* about right before you drink? | 1. *What* do you usually drink? | 1. What do you like about drinking with (who)? | 1. What are the negative results of your drinking in each of these areas? |
| | | | 2. What do you like about drinking (where)? | a) Interpersonal: |
| | | | | b) Physical: |
| 2. *Where* do you usually drink? | 2. What are you usually *feeling physically* right before you drink? | 2. *How much* do you usually drink? | 3. What do you like about drinking (when)? | c) Emotional: |
| | | | | d) Legal: |
| | | | 4. Name the pleasant *thoughts* while drinking. | e) Job: |
| | | | | f) Financial: |
| 3. *When* do you usually drink? | 3. What are you usually *feeling emotionally* right before you drink? | 3. Over *how long* a period of time do you usually drink? | 5. Name the pleasant *physical feelings* while drinking | g) Other: |
| | | | 6. Name the pleasant *emotions* while drinking. | |

From *Clinical guide to alcohol treatment: The community reinforcement approach* (pp. 34–35) by R. J. Meyers & J. E. Smith, 1995, New York: Guilford Press. Copyright 1995 by Guilford Press. Adapted by permission.

**TABLE 12.3 CRA Functional Analysis for Nondrinking Behavior (Activity)**

| External Triggers | Internal Triggers | Nondrinking Behavior | Short-Term Negative Consequences | Long-Term Positive Consequences |
|---|---|---|---|---|
| 1. *Who* are you usually with when you (activity)? | 1. What are you usually *thinking* about right before you (activity)? | 1. *What* is the non-drinking behavior/activity? | 1. What do you dislike about (activity) with who? | 1. What are the positive results of (activity) in each of these areas?<br><br>a) Interpersonal:<br><br>b) Physical:<br><br>c) Emotional:<br><br>d) Legal:<br><br>e) Job:<br><br>f) Financial:<br><br>g) Other: |
| 2. *Where* do you usually (activity)? | 2. What are you usually *feeling physically* right before you (activity)? | 2. *How often* do you do it? | 2. What do you dislike about (activity) (where)? | |
| 3. *When* do you usually (activity)? | 3. What are you usually *feeling emotionally* right before you (activity)? | 3. *How long* does it usually last? | 3. What do you dislike about (activity) when? | |

*(continued)*

**TABLE 12.3   CRA Functional Analysis for Nondrinking Behavior (Activity) (continued)**

| External Triggers | Internal Triggers | Nondrinking Behavior | Short-Term Negative Consequences | Long-Term Positive Consequences |
|---|---|---|---|---|
| | | | 4. Name the unpleasant *thoughts* while you are (activity). | |
| | | | 5. Name the unpleasant *physical feelings* while you are (activity). | |
| | | | 6. Name the unpleasant emotions while you are (activity). | |

From *Clinical guide to alcohol treatment: The community reinforcement approach* (pp. 38–39) by R. J. Meyers & J. E. Smith, 1995, New York: Guilford Press. Copyright 1995 by Guilford Press. Adapted by permission.

As noted earlier, additional CRA assessment information is contained in the Happiness Scale. The family relationships category would be given careful scrutiny, to explore Paul's satisfaction with his relationship with his children. The therapist could follow up on this with questions about how Paul would like that relationship to change. In some cases the therapist might ask Paul to bring the children to a session so that his interactions with them could be observed. Finally, given Paul's history of head trauma, and the fact that some of his symptoms might be suggestive of minimal brain damage (e.g., difficulty with written assignments, confusion during groups, impulsive behavior), a basic neuropsychological battery would be considered. However, since many of these symptoms seemed to disappear as Paul settled into a routine in the past and stopped using, the battery would only be introduced if there appeared to be new evidence to support the idea of cognitive deficits.

*3. What is your conceptualization of this patient's personality, behavior, affective state, and cognitions?*

Paul's developmental history, his pattern of substance abuse, treatment, and relapse, as well as the results of his psychological testing all point to consistent patterns that suggest a certain cognitive style. His depression scores on both the MMPI and the BDI are typical of the dysthymic mood often seen in alcohol abusers, and likely reflect a fairly concrete, rigid, and egocentric thinking style that could hinder his ability to accept personal responsibility for his predicaments in any consistent manner.

However, his profile also points to several aspects of his personality that make CRA an appropriate and potentially successful intervention strategy. For example, his very high Neuroticism score on the NEO-PI is typical of individuals who are emotional, highly sensitive, and overrun with negative feelings. While at first glance this may appear to be a negative aspect, CRA could capitalize on his sensitivity with its consistent use of positive reinforcement. For example, if his behaviors could be reframed as understandable given his learning history, then the problem would be posed as one of training, not of inherent character defect. Since CRA's emphasis is on learning new behaviors, Paul could be taught more effective coping strategies without having to feel embarrassed or ashamed that he has had difficulty staying sober in the past. This also would address the hopelessness evidenced on the BHI, as most aspects of CRA would be new and different from previous strategies he has used and been unable to maintain.

CRA also is particularly appropriate for individuals whose testing indicates an overall cognitive style similar to Paul's. Based on his school performance, history of impulsivity, and low scores on the NEO-PI subscales of Openness, Agreeableness, and Conscientiousness, it is likely that Paul utilizes a relatively inflexible thinking style that lacks abstractive ability or insight. This tends to lead to poor inherent problem-solving or planning capacity. Fortunately, these are the skills explicitly trained in the comprehensive format of CRA. Additionally, as CRA is a skills-based intervention, it does not demand any higher-order moral reasoning from its clients, although if that capacity is present it can certainly be utilized. In Paul's case, it is sufficient that he can begin to associate certain behavioral choices with particular outcomes. Once his preferred outcomes have been uncovered, a concrete thinking style is adequate to plan behavioral strategies that will allow for the highest probability of obtaining the desired consequences.

*4. What potential pitfalls would you envision in this therapy? What would the difficulties be and what would you envision to be the source(s) of the difficulties?*

Problems associated with the successful implementation of CRA come from two possible sources: the client or the therapist. Client difficulties arise when he or she is uncomfortable with CRA's action-oriented style. Particularly passive clients who look outside themselves for answers and are incapable of joining the therapist in active problem-solving may feel overwhelmed. Similarly, clients who are primarily seeking long-term support, rather than change, will be disappointed. In Paul's case, his voluntary decision to enter therapy and his clearly defined wish to reestablish meaningful relationships with his family suggest that he is indeed motivated to make the kind of changes that CRA demands.

Therapist-centered difficulties tend to arise when therapists become overly focused on the CRA "techniques" to the exclusion of other important issues. First and foremost is the problem that occurs when a poorly trained therapist confuses the behavioral component of the therapy for the whole therapy. Specifically, an over emphasis on implementing operant principles without equal emphasis on the human aspects of counseling (i.e., warmth, empathy, unconditional positive regard) relegates the therapy to just another skills-training program. It is the combination of compassion and skill that makes the CRA therapist effective.

The second common therapist-centered difficulty involves the therapist who becomes a prisoner of the CRA techniques and loses sight of the "real" issues in the process. For example, it is not uncommon to find a new therapist launch with zeal into weeks of problem-solving training using artificial problems, while missing the opportunity to address the fact that the client is continually late for sessions because of a transportation problem. The therapist needs to model how these generic skills are applied to the client's real-world difficulties. If this is accomplished, the client is more likely to be interested in further training and to generalize those skills to other behavioral domains. Finally, some therapists can perfectly execute the skills training components, but they overlook the importance of linking behavioral changes with the client's reinforcers. In other words, if the changes are not reinforcing to the individual, or if the client's "community" does not support them in some way, their effectiveness will be short-lived. In Paul's case, it will be important to ensure that his efforts toward sobriety, anger management, and the like are closely coupled with desirable familial and job interactions, and an increase in general nondrinking pleasurable activities.

*5. To what level of coping, adaptation, or function would you see this patient reaching as an immediate result of therapy? What result would be long-term subsequent to the ending of therapy (i.e., prognosis for adaptive change)?*

While it is true that Paul has returned for treatment once again due to an exacerbation of his substance abuse problem, there is reason in his history to expect some immediate positive results. For example, Paul's difficulties with sobriety consistently have occurred during the aftercare period and not at the point of immediate follow-up. Therefore, there is evidence to predict that even within the first phase of CRA treatment he can maintain his work and make some amends in his relationships with his ex-wife and children. This seems particularly likely given the fact that Paul has returned for treatment voluntarily, not as the result of a court order, with the recognition that two of his major life reinforcers are at risk. Although divorced, it appears his relationship with his ex-wife is very important to him, so its enhancement can be used to motivate change. As Paul found his own father's abusive acts so disturbing, CRA may capitalize on this fact and use it to reinforce the deescalation of his anger and violence.

Additionally, Paul stated that working made him feel good about himself, so with his job at stake it suggests that another powerful reinforcer is available to support immediate change. The fact that CRA is so effective in an outpatient setting gives Paul the chance to work with a treatment program that supports his sobriety without putting his employment at risk. In turn, this fosters Paul's self-esteem, because by maintaining his employment he will be able to remain "one of the guys." Also, he will be better able to provide financially for the family from which he is now estranged.

While other approaches to substance abuse treatment may view Paul's previous "failed" attempts as a poor prognostic indicator, CRA does not. For example, his first attempt was in a residential care setting where patients often do well while retained, but suffer once the structure imposed by such approaches is gone. Furthermore, while it is true that Paul eventually resumed his substance use habits after his release, there is a positive pattern that must not be overlooked. After his initial treatment, Paul was able to remain completely abstinent for approximately nine months. There is strong support in the literature (Hunt, Barnett & Branch , 1971; Marlatt & Gordon, 1980) to suggest that it is during the first 90 days following treatment that relapse is most likely. Paul lasted a period three times that long. He also reports periods within the last six years during which he has remained abstinent for as long as ten months and had relapses as short as two days. Given CRA's emphasis on harm reduction, these more prolonged periods of abstinence and abbreviated relapses can be reframed as evidence that Paul has the capacity to attain sobriety and that the focus needs to be shifted to its maintenance.

*6. What would be your time line (duration) for therapy? What would be your frequency and duration of the sessions?*

Although several randomized clinical trials have shown CRA to be effective within a relatively short 3-month period, it is structured in an open-ended format. Given the objective of helping clients master a specific set of skills necessary to achieve their goals, therapy is not complete until those skills are mastered and a reasonable degree of progress has been made toward obtaining their goals. With this in mind, the amount of time that is required varies from client to client.

In addition to client variables affecting the length of therapy, the therapist's ability to structure successes early in treatment is also a factor. By carefully selecting initial treatment goals well within the client's capability (e.g., showing up for the next session), self-efficacy is enhanced, the therapeutic relationship is strengthened, and the client continues to attend. In turn, the therapist has the opportunity to help the client learn to identify his or her behavioral contingencies and to begin to increase the number of pro-social behaviors in his or her repertoire, while decreasing drinking activities.

Treatment frequency is dictated by the client's motivation and progress. Although a CRA therapist normally would have sessions once weekly, the decision may be made to hold several sessions within the first week or two of treatment if a client is ambivalent or if there is concern about an impending relapse. During this period it would be important to apply proper positive reinforcement so as to make attendance and compliance with homework as rewarding as possible. As already noted, by structuring early successes, the therapist ensures that the client will be around for later ones! As therapy progresses and both therapist and client agree that the client is ready to become more independent, a "weaning" process is introduced. Essentially, sessions are scheduled every 2 weeks, then once a month, and so on. In this fashion the client-therapist relationship remains strong, and the client feels welcome to resume the regular sessions if difficulties arise.

As for session duration, an hour is usually adequate for an individual treatment session. If CRA is offered in a group format, duration runs easily to 1½ hours per session. Typically, only the first individual session runs as long as 1½–2 hours. During this time, assessment material is obtained, the program is explained, and strategies for maintaining sobriety until the next session are planned.

*7. Are there specific or special techniques that you would implement in the therapy? What would they be?*
Two of CRA's key techniques have already been explained in some detail: CRA Functional Analyses and Sobriety Sampling. The remaining techniques that would be most useful for this client fall into the behavioral skills training category: Problem-solving, communication skills, and drink/drug-refusal. As noted earlier, problem-solving is a step-by-step method for defining a problem, generating potential solutions, and devising a specific plan for implementing the desired solution. The procedure can be applied to virtually any type of problem. In Paul's case, problem-solving would be used to address his difficulty controlling his anger, both at home and at work. An illustration of the technique for one of these situations follows:

1. Define problem:
Yelling at co-workers when upset, and sometimes even hitting them.

2. Brainstorm potential solutions (therapist does not criticize any):
- bite my tongue
- put hands in pockets
- shove but don't punch
- call names only
- never get angry
- leave room after yelling
- leave room when first upset
- call a friend
- count to 10
- learn assertiveness
- work off anger at gym
- go smoke a cigarette
- shake hands instead
- talk calmly about problem
- sit & say nothing
- watch for signs of getting upset

3. Eliminate any undesired solutions (ones that the client cannot picture himself trying in the upcoming week):
Paul crosses out approximately half of the solutions.

4. Select 1–2 potential solutions and determine if feasible:
- put hands in pockets
- leave room when first upset

5. Identify any obstacles to implementing the solutions:

Paul says he is not sure that he can recognize when he is first getting upset.

6. Address each obstacle:
The therapist helps Paul identify signs of his anger building up, so that he will know when to leave the room.

7. Therapist checks on the outcome at the next session:
The therapist inquires about whether Paul attempted his plan, and whether it worked. Paul's plan is modified somewhat for the next week.

Note that the solution for dealing with anger is only a simple one that does not take into consideration the fact that Paul needs communication skills and impulse control training. Nevertheless, this solution provides an important temporary tool for Paul to use until there is sufficient time to teach him the necessary skills to more appropriately express his anger. If Paul had selected solutions from his list that were too difficult for him to actually utilize without much training (e.g., talk calmly about problem), this would have become apparent during steps #5 and #6, and the therapist would have coached him to select something else. Problem-solving eventually would be introduced to work on Paul's social life, given that he appears to have virtually no nondrinking social activities and few nondrinking friends. His job satisfaction would also be explored (Happiness Scale), and the relevant issues addressed as well. If Paul decided that he was interested in finding another job, CRA's job-finding component (Azrin & Besalel, 1980) would be utilized.

Communication skills training would be taught primarily in terms of the appropriate expression of anger toward both his co-workers and loved ones. Additionally, couples' communication skills would be introduced if his ex-wife attended any sessions (see question 13). Furthermore, drink/drug-refusal skills, a type of behavioral assertiveness training, would be an essential part of Paul's program. Finally, CRA routinely emphasizes relapse prevention throughout the program in several formats. It begins with the identification of triggers on the functional analysis and continues with the use of problem-solving to address urges. Also, since the CRA program attempts to make a nondrinking life style as reinforcing as a drinking life style, relapse prevention is an automatic focus.

*8. Are there special cautions to be observed in working with this patient (e.g., danger to self or others, transference, counter-transference)? Are there any particular resistances you would expect and how would you deal with them?*
Although Paul's testing indicates that he is moderately depressed and hopeless, there is no overt indication of suicidality or homicidality.

While it is true that he has impulse control difficulties as indicated by a history of violent outbursts against his wife and co-workers, those seem to be particularly exacerbated by his substance abuse patterns. Given that assertiveness training and anger-management skills are an integral part of CRA, Paul would not be considered to be highly dangerous based on his past behaviors.

With regard to resistance, the fact that CRA will be largely new to Paul will make rolling with any resistance much easier. This is especially true since CRA does not attack resistant behavior head-on. Instead, it focuses on looking at the meaning of the resistance as it relates to the functional analysis of the substance use behavior. For example, Paul's hopelessness could be addressed immediately with the use of a positive reframe of the times he has stayed sober in the past, and the fact that this time treatment is sought on his own initiative. Additionally, patients such as Paul often have been bombarded with litanies of what they have failed to do, whereas CRA would focus exclusively on what Paul is capable of doing at this moment. Furthermore, the CRA therapist would remind Paul of the "rewards" (reinforcers) that he has already stated will be available to him once he makes some difficult changes. Thus, resistance to treatment is sidestepped, so to speak, by emphasizing Paul's own reasons for seeking treatment and by not forcing him into behaviors he is not ready to adopt.

*9. Are there any areas that you would choose to avoid or not address with this patient? Why?*

Although CRA is designed to handle virtually any problem area, certain issues may temporarily be avoided until some basic skills are taught. For example, if Paul decides that he wants to try a new social activity, but the therapist is convinced that communication and drink-refusal skills need to be taught first, Paul would be advised to put his plan on hold. He would still actively work on his social life, but through a different avenue for a few sessions. Also, if Paul decided that he wanted to work on the relationship with his ex-wife, but he either still was drinking or had not yet learned how to control his anger, the therapist would encourage him to start by addressing these other critical issues first.

A very different scenario would emerge if a client reluctantly began therapy, insisting he or she had no drug problem. The therapist might "back door" the substance abuse issue by focusing on other problem areas first. Eventually, all roads tend to lead back to the need to reduce alcohol or drug use. The CRA therapist simply would allow the client to arrive at this conclusion without undue pressure.

*10. Is medication warranted for this patient? What effect would you hope or expect the medication to have?*

The use of medication to address withdrawal symptomatology during alcohol detoxification for all but the most severe cases is controversial. In our own work with chronic alcohol abusers within a homeless population (Smith et al., 1998), anti-anxiety agents were only rarely required and ambulatory detox was possible for all of the over 100 participants. This is not to suggest that uncomfortable withdrawal symptoms were absent, only that nonpharmaceutical interventions were available and effective. This seems an especially appropriate approach given that the goal of most substance abuse treatments is to show that uncomfortable emotions and situations can be dealt with in a manner that does not include ingestion of an outside agent.

Some providers might be prone to suggest an antidepressant agent given Paul's moderately high level of depression and hopelessness. However, in a comprehensive review of both the psychiatric and psychological literature on the effectiveness of medication versus cognitive-behavioral therapy, which could include CRA (Antonuccio, Danton, & De Nelsky, 1995), it was determined that medication should not be the first-line treatment approach. This would appear appropriate in this case as well.

One medication that might be considered in Paul's case would be disulfiram (Antabuse). While the CRA approach to the use of disulfiram is outlined elsewhere in this chapter, it is important to note the particular reasons this medication might be especially useful for Paul at this stage in his treatment. First, unless there have been drastic changes in Paul's blood chemistry or liver function over the last 6 years, his history indicates that his system can tolerate disulfiram without any specific side effects. Also, Paul's own experience provides potent evidence of how his drinking was better controlled when on the medication than when not. This argues further for its use as an immediate tool so that Paul may successfully sample sobriety for at least a 90-day period. Given that Paul's significant others may doubt his current willingness or ability to remain abstinent, the use of disulfiram has the additional benefit of demonstrating a good faith effort on Paul's part to utilize all strategies available to him. Finally, since the CRA program only advocates the use of disulfiram in the context of a supportive monitor, Paul would be more likely to remain on it longer. Another medication to consider at the point of aftercare is naltrexone, since this opioid antagonist has shown some promise in reducing binges if an individual starts to drink again (O'Malley et al., 1992; Volpicelli, Alterman, Hayashida, & O'Brien, 1992). To date, it has not been utilized in a controlled trial with CRA.

*11. What are the strengths of the patient that can be used in the therapy?*
Paul's major strength is the pride he takes in his work, and the fact that he has been viewed by co-workers as fair, hard working, and conscientious.

Since Paul experiences a sense of dignity and self-esteem associated with his work, his job would be considered a powerful reinforcer for him. Consequently, a CRA therapist would link Paul's efforts toward sobriety with doing well at work. Similarly, Paul would be reminded that he stood to lose something of great value to him (his job) if he continued to drink.

Another of Paul's strengths is his feelings for his children, and his desire to be a good father. Having access to his children is reinforcing, and so the therapist would assist Paul in devising a plan that would make this likely to happen. Sobriety would top the list, since in a nondrinking state he would be less apt to be denied visitation. The connection could also be made between Paul's desire to be a good father and his job performance. In other words, the therapist might point out that maintaining a steady job would not only provide financially for his children, but would set him up as a good role model for them as well. A final strength is the fact that Paul has had some success with sobriety in the past, particularly when he has maintained contact with a program. This information would be used to guide the development of his aftercare plan.

*12. How would you address limits, boundaries, and limit-setting with this patient?*

In terms of setting limits and boundaries within the therapeutic relationship, CRA operates in accordance with most standard clinical treatments. This includes establishing clear expectations for starting and ending sessions on time, and for paying in a timely fashion. The professional nature of the therapeutic relationship is also discussed. If Paul violated any of these boundaries the CRA therapist would raise the issue, discuss it with Paul so as to understand his feelings and motives, and then move toward a positive solution of the problem.

Getting the client to adhere to boundaries outside of therapy can be facilitated by using his or her reinforcers. For example, assume that Paul insisted he was going to see his children whenever he pleased, even though the divorce specified that he only could see them at certain prearranged times. A CRA therapist would proceed in the following fashion:

Paul:   I need to see my kids more. I'm just going to go over there whenever I have time. She can't stop me.

T:   I'm confused, I thought you wanted to see your children more, not less?

Paul:   I do. I want to spend more time with them. I just told you I was going to go over there.

T:   But if you go barging in on your ex-wife and the kids, she may go to her lawyer and have your time with the kids reduced.

Paul:  I don't care. They're my kids too and I should be able to see them whenever I want.

T:     You really miss your children, don't you Paul?

Paul:  I just said that. I need to see my kids.

T:     You're right, you do need to see your kids. That's why you need to be calm and think about what you are saying. If you cooperate, your ex-wife may let you spend more time with the kids. If you become angry and threaten her, you may hurt your chances of seeing your kids more.

Paul:  OK. I see your point.

*13. Would you want to involve significant others in the treatment? Would you use out-of-session work (homework) with this patient? What homework would you use?*

CRA always has viewed problem users' significant others as important collaborators in the treatment of substance abuse, and has included them successfully as disulfiram monitors, partners in marital counseling, active agents in resocialization and reinforcement programs, and relapse or problem detectors (Azrin et al., 1982; Meyers, Dominguez, & Smith, 1996; Meyers & Smith, 1995; 1997; Miller, Meyers, & Tonigan, in press). At some point during treatment the therapist would want to work on the relationship between Paul and his ex-wife, regardless of whether they get back together. The fact that they have small children means that they will be in contact for many years. Consequently, it may be helpful to teach them how to communicate as a couple and problem-solve, especially in the areas of child rearing and visitation privileges.

There are three CRA tools that may be useful for this couples work. The Relationship Happiness Scale would be given to both Paul and his ex-wife independently, in an effort to have them identify problem areas in their relationship. This would be followed by the Perfect Relationship form, which allows for specification of their behavioral goals and strategies. Finally, the Daily Reminder To Be Nice chart would be introduced so that an emphasis could be placed on increasing the frequency of positive interactions between Paul and his ex-wife. This type of relationship therapy would be done after Paul had already had some individual therapy to work on his sobriety.

Out-of-session homework is essential to CRA, since only 1–2 hours of therapy a week will not change a pattern that has taken years to develop. Assignments are often written onto the Goals of Counseling form in the strategies column. A basic consideration when assigning homework is to make sure that the client has the skills to be successful. In Paul's case, one assignment in the social life category might be to make a list of non-drinking social activities, and a second would be to try one. Paul would be verbally reinforced for any progress toward these goals. In the event that he did not complete an assignment, the CRA therapist would explore the reason, as opposed to questioning his commitment. This would then be followed by problem-solving, or the assignment would be tackled right in the session.

*14. What would be the issues to be addressed in termination? How would termination and relapse prevention be structured?*

Relapse-prevention work is critical in Paul's case, as the period after acute care has been most problematic for him historically. The integration of relapse prevention throughout all CRA interventions has been outlined in detail already. In general, it will be important to see that Paul has been trained in the necessary behavioral skill areas, and that he utilizes these new skills appropriately in his community (job, home). Since his continued use of those skills is dependent on him being reinforced for doing so, the CRA therapist must check on this regularly.

An additional issue in the termination process is the importance of establishing positive expectations for treatment success, with a clear understanding of what this would mean specifically for Paul. CRA strongly emphasizes that recovery is an ongoing process, and that while slips are not desired, they can be used as a source of valuable information in the determination of unforeseen high-risk situations. Therefore, Paul would be invited to return to therapy if needed. This would not be viewed as evidence of failure, but as a recognition of the need for more intense treatment involvement than perhaps he had been able to obtain in AA. This would not only allow Paul to seek additional treatment with some pride in his judgment, but it could also foster the idea that any further intervention will be viewed within a continuum of care. Hopefully this would encourage Paul in the future to access professional or peer support resources immediately upon recognition of a decline in function.

*15. What do you see as the hoped-for mechanisms of change for this patient, in order of importance?*

The most important mechanism of change for any patient being treated with CRA is the individual's own set of reinforcers, most of which are inaccessible as a result of his or her use of substances. Paul has returned to treatment with a clear statement about what is important to him and what is at stake if his substance use behavior does not change. The possibility of a reconciliation with his family and the maintenance of his job serve as powerful motivators to try different strategies for changing his behaviors.

The second mechanism of change is inherent in CRA's largely nonconfrontational format. At no time will Paul be told that he is required to quit drinking. It will be made absolutely clear that the choice is his, but he will be invited to sample sobriety. Simultaneously, through the strategies described earlier, Paul will learn that the things he values (i.e., family and job) are completely incompatible with drinking behaviors, but are well suited to nondrinking behaviors that will be reinforced consistently. One positive potential outcome would be the re-establishment of a relationship with his father, which might foster rewarding nondrinking activities (e.g., fishing) that Paul has abandoned. Other behaviors that likely will be inherently rewarding are sober time spent with his children, positive reinforcement for his job performance, more financial stability, and perhaps even some type of renewed relationship with his ex-wife.

In essence, the most powerful mechanism of change, whether accessed through CRA or another approach, is the set of natural consequences of positive behavior. This is true across a wide range of behaviors, across persons of different personalities and cognitive styles, and regardless of previous failed attempts to change. It is at the foundation of any change strategy such as CRA that has been based on a thorough understanding of behavioral science, and it will continue to prove effective in Paul's case as well.

# REFERENCES

Antonuccio, D. O., Danton, W. G., & DeNesky, G. Y. (1995). Psychotherapy versus medication for depression: Challenging the conventional wisdom with data. *Professional Psychology: Research and Practice, 26,* 574–585.

Azrin, N. H. (1976). Improvements in the community reinforcement approach to alcoholism. *Behaviour Research and Therapy, 14,* 339–348.

Azrin, N. H., & Besalel, V. A. (1980). *Job club counselor's manual.* Baltimore, MD: Pro-Ed., Inc.

Azrin, N. H., Sisson, R. W., Meyers, R. J., & Godley, M. D. (1982). Alcoholism treatment by disulfiram and community reinforcement therapy. *Journal of Behavior Therapy and Experimental Psychiatry, 3,* 105–112.

D'Zurilla, T. J., & Goldfried, M. R. (1971). Problem solving and behavior modification. *Journal of Abnormal Psychology, 78,* 107–126.

Finney, J. W., & Monahan, S. C. (1996). The cost-effectiveness of treatment for alcoholism: A second approximation. *Journal of Studies on Alcohol, 57,* 229–243.

Holder, H., Longabaugh, R., Miller, W., & Rubonis, A. (1991). The cost effectiveness of treatment for alcoholism: A first approximation. *Journal of Studies on Alcohol, 52,* 517–540.

Hunt, G. M., & Azrin, N. H. (1973). A community-reinforcement approach to alcoholism. *Behaviour Research and Therapy, 11,* 91–104.

Hunt, W. A., Barnett, L. S., & Branch, L. G. (1971). Relapse rates in addiction programs. *Journal of Clinical Psychology, 27,* 455–456.

Mallams, J. H., Godley, M. D., Hall, G. M., & Meyers, R. J. (1982). A social-systems approach to resocializing alcoholics in the community. *Journal of Studies on Alcohol, 43,* 1115–1123.

Marlatt, G. A. (1980). Relapse prevention: A self-control program for the treatment of addictive behaviors. Unpublished manuscript.

Marlatt, G. A., & Gordon, J. R. (1980). Determinants of relapse: Implications for the maintenance of behavior change. In P. O. Davidson & S. M. Davidson (Eds.), *Behavioral medicine: Changing health lifestyles.* New York: Brunner/Mazel.

Meyers, R. J., Dominguez, T., & Smith, J.E. (1996). Community reinforcement training with concerned others. In V. B. Hasselt & M. Hersen's (Eds.), *Sourcebook of psychological treatment manuals for adult disorders.* New York: Plenum Press.

Meyers, R. J., & Smith, J. E. (1995) *Clinical guide to alcohol treatment: The community reinforcement approach.* New York: Guilford Press.

Meyers, R. J., & Smith, J. E. (1997). Getting off the fence: Procedures to engage treatment-resistant drinkers. *Journal of Substance Abuse Treatment, 14,* 467–472.

Miller, W. R., Brown, J. M., Simpson, T. L., Handmaker, N. S., Bein, T. H., Luckie, L. F., Montgomery, H. A., Hester, R. K., & Tonigan, J. S. (1995). What works? A methodological analysis of the alcohol treatment outcome literature. In R. K. Hester & W. R. Miller (Eds.), *Handbook of alcoholism treatment approaches: Effective alternatives* (2nd edition). Needham, MA: Allyn & Bacon.

Miller, W. R., Meyers, R. J., & Tonigan, J. S. (in press). Engaging the unmotivated in treatment for alcohol problems: A comparison of three intervention strategies. *Journal of Consulting and Clinical Psychology.*

Monti, P. M., Abrams, D. B., Kadden, R. M., & Cooney, N. L. (1989). *Treating alcohol dependence: A coping skills training guide.* New York: Guilford Press.

O'Malley, S. S., Jaffe, A. J., Chang, G., Schottenfeld, R. S., Meyers, R. J., & Rounsaville, B. (1992). Naltrexone and coping skills therapy for alcohol dependence: A controlled study. *Archives of General Psychiatry, 49,* 881–887.

Smith, J. E., Meyers, R. J., & Delaney, H. (1998). The community reinforcement approach with homeless alcohol-dependent individuals. *Journal of Consulting and Clinical Psychology, 66,* 541–548.

Volpicelli, J. R., Alternan, A. I., Hayashida, M., & O'Brien, C. P. (1992). Naltrexone in the treatment of alcohol dependence. *Archives of General Psychiatry, 49,* 876–880.

# 13

# The Case of Paul:
# A Systematic Approach
# to Ericksonian Utilization
# and Therapeutic Change

## *William J. Matthews*

## I. THE TREATMENT MODEL

My basic approach to psychotherapy is influenced by the work of Milton Erickson. For Erickson (1901–1980), therapy was a way of helping people extend their perceived limits. Ericksonian therapy is formulated on the basis of various assumptions about people, health, learning, and the process of growth and change. The actual process of therapy will likely vary in each instance and each case. There are however, a number of basic principles which underly the Ericksonian approach (Lankton, Lankton, & Matthews, 1991; Matthews, Lankton, & Lankton, 1993, 1996 ). Foremost among these is an emphasis on the unique life circumstances of each individual and a belief that therapy needs to be tailored to fit that person's needs. Similarly, there is an emphasis on the innate health seeking motivation that even unpleasant symptoms can be taken as somehow representing. Each symptom or problem is examined in terms of how this is an effort to solve some developmental or interpersonal challenge. People are seen as having many resource experiences available to them, simply by virtue of being alive, and the goal of therapy is to help retrieve, develop, reinforce, and associate or reassociate these to relevant contexts.

Clients are seen as having the ability to identify and create solutions to various life challenges, drawing from resources (i.e., previous life experiences) within themselves. Therapists assist in this process by stimulating thinking that creates a context for these solutions to be developed. The most effective solutions are those that emphasize action. Insight and understanding are optional and certainly not a prerequisite for change. Change is at the psychological level when a reassociation in experiences results in a person having the desired psychological traits available and organized such that productive action is a new option. People can be expected to use better options once they are developed. It is not necessary to take something away or reduce behaviors that had been relied upon. It is not necessary to analyze past conflicts per se, only understand what the person is trying to accomplish in the present. Let us consider the key principles of this approach with specific reference to Paul.

## Guiding Principles

### Expectancy
An overarching theme in this approach is the important element of expectancy, the significance of which, and its effect on treatment outcome, cannot be overstated (cf. Kirsch, 1990). In this approach, expectancy is considered in two ways: (1) disrupting negative client expectancies; and (2) creating positive beliefs/expectancies that change will occur.

Both Paul and his wife have had a history of alcoholism within each family and related abuse. This previous experience has no doubt contributed to Paul and his wife's[1] expectancy of what occurs within a family. More significant is the likely assumption held by Paul that his failure to maintain his sobriety is both inevitable, and a function of some pathological unchangeable character trait, i.e., a negative expectation for change. A goal within and across sessions is to challenge this negative expectancy (perhaps directly, most likely indirectly) with a different perspective, e.g., that he is quite successful at achieving sobriety for a given period of time. Paul has both the expertise and resources necessary for change.

### Action vs. Insight
Ericksonian therapy is interested in getting clients active and moving (Zeig, 1980). This movement must be in their lives outside the office. Homework assignments are often given in order to have clients carry out

[1] The term 'wife' is technically incorrect as Paul is divorced. However, he lives with and seems quite connected to her. As such, 'ex-wife' also fails to adequately describe their relationship. Since for all intents and purposes they are more married than not, I will use the term 'wife' throughout the remainder of this chapter.

agreed upon behaviors between the sessions. Hypnotherapy and the use of anecdotes, therapeutic metaphors, and indirect suggestions are ways of conversing with clients to help create the impetus during sessions to carry out new relational behaviors or congruently engage in the homework assignments. It is from the learning brought by new actions, as opposed to insight, that change develops (Haley, 1976). The matter of importance is the clients' *participation* in new experiences and transactions in which the opportunity to develop new appropriate relational patterns can occur.

Paul has indicated that: (1) when he is working he feels better; (2) that active involvement in therapy assignments (e.g., writing about his feelings) was useful; (3) active participation in his treatment (i.e., attending AA meetings, taking medication, etc.) contributed to his sobriety. These behaviors are directly related to the desired therapeutic change. The issue of participation is further discussed in Questions 7 and 13.

### Expanding Perceived Limitations
Clients come to therapy typically having employed their most adaptive solutions available to their conscious minds. However, the problem(s) persist as a function of the limitations imposed by the client's conscious mind. A major focus of therapy then may be to overload, bypass, confuse, or otherwise engage the conscious mind in an effort to retrieve, organize, and associate to relevant contexts, resources of which the client may be unaware. The underlying idea is creating a positive expectancy for change by reminding the client of resources (i.e., strengths, abilities, previous accomplishments, achievements, etc.) that he or she may not have thought related to the presenting problem. Hypnosis and the use of metaphor (as indirect procedures), as well as direct suggestions, may be useful methods to achieve this goal.

My assumption is that Paul perceives his lack of sobriety as essentially outside of his control. One notion would be to investigate with him exactly how he stayed sober at any given point in time. What was different when he was sober? What did he do? What didn't he do, etc.? See Question 7 on treatment.

### Health vs. Pathology
Related to the previous principle is the idea that problems are not thought to be the result of the client's intrapsychic mechanisms gone awry, but rather the result of a difficulty of transitioning in the developmental life cycle (Haley, 1973). Consequently, the emphasis is to depathologize the client. Assessment is an activity which frames the presenting problem in terms of the developmental and interpersonal climate experienced by individuals alone or in a family. Directly connected to the process of assess-

ment is the co-development (i.e., with the client) of treatment goals and employment of whatever interventions work, such as hypnosis, to achieve the identified treatment goals (Lankton, Lankton, & Matthews, 1991). This process of assessment is nonpathological in its orientation, as the goal is to identify and/or rename (i.e., create a different story) behaviors or beliefs that are part of the client's strength.

On numerous occasions, Paul has demonstrated his ability to persevere, to make adaptive choices, to show concern for others (i.e., family). Given his past experiences, emphasizing his strengths and building on them has more likelihood of success, at this point, than focusing on his weaknesses.

### Therapeutic Change

From this perspective, change, rather than cure, is based on retrieving the resources within the individual and creating a shift in client expectancy toward the belief that change *is* possible. One might ask what if the client does not have the resources within himself for therapeutic change? In many ways, this is the crux of Ericksonian therapy. Most people tend to underrate their natural abilities and resources. They take for granted abilities that they perceive to be outside their conscious control (e.g., the perseverance and endurance required as a child to learn to ride a bicycle, going on a job interview, a first date, etc.). Most clients have at least some of the resources, abilities, affect, and behaviors that could be used to solve a current problem. The goal of Ericksonian therapy is to create the context in which clients can realize how much they already know and then use these abilities in a directed fashion for their own betterment.

With regard to drinking, Paul has clearly demonstrated the ability to make the desired changes. The goal of therapy is to increase the length of duration of change, and should relapse occur (a not unlikely event), a method to shorten and manage it. Additionally, in the absence of drinking, Paul has demonstrated a range of positive resources which can be developed to further enhance his social interactions.

### Present and Developmentally Oriented

What the client needs and wants to accomplish in the present is of utmost importance in this approach. While this sometimes is examined in the context of past or changing needs, the primary attention is focused on immediate and upcoming developmental demands. While a client's problem, by definition, had to have developed in the past, how it is maintained in the present and is problematic for the future becomes the focus of this approach.

With regard to Paul, future-oriented change may be quite significant and important to consider. In conjunction with sobriety, he needs more developmentally appropriate ways of being in an intimate relationships with his wife, family, and colleagues. Remaining connected to his family of origin model of being in the world has not been particularly useful. New skills for dealing with various emotional demands will need to be developed and utilized. Such new skills and resources in turn will likely contribute to increased control over his sobriety.

### Strategic

Finally, the therapist is active and shares responsibility for initiating therapeutic movement and creating a context in which change can take place. This is often facilitated by introducing conversational material into the therapy session and by the use of extramural assignments. That is, the therapist may not wait until clients spontaneously bring up material, but rather, may invite or challenge clients to grow and change by creating a context in which change can occur. Behaviorally oriented homework is important for the client to experience thoughts, behaviors, affect, attitudes, and self-image connected to the treatment goals (Lankton, Lankton, & Matthews, 1991; Matthews, Lankton, & Lankton, 1993). In this way, each session becomes a foundation to consolidate previous learnings to further movement toward established goals.

## II.  ESSENTIAL CLINICAL SKILLS AND ATTRIBUTES

### The Therapist's Role as Scientist

Making a strategic and therapeutic difference without imposing control is a balance one needs to maintain throughout therapy. In Paul's case, trying to exert control over him is not likely to meet with success. My goal is to be somewhat peripheral at all times, minimizing the importance of the therapist while emphasizing that the power and the credit for change belong to the client. This balance is as important during the course of therapy as at termination. While the therapeutic conversation will introduce memories, ideas, understandings, and so on, these suggestions must be in accord with the client's understandings, desires, and goals.

Additionally, I would contend that the therapist should provide a role model of active scientist for the client. Which is to say, that the therapist needs to hypothesize, empirically test various hypotheses/interventions (via observation), and revise said hypotheses/interventions based on the observed data. In essence, this is exactly what I would be asking of Paul with regard to his life experience, i.e., state his theory regarding his behavior, empirically test the validity of a given theory, and revise said theory based on data. Modeling this behavior becomes an indirect suggestion for both behavioral and attitudinal change for Paul.

# General Clinical Skills

Observational skills are one of the most basic requirements for a therapist to be successful in this, or in any, approach. Erickson's own children report that "observe, observe, observe" was one of their father's most consistent pieces of advice. This observing (both of verbal and nonverbal behavior) is not designed to derive an immutable truth about a client or family, but rather to be certain to receive as much relevant information from clients as possible to form working hypotheses. It can be quite useful to be able to observe the client and family members (where possible) and experience the dynamics or characteristics of the family system. Observing Paul with his immediate family and family of origin would be of value in ascertaining what new learning, roles, and skills will be necessary to maintain extended future change.

In addition to observational skills, other therapist attributes such as flexibility, willingness for self- disclosure when appropriate, active participation, and speaking the client's experiential language, as well as the obvious qualities of intelligence, patience, empathy, genuineness, and honesty, provide the therapist with the interpersonal foundation in which to use therapeutic creativity.

## Specific Clinical Skills

While the above interpersonal skills are necessary for the therapeutic process to occur, they alone are not sufficient. This therapeutic approach is based on a general cognitive-behavioral (CBT) oriented approach to therapy. As such, therapists need to have expertise in the use of six specific clinical skills (Kirsch, 1993). What makes this approach Ericksonian is perhaps in the creative application of these skills.

### Relaxation Training
Typically, a key component of most cognitive-behavioral treatments, relaxation is frequently paired with systematic desensitization training or used as a method of reducing anxiety associated with the various stressors of daily life. The ability to develop a relaxation response to a specific real-life stressor can be put into the form of a posthypnotic suggestion, thus increasing the likelihood of increasing the client's ability to produce relaxation as needed.

### Guided Imagery
Often paired with relaxation and/or desensitization technique, the use of imagery provides the client an opportunity to pair relaxation with a heretofore anxiety-provoking image. One can also suggest an image which

provokes relaxation and pair it with a previously negative scene as a method of further increasing the relaxation response. Imagery, of course, can be used without the relaxation response when a more physiologically active response is called for such as assertiveness.

## Behavioral Practice
Actual experience or exposure to real life situations is a central component in CBT which is designed to promote mastery and increase self-esteem. There are consistent research findings that behavioral practice is superior to vicarious learning in relation to behavior change (Wickless & Kirsch, 1989).

## Successive Approximations
The principle of shaping a desired response or graduated practice is a key aspect of CBT. Increasing exposure to anxiety-inducing stimuli, asking depressed clients for increasing yet minimal changes, practicing small changes in the direction of the therapeutic goals, etc., are all part of a shaping procedure.

## Cognitive Restructuring
The purpose of cognitive restructuring is to identify and modify patterns of thoughts and beliefs that contribute to the client's emotional and behavioral dysfunctions. Such beliefs are typically maintained, regardless of the evidence to the contrary, by the client's logical distortions. The goal in this process is to have the client invalidate through behavioral experience (e.g., imagery, successive approximations, practice, etc.,) previously held beliefs, attitudes, and thoughts.

## Hypnosis
CBT can, of course, be done without hypnosis. The implication is that hypnosis is not a special state or condition (Kirsch,1993). However, many clients typically hold positive expectations regarding the benefits of hypnosis and as such become good candidates for its use. Hypnosis has been empirically demonstrated to be effective in altering a person's sensations, perceptions, thoughts, and behavior and as such can be useful as an ancillary aspect of treatment (Kirsch, Montgomery, & Sapirstein, 1995). Depending on Paul's overall responsiveness, hypnosis may provide a useful technique to promote attitudinal and behavior change.

## III. THE CASE OF "PAUL": 15 CLINICAL QUESTIONS

1. *What would be your therapeutic goals for this patient? What are the primary and secondary goals?*

Within this treatment model, clear, identifiable, and achievable therapeutic goals are useful parameters by which both the client and therapist can evaluate the effectiveness of the work. Certainly a primary goal is to help Paul gain control over his abuse of substance. However, a change in his behavior concerning substance raises equally valid questions about other aspects of Paul and his interpersonal interactions. Thus, in my approach to the primary goal of a change in Paul's abuse of substance, I will consider Paul's treatment from the perspective of six general treatment goals in which change can be expected to be of benefit. They are changes in: (1) affect; (2) attitudes; (3) behavior; (4) self-image; (5) social network; and an (6) increase in discipline and enjoyment in living. In each of these areas, from my perspective, treatment goals must be codeveloped with the client as a result of the therapeutic conversation and ought not be imposed unilaterally on the client. In the following discussion, I would ask the reader to assume that the specifics of each goal is the end result of this joint conversation in which there was agreement between the therapist and client.

## Affect
Paul needs to increase his sense of well-being, feelings of competence, general level of comfort in social interactions, and feelings of self-worth, providing a hopefulness for the future which, by definition, will reduce feelings of anxiety, depression, and hopelessness. It would not be unreasonable to consider anxiety to be a particular problem for Paul such that increased feelings of comfort, relaxation, and security in a range of contexts would be of clear therapeutic value.

## Attitude
It is important to ascertain what is Paul's overarching or prevailing view of the world in relationship to himself. He might reasonably be expected to say "The world is a scary place and I am a hopeless failure in it." With further questioning I would state that when his problems are resolved and he is sober (use of positive expectancy), he might suggest "I feel good about my strengths and I know my limitations. I can be in charge."

## Behavior
What specific behavior in what context would be an indication for Paul that he was making the desirable changes?, i.e., with his wife?; his children?; in the workplace?; with former drinking associates? Specifically, Paul will need to not drink and to develop a range of socially appropriate behaviors in the absence of drinking. Additionally, in the absence of drinking Paul will need to be able to show developmentally appropriate behaviors of intimacy, tenderness, control of temper, parenting, and so forth.

## Self-Image

As the result of the assessment process, one is likely to conclude that Paul has a poor image of himself in terms of his self-control around drinking, and in his interactions with others. Based on his perception of his past experience, Paul is likely to see an internal representation of himself as ultimately failing in a range of social interactions (e.g., drinking, violence, dealing with co-workers, etc.). This negative self-image contributes to a negative and self-fulfilling expectancy for change. A therapeutic goal for Paul would be to develop a positive self-image and "see" (i.e., internally represent) himself succeeding in a range of scenes in which he had not been successful in the past. Such a positive internal representation becomes predictive for future success.

## Social Network

Paul has learned and developed a certain role in his family which in turn has placed limits on the range of his social behavior and communication style (Lankton, Lankton, & Matthews, 1991). His present way of relating to his family may no longer be of value which may necessitate developing new role-taking behavior and a different style of communication. This frame is perhaps even more relevant for his social network involving his drinking behavior.

## Enjoyment and Discipline in Life

An important question for Paul is "In the absence of drinking, what would you do?" An extended and in-depth conversation on his interests and strengths will determine a range of possible activities that will be important to reinforce during the course of treatment. This treatment goal is consistent with the notion that Paul will need to further develop behaviors that are active and positive, and that will increase the likelihood of his experiencing nondestructive pleasurable activities.

The essence of this approach is to develop, in concert with Paul, treatment goals that are mutually interactive, i.e., that inform and are informed by each other. Thus, Paul needs to experience the affect and beliefs necessary for change, which need to be connected to specific behaviors which in turn will reinforce these more productive affect and attitudes. Additionally, the client needs to have a positive internal image of himself succeeding in various stressful contexts as a prelude to actually operating in these various contexts. An overarching theme is not just stopping his negative behaviors but increasing various opportunities for self-discipline to enjoy his life.

*2. What Further Information would you want to have to assist you in structuring this patient's treatment? Are there specific tools you would use? What would be the rational for using those tools.*

In this therapeutic model, the value of assessment must be its link with intervention. Any assessment inventory should provide clear direction for the clinician to develop a treatment plan for a given therapy session and across the course of therapy. Paul was given a number of assessment inventories (e.g., MMPI, NEO-PI, BDI, BHI, BIS, and the Spielberger S-TAS). While these inventories certainly provide useful information, in my clinical practice I have used primarily the BDI and the Interpersonal Check List (Leary, 1957). The issue for me is a cost-benefit analysis of what I will gain from these inventories versus the time and effort for both the client and me to fill them out and score the scales, respectively.

I find the Beck Depression Inventory, and the Leary Interpersonal Check List (ICL) (Leary, 1957) to be particularly useful, easy to administer, and easy to discuss directly with clients. I use the ICL essentially with all clients as it, relative to my therapeutic approach, is clearly linked with clinical intervention. The ICL is based on the client's self-report interactions in the *social context*. It is constructed with 128 weighted items covering 4 quadrants (i.e., managerial/autocratic vs. self-effacing/dependent; friendly/cooperative vs. aggressive/distrustful. I will ask the client to fill out the ICL following the initial session or to fill out the questionnaire and return it prior to the initial session depending on the time frame involved. At the beginning of the second session, I will discuss the results of the inventory and their implication for our treatment plan. Since the ICL is presented in graphic form, it tends to be easily understood by most clients.

As I use this inventory, the ICL allows me to emphasize the client's strengths, and to assess his or her interpersonal strategies that may (or may not) have been successful in the past but are less so in the present. Additionally, the ICL allows me to emphasize those skills and behaviors that the client might add to his or her repertoire. For example, I would expect Paul to score fairly high (based on the results of the above inventories) on the aggressive, rebellious, and competitive scales and relatively low on the responsible, cooperative, dependent scales. In the clinical setting, the absolute value of each scale (0, reports showing no behavior in a given category, to 20, an extreme presentation in a given category) is of less importance than the relationship of the scales to each other. Being aggressive, competitive, etc. is not, per se, or in all instances, negative; however, as a singular way of relating to others (particularly his wife), he is unlikely to achieve his desired goals of intimacy either as a partner or parent.

*3. What is your conceptualization of this patient's personality, behavior, affective state, and cognitions? What are the strengths of the patient that can be used in therapy?*

The data from the various assessments suggest that, in various interpersonal interactions, Paul is anxious, not particularly open or friendly, and not particularly conscientious. He has shown a tendency to openly and consistently express anger, whether legitimate or not, and is impulsive. Paul also reports a moderate to severe level of depression and hopelessness.

Put in a more narrative and interactional form (i.e., how Paul relates to others), I would hypothesize that Paul has a limited set of social skills such that when his interactions with others are not successful he may show anxious, hostile, and generally unfriendly and uncooperative behavior, the result of which leaves him feeling depressed and hopeless which further reduces the likelihood of achieving future successful interactions. The abuse of substance is most likely simultaneously causal and the result of Paul's social limitations and is a combination of genetics and family learning history. We might surmise that his use of substance is a form of self-medication with limited short-term benefits with regard to reducing anxiety, depression, and hopelessness and disastrous long-term effects on his ultimate well being, health, and safety. With regard to drinking, Paul is caught in a drinker's paradox which is: (a) "I am sober." leading to (b) "I can drink." leading to (c) "I am drunk." leading to (d) "I can't drink." which loops back to (a) "I am sober." and so on. A major goal of therapy is to assist Paul to step out of, break, or reframe this paradoxical loop in which he appears stuck.

Most importantly, however, Paul has shown a number of strengths upon which successful treatment will depend. He has shown a history of willingness to work and take pride in his efforts. He was able to initiate and maintain some level of intimacy with his wife, up to a certain point. He has clearly shown the ability to maintain his sobriety for an extended period. Additionally, his father has been able to maintain his own sobriety through his efforts in AA which may provide a larger supportive context for Paul's desired behavioral change. An emphasis on Paul's strengths is a key notion in a solution-focused approach, as the goal is to increase what he does well over longer periods of time.

*4. What potential pitfall would you envision in this therapy? What would the difficulties be and what would you envision to be the source(s) of the difficulties?*

Without question, the case of Paul has been and is likely to be quite difficult. For him, the potential consequences of continued substance abuse are substantial, i.e., loss of family, job, self-esteem. His substance abuse has resulted in, on more than one occasion, driving an automobile while under the influence and violence inside and outside of the home. Continued repetition of these behaviors could very well result in Paul's death, the death of other(s), and/or incarceration. Paul perceives his life as not under his control and is hoping against hope that in some manner a therapist can deliver that which he has been unable to achieve on his own. The therapist treating Paul is faced with the heretofore repeating behavioral cycle of sobriety, failure, sobriety, and so on. Both therapist and client (and his family) experience the emotional cycle of hope, despair, frustration, anger, hope, etc.

The most significant pitfall over the course of therapy is likely to be a relapse in Paul's substance abuse. Concomitantly with a substance relapse, his engaging in aggressive or violent behavior within his family or toward nonfamily members will present a significant challenge to the therapeutic treatment plan. Treatment, which will be discussed later, will need to assess and then preempt the likely antecedents (e.g., time, context, cognitions, and/or feelings) of his use of substance and of violent behavior. The emotional strain on the therapist of working with a high-risk client such as Paul can be significant. Since the desirable goal of therapy would be for Paul to be substance free (or a social drinker, if possible), and since he previously has achieved sobriety for an extended period of time, the therapist may feel extremely disappointed or depressed should Paul relapse. In this situation, I would need to guard against the belief that I can cause or somehow force Paul to be substance free.

*5. To what level of coping, adaptation, or function would you see this patient reaching as an immediate result of therapy? What is the prognosis for adaptive change?*

Individual prognosis questions in psychotherapy, while certainly legitimate, are, for the most part, quite difficult to answer. In clinical effectiveness or efficacy studies with large samples, dependent measure mean scores of one treatment condition in comparison to another treatment or no-treatment condition will typically allow for some level of prediction based on within- and between-group variability. However, in the clinical context with a sample size of one, we are dealing primarily with error variance, and therein lies the problem of prognosis. With that significant hedge on my part, I take the position that the prognosis with Paul has a clear potential for success. As I stated earlier, Paul, in spite of his repeated relapses, has shown an ability to maintain sobriety (for 9 months at one point), positively interact with his wife and children, and be productive in work. A positive outcome with Paul is dependent upon determining and managing the antecedents, behaviorally and cognitively, that trigger his relapses. Equally as important as determining the negative triggering stimuli for Paul is helping him maintain that which is working well for him (i.e., attending AA meetings, church with his ex-wife and children, going to work).

If Paul is able to control, manage, or avoid the negative triggers for his undesired behavior and continue to show the positive behaviors, then the prognosis is obviously positive. From my perspective, the key to a positive prognosis is expanding the support system for Paul such that when stress does occur, he perceives options other than loss of sobriety and/or engaging in violent behavior, specifically, expanding and involving his family system, AA, and workplace such that a context of support can be in place as an alternative to non-sobriety-based attempts at anxiety or depression management. In this context, prognosis is positive but not inconsistent with the notion that relapse is a probable event.

*6. What would be your time line for therapy? What would be your frequency and duration of sessions?*

A therapy time line, particularly in this time of managed care, seems necessarily, rightly or wrongly, connected to the cost of therapy. In answering this question, let us assume that Paul is not covered by a managed care organization that might place arbitrary limits on treatment and/or limit the frequency of treatment sessions. As such, some schedule of payment will need to be worked out for Paul, as his treatment is likely to exceed the minimal psychotherapy limits (time and cost) of a non-HMO insurance plan. Discussion of these issues with Paul can be quite important as it deals with his motivation and commitment to the desired goals of therapy. With any change there is some cost (financial and emotional) attached. This notion of cost, in my approach, is discussed early and is part of the assessment of Paul's motivation to change. That his commitment to change is likely to exceed his financial ability to pay is not necessarily a problem. Some arrangements will need to be made for a sliding fee scale which may be made contingent on his ability to show the desired behaviors, i.e., if he were to maintain his sobriety for a given time period the reduced fee would continue. If he were to lose his sobriety, the cost of each session would be increased based on a prearranged scale.

Once the financial arrangements have been established, the schedule of visits can then be negotiated. Given Paul's shaky condition, I would choose to see him, initially, every day. Paul will need a significant amount of positive reinforcement to maintain his sobriety, and reduction of his anxiety. During the early stages of therapy, I think that a once-a-week session may be insufficient to create the context for the desired changes. In lieu of hospitalization, brief daily visits (15–20 minutes) may provide an adequate context for the reinforcement of the desired behaviors. As the desired behavior increases, then the sessions can be lengthened as can the time between sessions. The key notion here is to increase Paul's focus and confidence to maintain the desired changes. Initially, I would suggest that treatment contact will be frequent with a reduction over time depending on Paul's success. At some point therapy may take the appearance of a "long-brief therapy," which is to say Paul may eventually be seen once every month, once every 2 months etc., for an extended period of time. His longest period of sobriety reported was 9 months, after which he relapsed. As such, I would be interested in maintaining contact with Paul at the 9-month mark and for some period beyond.

The responsibility, format, and purpose of each session lies, to a great extent, with Paul. Thus if Paul were to say, "We need to meet tomorrow" or "I would like to increase (or decrease) the frequency of sessions" my basic question to him would be "How does this request effect your treatment goals?" "How would we use this extra session?" If he were to request a decrease in the frequency of contact, I might ask "What has changed for you that makes sense to have fewer sessions?" Questions such as these seek to remind Paul that he has significant responsibility for the direction and accomplishments of the therapeutic process. In essence, the time line of therapy is a negotiated process between Paul and me always in relation to the stated goals of therapy.

*7. Are there specific or special techniques that you would implement in the therapy?*

My treatment approach with Paul will focus both on his conscious overt behavior and his less conscious cognitions. As such, I would employ the techniques associated with Solution-Focused therapy (O'Hanlon & Weiner-Davis, 1989) and hypnosis.

## A Solution-Focused Approach

Certainly a major focus will be to develop some initial control of Paul's drinking in connection with the other changes (e.g., the ability to maintain friendly cooperative relationships with his wife, children, family of origin, and co-workers) previously discussed. Central questions for Paul, with regard to his drinking and positive social interactions, will be "What has worked in the past?" "What would it take for you to do that now?" "What is different for you when you are not drinking (fighting/arguing) than when you are?" "Who else would notice these changes?" I would be looking for exceptions to the presenting problem and previous success (which he clearly has had). My intention will be to: (1) find the positive change that Paul has already made; (2) to maintain it, and; (3) then amplify it. The actual intervention method will vary according to Paul's needs and expectations. Specifically, the central elements of a cognitive-behavioral or a solution-focused approach (de Shazer, 1985; O'Hanlon & Weiner-Davis,1989) will be employed.

As has been discussed, the emphasis will be on accomplishing consistent, achievable changes (i.e., in affect, attitude, self-image, social network, and behavior). Behavioral practice and homework assignments to be accomplished between therapy sessions will be developed conjointly with Paul. For example, based on a previous positive interaction with his wife, Paul might be asked to specifically repeat his behavior (or a segment thereof) in an upcoming interaction with her. He may be asked to observe and record how other people resolve conflictual interactions without extreme anger, or how people can show tenderness and civility toward each other as precursors to his actually practicing similar behaviors.

A key question within this framework is the "miracle question" (de Shazer, 1985). The basic miracle question is "Suppose that one night, while you were asleep, there was a miracle and this problem (sobriety, anxiety, hopelessness, etc.) were solved. How would you know? What would be different? What would you do? Who would notice?" These questions will help Paul to focus on what works and to change rather than getting rid of the problem, per se. This question itself becomes an indirect suggestion for future change. In thinking about the answer Paul has to contemplate his future from a positive perspective. In answering the questions Paul will describe a range of behaviors (e.g., saying "no" to drugs, smiling at his wife or children, holding his temper, etc.) that I can then prescribe at the end of each session. Each session is an opportunity to note what Paul did well and find a way in which he can repeat the positive behavior.

## Hypnosis

As stated earlier, hypnosis has been shown to be significantly effective as an ancillary aspect of treatment. One reason for its effectiveness is that hypnosis typically carries with it high expectations by the client for positive therapeutic change. If Paul were to hold this expectation, then hypnosis as a method for creating change could be quite valuable. Specifically, the use of relaxation, positive imagery and beliefs can be suggested and then associated or linked with the occurrence of predicted stimuli in Paul's daily life. For example, feelings of tenderness and warmth can be accessed, developed, and associated to an upcoming interaction with his ex-wife. Feelings of competence, pride, and confidence could be accessed, developed, and associated to certain workplace scenes. The feelings and cognitions that Paul has had when he was not drinking need to be reaccessed and associated with his daily behavior particularly in relationship to previously negative environmental stimuli. The overall goal is to build and link mental images and associated physical feelings with the positive behaviors of change.

*8. Are there special cautions to be observed in working with this patient? Are there any specific resistances you would expect and how would you deal with them?*

Questions of the ethical responsibility of the therapist (e.g., duty to warn in the case of possible violence) are likely (ought) to be at least partially present in the therapist's mind. What if, during the course of treatment, Paul's substance abuse results in the death of a family member or a stranger? (See Question 12 for a specific discussion of limit setting with Paul.) However, while considering these issues in Paul's treatment, I am struck by the tragedy and pain of his life and his inability to achieve control over his behavior. My overarching question is how best can I be of help and in what way. Secondarily, should Paul and I experience stuckness in our work together, I will need to ask in what ways do my thinking and assumptions contribute to this stuckness. Resources of patience, flexibility, and creativity will be needed by both the therapist and client.

Given the initial assessment data discussed in Question 2 and the predicted data from the ICL, I would expect Paul to be somewhat oppositional, challenging, and distrustful, what is typically referred to as resistant client behavior. If I choose to view his behavior as resistant, then I am likely to: (a) see and experience resistance in our interactions, and; (b) experience frustration and annoyance with Paul. A key Ericksonian notion in working with all clients is the idea of utilization, to accept what the client brings into the therapeutic context and utilize that presentation as part of the change process. If Paul is being oppositional or rebellious, then my task is to engage his oppositionalism in a positive manner, i.e., to present a challenge that he is willing to accept to defeat or prove me wrong. The issue for me in regards to resistance from Paul is to accept and use it for his therapeutic benefit.

*9. Are there any areas that you would choose to avoid or not address with this patient?*

At this point in the assessment and treatment, I see no areas for which there would be specific prohibitions to address. During the course of treatment, however, some issue that is of particular concern to Paul may arise (e.g., sexual abuse). He may choose not to discuss, or indicate significant difficulty in discussing, this topic. In the case of sexual abuse, a prior experience of this type may have negatively effected his ability to trust others, creating feelings of anxiety or depression which he seeks to avoid by the use of substance. If this scenario were to emerge, then some resolution regarding his behavior, sense of responsibility, and experience would likely be beneficial. The use of hypnosis, specifically the use of metaphors or stories during hypnosis may be quite useful in providing a nonthreatening and indirect stimulation of his thinking and possible resolutions to his problem which had been difficult to discuss directly (Donnelly & Dumas, 1997; Martin, Cummings, & Hallberg, 1992).

*10. Is medication warranted for this patient? What effect would you hope medication to have?*

Paul indicated that the use of Antabuse was successful in helping him not to drink. However, sobriety within the context of the drinker's paradox previously discussed may actually contribute to a new cycle of drinking. A shift from this repetitive cycle is obviously necessary for Paul to make significant changes in his behavior. In this approach, I would not directly require that Paul reinstitute Antabuse (or attend AA for that matter), as such a requirement is likely to be met with noncompliance. However, I would engage in a conversation about how he felt while taking it (or attending AA, etc.); how he felt when not taking it; how it helped or not; how he decided to not take it; under what conditions (if any) would he take it (attend AA) again; what would happen if he took it; what would happen if he continued not to take it, etc. Through this conversation Paul may be able to make a clear choice regarding this medication and the consequences of taking or not taking it.

For a client with a problem of substance abuse, there is a contradictory quality of suggesting psychotropic medications to reduce negative feelings while condemning self-prescribed medications for the same purpose. Additionally, the use of antidepressants, in general, is problematic as the effect of expectancy and placebo may, in fact, produce most of the effect (Kirsch & Sapirstein, in press). Therein lies the dilemma. If I were to suggest to Paul that he take an antidepressant, he may accede to my request, take the medications, and report a positive change. However, the change may be a function of expectancy/placebo which may be achievable without medications. Clearly, my choice would be to enhance his expectancy for change without the use of psychotropic medications. The overarching theme of this treatment approach is helping Paul create a positive expectancy, belief, attitude that he is capable of lasting positive change.

*11. What are the strengths of the patient that can be used in therapy?*

Within this model, strengths of the patient is a central notion that is linked to intervention and positive change. If one were only to consider the client's weaknesses or shortcomings, there would be tendency to consciously or unconsciously reinforce the negative. The analogy is to the procedure of systematic desensitization in which the relaxation response reciprocally inhibits the anxiety response in relation to a perceived threatening stimulus. My approach with Paul, based on the previously stated principles of Ericksonian and Solution-Focused Therapy, is to emphasize the positive behaviors for which he is capable such that when he is showing these behaviors he is, by definition, not showing the negative behaviors. Only focusing on his negative behaviors has little likelihood of producing the positive behaviors required for change.

As I stated in Question 3, Paul has demonstrated a number of strengths. He has been able to remain sober for nine months, he was willing to complete therapy tasks such as talking and writing about difficult issues, he takes pride in working and being productive, and he loves his children. As discussed in Question 7 on treatment, each of these behaviors needs to be reinforced, stabilized, and amplified for positive change to occur. It is likely that Paul experiences himself as a failure as a worker, at being sober, as a husband, and as a father. Yet he has been able to succeed in each of these areas, albeit for a limited time. The goal of therapy is to extend the duration of each of these desired behaviors.

*12. How would you address the limits, boundaries, and limit setting with this patient?*

As discussed in Questions 4 and 8, there are definite pitfalls particularly in working with a substance abuse client. From my perspective it is important to model clear boundaries, expectations, and consequences for Paul should (which is likely) unacceptable behavior occur. There are three areas of concern which will need to be discussed with Paul: (1) issues dealing with a duty to warn others should he present a clear and directed danger; relatedly (2) the issue of domestic violence; and (3) relapse in the use of substance.

In instances 1 and 2, Paul needs to understand that these behaviors are unacceptable in all cases regardless of his emotional or physical state. The early establishment of rapport is important as it will provide a supportive context for discussing any violation of these behavioral requirements. However, even if rapport were slow to develop, I would not wait to make clear the expectations regarding unacceptable behaviors. The likely problems in doing so should be obvious to the reader.

Finally, issue 3, of what to do should a relapse occur is obviously important. Relapse prevention is integral to the treatment of clients dealing with substance abuse. Paul and the social network in which he operates (i.e., family of origin, nuclear family, and perhaps co-workers) will need to be involved in developing a plan should Paul show the signs of an impending relapse. I will discuss the involvement of significant others and issues of relapse and relapse prevention in subsequent questions.

*13. Would you want to involve significant others in the treatment? Would you use out-of-session homework with this patient? What homework would you use?*

The above treatment plan presupposes that Paul exists within a given social system. Of particular interest is his nuclear family and family of origin. Depending on the direction of the therapy, a consultation with all or parts of his family system is likely to be of clinical value. For example, since Paul's father is currently in AA and sober, a family meeting with Paul and his father may be useful to consider the meaning of past behaviors along with current and future expectations for change. In session, behaviorally oriented work dealing with the appropriate range of affective expression with his wife and children will provide a significant opportunity for Paul to develop new behaviors. A determining factor on direct involvement of family members is the measurable success of treatment based on the defined goals. If therapy without direct family involvement is productive, then continuation is reasonable. However, if therapy is not successful then change (e.g., expanding the field and including family members) on my part may be warranted. It is quite likely that involving Paul's family in the treatment will be useful.

As discussed in Question 7 on treatment, homework is integral to this approach as assignments are likely to stimulate Paul's thinking and his considering other possible solutions. Homework assignment are analogous to posthypnotic suggestion in that a given assignment is designed to stimulate Paul's behavioral, affective, attitudinal, and self-image thinking in ways different from the past. The goal of therapy is for Paul to develop more useful behaviors relative to the demands of interpersonal intimacy, and to anxiety stimuli that in the past have been causal to his abuse of substance. As stated earlier, Paul needs specific practice in showing tenderness to his wife, to whom, although divorced, he seems quite connected. In the therapeutic context with his wife, a given session(s) is likely to involve specific practice in showing tenderness. Clearly he needs to practice the skills and behaviors associated with fatherhood. Once a baseline of behavior has been established (i.e., he can actually do the desired behaviors), he is ready for practice outside of the treatment session. Homework in these areas will typically involve observing others who show these behaviors (i.e., in real life, in a specific video, movie, or book) and practicing these behaviors in appropriate contexts in specific ways for a time-limited period.

*14. What would be the issues to be addressed in termination? How would termination and relapse prevention be structured?*

The length of treatment (and therefore, termination) is defined in this model by the achievement of mutually agreed upon goals. When the therapeutic goals are accomplished, then therapy is ended. However, if after a given set of goals are achieved, Paul wanted to continue in treatment, then new therapeutic goals would be codefined and work would proceed relative to the new goals. If there was no progress in treatment (i.e., the defined goals are not being achieved), the central question would be "Given no change as defined by us has occurred, why should we continue?" I should note that relapse or even continued drinking would not necessarily be the basis of termination. As discussed in Question 6 regarding the time line of therapy, the frequency and duration of the therapy sessions is variable and would depend on the specific treatment goals and assigned behavioral homework. Also as mentioned earlier, initial treatment is likely to involve some daily check-in, followed by reducing the frequency and lengthening the session over time.

It is conceivable that termination (i.e., the cessation of therapeutic contact) might never specifically occur. It may be of benefit for Paul to have an ongoing series of follow-up sessions (spread out over time). Paul has experienced a series of failures regarding his personal life, work life, and control over substance. Treatment not only involves a change in these behaviors but a maintenance and continuance of this change. Once the initial treatment goals have been achieved, I would recommend to Paul that some therapeutic connection over time be continued, e.g., initial monthly follow-up, a six-month follow-up, etc., explicitly for maintenance purposes. These follow-ups could, at some point, be conducted by telephone and not involve payment. It would be important that Paul perceive himself to be connected to the therapist even over extended periods of time.

Relapse is frequently a fact of life in dealing with substance abuse. As the desired change is increasing, it would be important not to deny, or fear, the possibility of relapse. A major of focus of this work would be to identify the stimulus contingencies that are likely to predict a relapse. Paul is either unaware of these contingencies or feels them to be completely out of his control. Successful therapeutic change would place relapse prediction and prevention under Paul's conscious control. The focus in treatment has been to maintain then amplify positive change directly through CBT/SFT and/or indirectly via hypnosis. Once this behavioral shift has occurred, I would engage Paul in a conversation about this change. "What has he done differently?" "How is not drinking useful?" "What is different now than in the past with respect to drinking?" "In the past if you yelled at a co-worker (wife, children), you might end up drinking at the end of the day. What is different now?" More specifically, I have found it useful to ask the client, "If you wanted to start down the road to drinking, what would be your first step, next step, etc." A continuation of this theme would be to ask "If you were to relapse, exactly when, under what conditions would this occur?" These questions seek to identify the stimuli that have historically provoked a drinking response and seek to place control of these anticipatory stimuli within Paul's affective, attitudinal, and behavioral choices.

*15. What do you see as the hoped-for mechanisms of change for this patient, in order of importance?*

The primary mechanism of change for Paul, in this model, is the interaction between his beliefs, attitudes, or expectancies about his ability to change as they inform and are informed by his actual behavior. Paul has had a series of negative experiences which contribute to a belief and a negative self-image that he is a failure and not likely to change. He has collected plenty of empirical data to support his belief system. As this belief continues, it of course becomes a self-fulfilling prophecy in which he will find more data to support his belief system ad infinitum, to his own detriment and the detriment of his family. I refer to my earlier notion of "therapist as scientist" as a model for the "client as scientist." The primary mechanism of change is creating behavioral experiences (i.e., data) that challenge his negative expectancies, which as these expectancies change, allow Paul to observe positively oriented behavioral experiences (i.e., new data). With regard to substance, when faced with feelings of anxiety in a given social context, therapeutic success occurs when he does not perceive his response to this anxiety as hard-wired and therefore as inevitable that he will drink. That which he formally perceived as involuntary has now become voluntary, i.e., under his control. Change for Paul becomes a positive self-fulfilling prophecy based on a definable shift in beliefs and behavior.

## CONCLUSION

Working with Paul is complex and challenging with likely periods of frustration and disappointment by both the therapist and the client. My approach to Paul is to find the client's strengths and resources for change(which may include his nuclear and or family of origin) and associate them to the contexts that are needed. Within this modality, it is likely that changes in affect, attitude, self-image, and behavior will be important components for therapeutic success. The suffering of the client, within this approach, becomes less of a focus than finding ways in which he can increase his enjoyment and discipline in his life.

Once clearly defined, behavior-oriented treatment goals are established, treatment interventions can vary from the direct approaches of cognitive-behavioral or solution-focused interventions to the more indirect approach of hypnosis, metaphor, and/or indirect suggestion. Both approaches are complementary to each other. Treatment success and termination is measured by the achievement of definable and observable goals. Underscoring this approach is a respect for and an emphasis on the client's strengths which are considered within a nonpathologizing, action-oriented perspective.

## REFERENCES

de Shazer, S. (1985). *Keys to solutions in brief therapy.* New York: Norton.
Donnelly, C. M., & Dumas, J. E. (1997) Use of analogies in therapeutic situations: An analogue study. *Psychotherapy, 2,* 124–132.

Haley, J. (1976). *Problem-solving therapy.* San Francisco: Josey Bass.

Haley, J. (1973). *Uncommon therapy: The psychiatric techniques of Milton H. Erickson, M.D.* New York: Norton.

Kirsch, I. (1993). Cognitive-behavioral hypnotherapy. In J. Rhue, I. Kirsch, & S. Weeks (Eds.), *Handbook of clinical hypnosis.* Washington, D.C.: APA.

Kirsch, I. (1990). *Changing expectations: A key to effective psychotherapy.* Pacific Grove, CA: Brooks/Cole Pub.

Kirsch, I., Montgomery, G., & Sapirstein, G. (1995). Hypnosis as an adjunct to cognitive-behavioral psychotherapy: A meta analysis. *Journal of Counseling and Clinical Psychology, 63*(2), 214–220.

Kirsch, I., & Sapirstein, G. (In Press). Listening to prozac but hearing placebo: A meta-analysis of antidepressant medication. *Treatment and Prevention.*

Lankton, S., Lankton, C., & Matthews, W. (1991). Ericksonian family therapy. In A. Gurman & D. Kniskern (Eds.), *Handbook of family therapy, vol. II.* New York: Brunner/Mazel.

Leary, T. (1957). *The interpersonal diagnosis of personality: A functional theory and methodology for personality evaluation.* New York: Ronald Press.

Martin, J., Cummings, A. L., & Hallberg, E. T. (1992). Therapists' intentional use of metaphor: Memorability, clinical impact, and possible epistemic/motivational functions. *New York Journal of Consulting and Clinical Psychology, 1,* 143–145.

Matthews, W., Lankton, S. & Lankton, C. ( 1993). Ericksonian approaches to hypnotherapy. In J. Rhue, I. Kirsch, & S. Weeks (Eds.), *New York handbook of clinical hypnosis.* Washington, D.C.: APA.

Matthews, W., Lankton, S., & Lankton, C. (1996). Ericksonian hypnotherapy: A case study. In J. Rhue, I. Kirsch, & S. Weeks (Eds.), *Handbook of clinical hypnosis: Case Studies.* Washington, D.C.: APA.

O'Hanlon, W., & Weiner-Davis, M. (1989). *In search of solutions: A new direction in psychotherapy.* San Francisco: Jossey-Bass.

Wickless, C., & Kirsch, I. (1989). The effects of verbal and experiential expectancy manipulations on hypnotic susceptibility. *Journal of Personality and Social Psychology, 57,* 762–768.

Zeig, J. (Ed.). (1980). *A teaching seminar with Milton H. Erickson.* New York: Brunner/Mazel.

# 14

## Comparative Treatments: Summary and Conclusions

*E. Thomas Dowd, Pamela J. Millas, and Loreen G. Rugle*

The case of "Paul" has been analyzed from ten different perspectives and a variety of assessment and treatment recommendations have been made. Some of the approaches are quite different in both conceptualization and treatment (e.g., psychodynamic and behavioral systems) while others are closer (e.g., behavioral family therapy and behavioral systems). The two harm reduction models appear to be variations on a similar theme. As is usual in these instances, there are both similarities and differences among the approaches. In this chapter we will summarize these similarities and differences for each question and then provide an overall integration.

### I. THE TREATMENT MODEL

The psychodynamic approach is based on the assumption that significant antecedent events and conflicts contribute to Paul's current use and abuse of substances and/or that the substance abuse itself creates psychological conflict. For this approach to be of use, Paul must consider these past and current intrapsychic conflicts to be important and be capable of making the connections between these conflicts and his current behaviors. It is helpful if these connections are more easily accessible because less accessible connections may be subject to distortions as Paul attempts to keep his defensive structure in place. Another assumption is that insight and awareness of these connections can itself alter current and future behavior.

The behavioral systems approach, on the other hand, locates the causal change agent in Paul's total environment rather than in his intrapsychic conflicts. It is based on a social learning framework focusing primarily on the ways in which current reciprocal interactions may precipitate and reinforce Paul's substance use. Although the past is important, it is an external, environmental past rather than an internal one. This model, unlike Skinner's earlier formulation, assumes that reinforcers *correspond to*, rather than *cause* behavior. Essentially various environmental factors *interact with* Paul's behavior rather than directly *cause* it.

The cognitive therapy model examines the role of maladaptive cognitions in the *maintenance* of substance abuse, the tendency towards *relapse*, and structures *interventions* with which to break the vicious cycles characteristic of the addiction process. Cognitive therapy may also help Paul to deal with his cravings and urges to use drugs. It does not postulate that faulty cognitions were responsible for the original substance use, which is seen as caused by a variety of internal and external factors but rather that they may maintain and exacerbate it. However, an analysis and modification of these cognitions can help in overcoming substance abuse.

The rational-emotive-behavior (REBT) approach can be seen as a variant of cognitive therapy, though probably not by REBT adherents. REBT's essential contribution is to examine the role of emotional dysfunction in psychological and behavioral problems, including substance abuse. It unhooks consequences from prior events, seeing the consequences as caused by Paul's belief system instead. Especially important for substance abusers like Paul, REBT attempts to increase *frustration tolerance* and *catastrophizing*.

The client-centered holistic approach would help Paul to set long- and short-term goals *of his choosing*. It is not necessary for the therapist to focus on stopping or reducing drinking or even focus on substance abuse and in that sense conceptually separates substance *use* from substance *abuse*. It is clearly the client who is in charge of treatment although Paul must agree to change his life to some extent. This model is extended in the client-driven harm reduction approach, which also stresses the client as the decision-maker who makes decisions about goals and progress. Thus, the therapist would help Paul decide which goals to work toward, which might not include total abstinence. Even a reduction in substance use would be seen as reducing the level of harm. This approach is at variance with the implicit or explicit abstinence assumption typical of substance abuse treatment programs and is highly pragmatic in setting a "low threshold" for entering treatment.

Harm reduction is also the key element in the relapse prevention model, although the term is used in a different sense. This approach has long recognized that relapse poses an unusually large threat to continued sobriety, in part because of negative internal cognitions and in part because of external social pressures. Like the client-centered models, it is process-oriented and like the behavioral systems approach, it stresses an examination of the client's total environmental context (under the rubric of harm reduction). But its major difference from other models is its emphasis on the management of relapse.

The family therapy approach is essentially a behavioral model, although interactive in nature and based on the role of Paul's family members in maintaining his dysfunctional substance abuse patterns. In one sense, it can be seen as a variant of the behavioral systems approach with the family as the major system. It also stresses relapse prevention.

In some ways, the community reinforcement approach combines elements of the behavioral systems, family therapy, and cognitive (via problem-solving) models, with aspects of relapse prevention as well as vocational and recreational training. In that sense it is the most comprehensive model examined and would see Paul as embedded within an environmental context that both supports and enables his substance abuse. The therapist would work with Paul's environment, as well as with Paul, to modify that context.

The treatment program based on Ericksonian therapeutic principles represents a somewhat unusual approach to substance abuse treatment. Like the psychodynamic model, it is essentially intrapsychic in orientation. It stresses the role of expectancy, action, and expanding perceived limitations. Somewhat like the client-centered approaches, it postulates that Paul already possesses the necessary skills and resources necessary to change and it is a matter of the therapist providing a context in which that change can take place. Like more behavioral approaches, however, the therapist is quite active. Thus, the Ericksonian model combines elements of both the intrapsychic and environmental models with an assumption of positive client resources added.

These models share some commonalities and differ on some elements and can be seen as differing primarily on the dimensions of locus of action and relative balance between therapist and client direction. Older models, such as the psychodynamic and behavioral, tend to stress one intervention point, for example Paul's internal state or the environmental press. Newer models, such as the community reinforcement approach, tend to be more comprehensive in considering various aspects of Paul's internal and external environment. In some approaches, such as the cognitive therapy and REBT approaches, the therapist tends to be active and directive; in other models, such as the client-centered holistic and Ericksonian models, Paul would be more involved in setting goals and therapeutic progress. These are relative emphases, however, since it is apparent that increasingly models draw on the strengths of each other; for example the relapse prevention model also includes cognitive and environmental elements. All except perhaps the client-centered holistic model explicitly or implicitly focus on the elimination of substance abuse and tend to equate use with abuse.

## II. CLINICAL SKILLS ESSENTIAL TO TREATMENT

Behind the different words and concepts used by the different authors, there was a remarkable consistency in this area. Essentially, the common skills needed can be conceptualized as belonging to two domains: knowledge of the theoretical background of the approach and good human relations skills. Each author stressed that therapists should know their particular theory well enough to be able to use it as an organizing principle in guiding their observations and analysis of Paul's situation. In other words, the theory provides a set of conceptual pegs upon which to hang one's assessment and intervention. No therapist can possibly pay attention to everything and theory at its best guides one in what to look for and what to ignore. The danger, as theories become more complex, is that—precisely for that reason—they will become less useful as guiding and organizing principles.

The authors were also remarkably consistent in stressing the nature of a good relationship or working alliance with Paul. If there is one finding in the empirical literature that is especially robust, it is the correlation between a good working alliance and positive therapeutic outcome. Even an approach that has been thought to derogate the importance of the therapeutic relationship (behavioral systems) argues for its necessity. Thus, although Ruben (this volume) states, ". . . establishing therapist-client rapport is not essential to imparting behavior change . . .," he also says immediately after, "What is essential are positive interpersonal skills."

There are some unique skills mentioned by some authors, some deriving from the particular model, though we suspect others might agree with them as well. For example, the REBT approach argues that therapists "had better" have high frustration tolerance when working with substance abusers. The community reinforcement approach mentioned knowledge of community resources as important. The family therapy approach mentioned knowledge of various substances and their effects as important. Therapist awareness of self is also mentioned by some authors.

## III.  SPECIFIC QUESTIONS

### 1.  Therapeutic Goals

Not surprisingly, the goal of abstinence from, or at least reduction in, the use of addicting substances was mentioned by every author. It was difficult in some instances for us to understand if only a reduction in use would be accepted, though all approaches seemed to advocate abstinence as the ideal goal. The REBT approach provided an extensive discussion of the pros and cons of this contentious issue. Even the client-centered holistic model, which earlier appeared to accept partial or even nonreduction of substance use as an acceptable goal, here suggested abstinence as a long-term goal. Thus, it appears that, while several authors may accept reduction in substance abuse as a short-term or partial goal, ultimate abstinence is seen as the ideal outcome.

Other, more secondary goals were also mentioned, such as a reduction in anger, impulsivity, and aggression, immediate instillation of hope, better family relationships, construction of a new social awareness, and an increase in job-related skills. Some of these, e.g., aggression and impulsivity, have been shown to be related to substance abuse (McCormick, Dowd, Quirk, & Zegarra, 1998; Putt, 1996). Interestingly, not all these additional goals followed directly from their respective models; for example the family therapy approach mentioned prevention of relapse, the client-centered holistic model and relapse prevention approaches mentioned overcoming depression, and the relapse prevention model mentioned family and marital work. Other goals, however, seemed to flow directly from the model; for example, the psychodynamic approach stressed achievement of insight, and the cognitive and REBT approaches mentioned changing cognitive dysfunctions. Thus, while there are differences among the approaches with regard to appropriate goals, there are also many similarities.

### 2.  Further Information

Every author, in one form or another, recommended the administration of additional standardized instruments. Usually these were more specific measures to assess substance-abuse-related behaviors and attitudes but occasionally they were more general tests of psychological distress. They included specific recommendations for structured interview assessment. In addition, several authors (not only those representing more environmental approaches) recommended assessing the level of social, including family, support. Likewise, several authors recommended assessing the "payoff" (i.e., reinforcing consequences) of using drugs, including the author of the client-centered holistic approach. The assessment of family dynamics was recommended by other authors than the representative of the family therapy approach. Several authors recommended assessment of Paul's level of motivation and self-efficacy. The community reinforcement approach was perhaps most closely tied to its model in recommending exclusively functional analyses of substance abuse behaviors and their triggers. There were other, more idiosyncratic recommendations, such as assessment of cigarette smoking and a physical assessment. In general, however, we were impressed with the degree of overlap in recommendations for further information among all the approaches as well as the heavy reliance on standardized tests.

## 3. Conceptualization of Personality, Behavior, Affective State, and Cognitions

To some extent, the conceptualization of Paul's personality and cognitions and the relative importance given to personality, cognition, and behavior depended on the model. Thus, the psychodynamic approach stressed unconscious duplication of the father and Paul's longstanding dysfunctional patterns, the behavioral systems approach looked at dysfunctional stimulus-response interactions and the effect of rule-governed statements, the cognitive approach examined the learning history of trauma and poor modeling from Paul's father, and the REBT approach saw Paul as engaging in irrational "musturbatory" beliefs and self-condemnation. Both the client-centered holistic and the Ericksonian approaches, true to their respective models, mentioned Paul's strengths. Some of the other approaches which lack more extensive theoretical development, such as the relapse prevention, harm reduction, and community reinforcement models, were more generically descriptive, stressing such behaviors as impulsivity, low self-efficacy, and a rigid style. Interestingly, not all approaches used the assessment data provided, including some for which it would seem natural, while several approaches such as the community reinforcement and Ericksonian models used it extensively. One approach, harm reduction, largely eschewed the use of personality tests. Different approaches sometimes made use of each other's concepts, for example the relapse prevention model suggested that Paul had replicated his family of origin. There were several concepts, perhaps gleaned from the assessment data, such as impulsivity, low self-efficacy, and depression, which were common across many approaches. Thus, it appears that, while some approaches maintain their unique conceptualizations, there is considerable and perhaps increasing overlap of concepts. Perhaps adherents of these schools read each other's literatures.

## 4. Potential Pitfalls

Although often phrased in different terminology, there were considerably more commonalities than differences among approaches in this area. Most of the models considered the possibility of relapse to be the greatest pitfall, not surprising in view of this history of it. Related to this was the perceived difficulty of keeping Paul in treatment. Many of the approaches mentioned Paul's social relationships as potentially problematical as well as his personal style of impulsivity, anxiety, and lack of openness. Both the cognitive therapy and REBT approaches, which stress the completion of inter-session homework as a powerful change agent, thought perhaps Paul would not complete such homework. There was some mention of Paul perhaps using substances because of anxiety generated by therapy itself.

## 5. Ultimate Level of Coping and Prognosis for Change

Perhaps operating from the principle that "The past is the best predictor of the future," most of the authors seemed at best to be only partially optimistic about Paul's chance for ultimate and continued sobriety. On the other hand, the client-centered holistic approach seemed to use the same principle to argue that Paul should be able to manage his substance abuse since he has done it before. Some authors appeared to describe an ideal prognosis rather than one to which Paul could reasonably aspire. Both the community reinforcement and the Ericksonian approaches, however, seemed quite optimistic about Paul's eventual recovery. The former pointed to Paul's voluntary return to therapy, perhaps indicating good motivation, and the external reinforcer of keeping his job. This approach does not even consider his previous "failed" attempts as a poor prognostic indicator and points to his periods of sobriety. The latter also stressed Paul's previous ability to maintain periods of sobriety and used a behavioral conceptualization in basing his recovery this time on his ability to manage the behavioral and cognitive antecedents that trigger substance abuse as well as develop a more positive social system. If the past is indeed the best predictor of the future, perhaps it depends on which aspect of the past we consider.

## 6. Duration of Therapy

There was reasonable consistency among the approaches that provided specific number of sessions regarding the duration of therapy, generally 20–40 sessions. It was common, however, to suggest that Paul be seen for a longer period of time on a reduced schedule, perhaps every 2 weeks or once a month. Surprisingly, the psychodynamic approach advocated the shortest number of sessions, though the author cautioned that maximum benefit would likely be obtained only by more sessions, and the behavioral systems approach, at over 50 sessions, was the longest! The client-centered holistic approach suggested over 40 sessions at first with further support as necessary. The relapse prevention approach advocated an intensive program at first, gradually tapering off by continuing about 2 years; not surprising considering Paul's history of relapse. Several approaches were more cautious, recommending that therapy continue until Paul's goals were reached.

Except for the family therapy approach (which specifically mentioned family therapy), the cognitive approach (which mentioned coping strategies), and the community reinforcement approach (which mentioned positive reinforcement and homework), the answers to this question did not appear to be derived from the model. However, there was evidence that most approaches used a comprehensive model and drew from concepts in other models.

## 7. Specific/Special Techniques

To some extent, the techniques suggested followed from the model. Thus, the psychodynamic approach discussed the therapeutic alliance, transference, and Paul's attending to circumscribed aspects of himself; the cognitive approach discussed several cognitive techniques, the REBT approach discussed preferential RET; and the Ericksonian approach suggested solution focused therapy and hypnosis. However, there were a number of techniques mentioned that appeared to be drawn from other models. The behavioral systems approach provided a very comprehensive list of techniques, drawn from a variety of approaches; the client-centered holistic approach mentioned cognitive behavioral relapse prevention; the harm reduction approach advocated a thorough functional analysis of Paul's substance use; the relapse prevention approach mentioned behavioral marital and family therapy; and the family therapy approach used self-monitoring. Generic techniques like the 12-step program and medication were also mentioned. Once again, it appeared that the different models have influenced each other.

## 8. Special Cautions and Resistances

Most of the authors mentioned Paul's impulsivity and anger as potential problems and some mentioned the possibility of suicide. On the other hand, one author did not see these attributes as problems and others did not see a danger of suicide. Resistances mentioned seemed to be related to Paul's defensive cognitive structure and lack of insight (regardless of how this concept was phrased) and how he would respond to being challenged. Generally, the authors saw him as responding by anger or by not completing homework assignments. The relapse prevention approach advocated setting boundaries and not meeting with Paul if he seemed high. Two, the community reinforcement and Ericksonian approaches, minimized the likely appearance of resistance, because their approach works with it and defuses it.

## 9. Areas to Avoid

In general, the authors did not see certain topics as areas to avoid. However, most did suggest that Paul's current substance abuse be the focus of attention and that more distal topics such as family-of-origin contributions to it be shelved for the moment. The REBT approach provides an explicit reason for this decision: "people with addictions often provide external reasons for their substance abuse." The psychodynamic approach advocated that more core issues of Paul's psychological life be avoided for the moment until a good therapeutic alliance has been established and the client-centered holistic approach thought some issues, such as anger management and marital counseling, might better be addressed in other contexts. The cognitive therapy and the harm reduction approaches suggested that the *manner* in which topics are introduced may be more important than the topic itself. These suggestions are well taken. Therapy with substance abusers is probably best addressed first to the abuse itself and only later to the contributions to it and underlying reasons for it.

## 10. Medication

The responses to this question were quite variable, illustrating perhaps the controversy in the field on this issue. Several of the authors recommended that Paul *not* be given medication, in an attitude captured best by Matthews (this volume, Chapter 13),

> "For a client with a problem of substance abuse, there is a contradictory quality of suggesting psychotropic medications to reduce negative feelings while condemning self-prescribed medications for the same purpose." (p. 250).

On the other hand, several authors recommended Antabuse for Paul, since it had been helpful before, and some recommended an antidepressant. Other less common medications were suggested along with problems associated with the medications he is currently taking. This appears to be an area of some controversy and divided opinion within the substance abuse field.

## 11. Patient Strengths

There is probably more agreement among the chapter authors in this area than in any other. They were essentially unanimous in seeing Paul as possessing many strengths and nearly so in identifying them. Foremost among Paul's strengths is the fact that he is self-referred and recognizes his need to change. Second, Paul has had success at work and has been able to hold a job, at least when not actively using substances. In addition to his work he has leisure activities that are important and interesting to him. Third, Paul appears capable of maintaining important relations with other people, including his ex-wife (they are still living together), his parents, friends, AA sponsors and other mentors, and children. Especially significant for some of the authors was his reaction to the fear he saw on his children's faces. In other words, Paul has empathy for and a history of demonstrated relations with other people. Finally, he has been able to maintain sobriety for periods of time in the past.

## 12. Limits and Boundaries

There was a high level of agreement among the authors in this area. Almost all explicitly mentioned explaining to Paul that he could not be seen if he came to the session drunk or high. There was less consensus, however, regarding his use of substances between sessions. Most of the authors mentioned an explicit contract against aggression or violence towards others, including the therapist. Interestingly, only two approaches (cognitive therapy and family therapy) explicitly mentioned the importance of not missing sessions. Other limits included the usual client socialization ("ground rules") process, in which issues such as coming to sessions on time, respecting therapist-client professional boundaries, confidentiality, fee-payment, homework, accuracy, and working towards change are discussed. With the exception of in-session substance abuse and possibly aggression, these are common limits and boundaries applicable to all therapy.

## 13. Involvement of Significant Others and Use of Homework

In general, the involvement of significant others in therapy followed the model presented. Thus, the psychodynamic approach advocated individual therapy now (and perhaps marital therapy later) and did not mention homework; the behavioral systems approach saw the involvement of others as providing useful data; the cognitive therapy and the REBT approaches advocated and described homework in detail; and the family therapy approach recommended family therapy including many of Paul's significant relationships. Several approaches besides cognitive therapy and REBT would use homework, though the homework exercises tended to be of the more generic substance abuse variety, such as identifying triggers, practicing drink refusal, and developing social assertiveness/communications skills. But it is apparent that many approaches would involve other people in Paul's treatment and make use of homework, though not necessarily to the same extent.

## 14. Termination Issues

Not surprisingly, the behavioral systems approach provided a detailed analysis of termination procedures. Most authors suggested an intensive treatment at first followed by a gradual fading of treatment, with increasing times between sessions and booster sessions provided if needed. Several also mentioned that Paul's ultimate recovery may be a long-term process. Adjunctive treatment formats such as 12-step programs were also mentioned. Perhaps reflecting the influence of relapse prevention or its placement in the question, most authors also advocated explicit attention to this, although the degree of specificity varied. However, Paul's repeated lapses may have indicated to the authors that relapse prevention was an important issue to be addressed. The cognitive therapy approach suggested that Paul not try to "test" his sobriety.

## 15. Mechanisms of Change

While the mechanisms for change were phrased in the language structure of each approach, there was a universal recognition that Paul's recovery, if successful, would involve a wide range of change mechanisms. Thus, the psychodynamic approach, while arguing that understanding what one does is a prerequisite for changing, also stated that behavior and psychological states exist and interact with each other in a bidirectional loop. Both the behavioral systems and the community reinforcement approach identified the learning and reinforcement of new skills as fundamental to change, but seemed to be aware that Paul's understanding of his behavior patterns in relation to new patterns is useful. Both the cognitive therapy and the REBT approaches focused on cognitive mechanisms of change but placed them within a behavioral context. Other approaches were comprehensive and included a variety of environmental changes (e.g., developing a new life plan) as well as changing internal states (e.g., learning how to deal better with anger and impulsivity, developing heightened self-efficacy). In essence, the mechanisms for change can be summarized as: the development of new behaviors in a comprehensive framework of change, fostered and followed by the development of new patterns of thinking, and supported by a new or improved social network. One could argue that such a comprehensive framework is behind all successful change.

## IV. CONCLUSION

While certain aspects of substance abuse treatment clearly depend on the particular model used, it is apparent that other aspects are common to all or most approaches. Over the years, the different models appear to have influenced each other and increasingly overlapped. Thus, for example, relapse prevention now appears to be a part of many approaches, not only the one from which it originated. Likewise, family therapy or at least the involvement of significant others, is used by a number of approaches. Environmental management is also part of several approaches, not only those that are explicitly behavioral.

At the same time, however, the answers to certain questions were clearly model-derived. This was most apparent in such question as the goals of treatment, conceptualizations of personality, ultimate level of coping, special techniques, and mechanisms of change. Even here, however, there were numerous commonalities. The remainder of the questions addressed perhaps more generic substance abuse treatment components and here the commonalities outweighed the differences.

In this regard, the treatment of substance abuse parallels the treatment of other disorders. Models of interventions that originally are developed in reaction to earlier models are demarcated sharply from their predecessors. Over time, however, it becomes apparent that the newer model, which possessing many strengths, cannot account alone for the complexity of human behavior. Newer models are then developed which either address deficits in the earlier models or provide an integration of previous models into more comprehensive ones. No one model can possibly account for the full range of human functioning, however, so the relative distinctions among the various approaches, though muted, still remain.

Substance abuse is an entrenched and destructive social problem, not only in the United States, but in many other nations. It is fostered and maintained by a wide variety of internal, environmental, and cultural factors. It will likewise take the combined efforts of many professionals utilizing a variety of approaches to eradicate or at least reduce it.

# REFERENCES

McCormick, R. A., Dowd, E. T., Quirk, S., & Zegarra, J. H. (1998). The relationship of NEO-PI performance to coping styles, patterns of use, and triggers for use among substance abusers. *Addictive Behaviors, 23,* 497–507.

Putt, C. A. (1996). *Relationship of preexisting levels of hostility and aggression to substance abuse and psychiatric symptom severity.* Unpublished doctoral dissertation, Kent State University.

# Appendix

## Comparison of Approaches to the Case of Paul: Responding to the Questions

1. Goals

| | |
|---|---|
| Psychodynamic Therapy | develop insight about intrapsychic forces behind drug use explore impulse conflicts, conflictual relations with father, and cycle of behaviors change response to conflict management, label affects/cognitions, strengthen ego functioning |
| Behavioral Systems | recidivism, control impulsivity, urges, anger and aggression increase prosocial behaviors, recovery inoculation skills |
| Cognitive Therapy | hope (commit to change), safety (violence, sex, driving), abstinence change beliefs about self, life, future, and drugs; relax to sleep; reduce anger use time constructively, problem solving, communication skills, appropriate peer relations |
| Rational Emotive Behavior Therapy | client's choice of abstinence or controlled abstinence replace negative with adaptive emotions |
| Client-Centered Holistic | gain control over abuse maintain job, mend family relations develop long-term goals, e.g., develop abstinence strategies, manage emotions and behavior, develop appropriate peer relations, and accept own history |
| Client-Driven, Research-Guided Treatment | discover causal factors commit to change develop plan of action, e.g., explore cost/benefit of use and option |
| Relapse Prevention | abstinence, reduce effect on self and others, understand family context reduce depression, eliminate violent behavior, increase self-efficacy |
| Family Therapy | abstinence strategies to maintain gains |
| Community Reinforcement Approach | gain control over abuse job progress, mend family relations anger management, appropriate peer relations |

| | |
|---|---|
| Erickson Utilization | gain control over abuse<br>changes in affect, attitude, behavior, social network, self-image, enjoyment and discipline |

2. Information Desired

| | |
|---|---|
| Psychodynamic Therapy | interview family to determine accuracy of narrative, techniques that enlist defenses, use of social support, relationship with father, role of ex-wife in use, and experience of events<br>measures: Rorschach, Thematic Apperception Test |
| Behavioral Systems | frequency of use, setting and people associated with use, reasons for periods of abstinence disposition prior to, during, and after use; other ways impulses satisfied; family involvement skills deficits and excesses, treatment history, recurrent factors derailing recovery<br>measures: Taylor-Johnson Temperament Analysis, Michigan Alcoholism Screening Test, Adult Child of Alcoholic Behavior Profile, Word Memory Test |
| Cognitive Therapy | records of past treatment<br>structured interview, interview wife and father<br>measures: Beck Depression Inventory, Beck Scales for Hopefulness and Suicidal Ideation Belief About Substance Use, Cravings Belief Questionnaire, Relapse Prevention Scale |
| Rational Emotive Behavior Therapy | frequency, amount, and benefits/costs of drug use, wife's attitude toward use thoughts prior to emotions and drug use, logs of emotional episodes and use self-report scales of irrational beliefs, Likert scenario measures of commitment to beliefs |
| Client-Centered Holistic | role, reasons for, and effect of alcohol abuse; role of spouse<br>measures: Inventory of Drinking Situations, Inventory of Drug Taking Situations, Situational Confidence Questionnaire, Drug Taking Confidence Questionnaire |
| Client-Driven, Research-Guided Treatment | structured interview: commitment to goals, use of tobacco products view of past treatments, support network<br>measures: Comprehensive Drinking Profile |

(continued)

## 2. Information Desired

| | 2. Information Desired | 4. Pitfalls |
|---|---|---|
| Relapse Prevention | interview wife to determine motivation for and losses/rewards of change<br>measures: decision matrix, Beck Depression Inventory, Addiction Severity Index<br>self-monitoring journal | therapist pushes too hard<br>inconsistent motivation<br>recurrence of problems<br>insight triggers use, depression, guilt |
| Family Therapy | appropriate level of care, environmental supports, effects of alcohol use, emotional disorders<br>family-skills deficits, communication, problem solving, and roles<br>measures: Michigan Alcoholism Screening Test, Annis' Inventory of Drinking Situations | |
| Community Reinforcement Approach | internal/external triggers, severity of problem, consequences of use, non-use pleasures<br>measures: Happiness Scale, neuropsychological tests | |
| Erickson Utilization | measures: Beck Depression Inventory, Leary Interpersonal Checklist | |

## 3. Conceptualization

| | 3. Conceptualization | 4. Pitfalls |
|---|---|---|
| Psychodynamic Therapy | replicating father's pattern, dysfunctional family of origin insightful about failures, conflict threatens view of self values own role in family, pride in work, conscientious periods of sobriety, sense of community, previous success drug use as self-medication | overconfidence, risky behavior<br>avoidance or escape behavior<br>substitute new addiction, defiance<br>defensiveness, dislike therapist<br>therapist expectations<br>family: distrust change, expectation, overprotection, resentment, resist or overdo own change |
| Behavioral Systems | pattern of anticipatory anxiety, inhibition, anger chronic interpersonal deficits, low frustration tolerance<br>inconsistent family support<br>feels shame, suicidality, depression<br>drug use to gain arousal, counter depression, self-medicate | |

| | | |
|---|---|---|
| Cognitive Therapy | self-absorbed, poor self-esteem, poor emotion regulation<br>disregards societal norms, grandiose, poor<br>limited ability to introspect, poor role models<br>positive regard<br>good employee, empathy for children<br>childhood-trauma, neglect, and failure<br>drug use as self-medication | dropout if overconfident<br>limited self-monitoring<br>mistrust authority, prior failed treatment,<br>homework noncompliance<br>not avoid risky situations<br>expectation of family outcome |
| Rational Emotive Behavior Therapy | impulsive, angry, aggressive, easily depressed, anxious<br>dependent personality, low frustration tolerance, labile<br>excessively desires social acceptance, attention<br>has many irrational beliefs<br>suffers from symptom stress producing cyclic behaviors | poor attendance, low tolerance for work<br>low levels of agreeableness, openness<br>failure to dispute irrational beliefs<br>anger, unable to deal with therapist confrontations |
| Client-Centered Holistic | impulsive, angry, anxious, depressed<br>good relations with others, resilient, work success<br>no excuses or blame, at risk to lose job and family | dropout<br>halt loss of job and family<br>lack of resources to treat holistically |
| Client-Driven, Research-Guided Treatment | impulsive, depressed, discouraged, lacks self-efficacy<br>poor decision making skills, some intimacy/ social support<br>capacity for self-examination | dropout if not gain hope<br>dropout if change not fast<br>finding appropriate peers |
| Relapse Prevention | impulsive, angry, depressed, distrustful, self-absorbed<br>lonely, violence-prone, uncertain of value in relations | dropout as crisis passes<br>unable to establish trust<br>unemployment<br>not finding appropriate peers |

(continued)

| | 3. Conceptualization | 4. Pitfalls | 5. Expected Results | 6. Time Line |
|---|---|---|---|---|
| Relapse Prevention (*continued*) | chaotic, abusive childhood, limited social/intimacy models<br>drug use as self-medication | drugs integral to functioning<br>ambivalence about abstinence<br>poor discipline, polysubstance use<br>forgetting negative effects | | |
| Family Therapy | impulsive, depressed, angry, rebellious, low self-efficacy<br>chaotic, abusive childhood, denial to cope with stress<br>functions well when abstinent<br>drug use as self-medication | poor or rigid therapist | | |
| Community Reinforcement Approach | impulsive, depressed<br>concrete, rigid, egocentric thought; lacks insight, sensitive<br>poor problem solving and planning | | | |
| Erickson Utilization | impulsive, angry, anxious, depressed<br>closed, limited social skills<br>drug use as self-medication | relapse<br>cycle of sobriety and failure<br>therapist reaction to relapse | | |
| Psychodynamic Therapy | | | prognosis guarded, tumultuous cycles likely, follow-up essential<br>reduce maladaptive behavior, regular employment<br>resume role as father, control anger and impulses | 20 session time frame<br>limited success expected |
| Behavioral Systems | | | poor prognosis without structured intervention | six months to one year<br>twice per week, decreasing |
| Cognitive Therapy | | | poor prognosis with brief period of sobriety<br>gain skills in self-monitoring, communication, | intensive, extensive<br>initial: two hours per week |

*(continued)*

| | | then diminishing AA attendance daily |
|---|---|---|
| Rational Emotive Behavior Therapy | problem solving, delay/distraction, evaluate thoughts/beliefs, reduce anxiety view recovery as process | 25 sessions |
| Client-Centered Holistic | abstinence or decreased frequency of use, near-term loneliness tolerate being alone, find better social supports learn coping strategies to deal with emotions | two years intensive one hour/week, decreasing 3–5 years supportive |
| Client-Driven, Research-Guided Treatment | manage use enough to maintain job and family long term: address issues to sustain change | open-ended, possibly short determined by client |
| Relapse Prevention | develop plan for change enhance self-efficacy | not specified first year intensive |
| Family Therapy | less depression, enhanced self-efficacy, better coping skills prevent serious relapse and violent behavior better family relations, better communication | inpatient care initially weekly family sessions monthly follow-up |
| Community Reinforcement Approach | relapse likely other issues depend on abstinence | open ended one hour per week then diminishing |
| Erickson Utilization | maintain employment mend family relations longer abstinence sobriety with relapse manage triggers, maintain successes, expand supports | minimum 9 months initially every day then once per week |

|  | 7. Techniques | 8. Cautions/Resistances | 9. Avoid To Areas |
|---|---|---|---|
| Psychodynamic Therapy | tell story at own pace<br>informal, verbal contracts<br>discuss expectations/process | maximize therapist safety<br>harm to self or others | areas outside approach<br>impulsivity, substance use, failure to cope |
| Behavioral Systems | stepwise learning of cues and urges, belief systems, social skills, life-style restructuring, marital and family skills, employment skills, community resources, relapse prevention |  | constructs: ego, libido, unconscious, hierarchy of self, transcendental states |
| Cognitive Therapy | activity scheduling, delay/distract, rational responding, problem solving<br>Daily Thought Record<br>relaxation, breathing control | harm to others (family, driving)<br>medical supervision<br>wary of therapist/therapy<br>inadequate feelings<br>underreporting and lying | none |
| Rational Emotive Behavior Therapy | change core philosophical beliefs by cognitive, emotive, behavior means<br>detect and debate irrational beliefs | threat of harm to others<br>sexual relations to escape fears<br>view therapy as disapproval | none |
| Client-Centered Holistic | Cognitive/Behavioral Relapse Prevention<br>explore learned behaviors<br>supportive therapy | drop out<br>transference if male therapist<br>group work too early | none |
| Client-Driven, Research-Guided Treatment | determined with client<br>include AA and anger management | harm to self or spouse<br>therapist frustration at progress | none |

| Approach | Techniques / Methods | 10. Medication | 11. Patient Strengths | 12. Limits/Limit-setting |
|---|---|---|---|---|
| Relapse Prevention | Cognitive/Behavioral Relapse Prevention; Family Therapy | | no session if intoxicated, harm to self or others, false confidence | none |
| Family Therapy | family therapy and feedback; daily self-monitoring sheet; behavioral contracting | | monitor suicidality, minimize cost of abuse, ambivalence to abstinence, transference - anger | distal causes of abuse, marital issues if wife not involved |
| Community Reinforcement Approach | CRA Functional Analysis; Sobriety Sampling; problem solving, communication; drink/drug-refusal | | hopelessness | none |
| Erickson Utilization | Solution-Focussed: find positive past change and amplify it; hypnosis, relaxation | | harm to others, oppositional behavior, distrustful behavior | blaming others, justification of use |
| Psychodynamic Therapy | | possibly antabuse | recognizes need to change, desire to be good father, religion | commitment to therapy, control of substance use |
| Behavioral Systems | | antabuse, BuSpar (anxiety) | insightful; pride, ambition in parenting, work, prior sobriety | clear expectations and methods |
| Cognitive Therapy | | not recommended, later consider: antidepressant, antabuse, find source of valium | voluntary treatment, learned from past treatment, capacity for empathy, maintain employment, has hobbies | bounds of confidentiality, no session if intoxicated, attendance in therapy and AA, efforts at work/homework, accurate reporting, commitment to change, no threat to harm therapist |

*(continued)*

| | 10. Medication | 11. Patient Strengths | 12. Limits/Limit-setting |
|---|---|---|---|
| Rational Emotive Behavior Therapy | not recommended | self-referred<br>recognized children's fear of him<br>desire to please | no session if intoxicated<br>keep therapy focussed<br>homework compliance |
| Client-Centered Holistic | antabuse<br>antidepressant | prior sobriety (short)<br>overcome other addiction<br>maintain employment<br>family/mentors relations<br>sensitivity to others<br>good physical health | no session if intoxicated<br>establish respectful, constructive process |
| Client-Driven, Research-Guided Treatment | decision is client's<br>antabuse or naltrexone<br>antidepressants | prior sobriety (long)<br>overcome other addiction<br>maintain employment<br>form/maintain relationships | bounds of confidentiality<br>limit therapist availability |
| Relapse Prevention | naltrexone<br>antidepresssants | overcome other addiction<br>perseverance, pride in work<br>possible marital bond<br>positive childhood | bounds of confidentiality<br>no session if intoxicated<br>spouse—set limit on violence<br>spouse—set drug-free home |
| Family Therapy | antabuse or naltrexone | desire to be good father<br>marital bond; maintain intimacy<br>maintain employment | importance of compliance<br>attendance<br>self-responsibility |
| Community Reinforcement Approach | antabuse | prior sobriety (long)<br>conscientious, pride in work<br>dignity, self-esteem in work<br>desire to be good father | attendance and payment<br>following visitation rules |

| | 13. Family/Homework | 14. Termination | 15. Mechanism of change |
|---|---|---|---|
| Erickson Utilization | decision is client's antabuse antidepressants | prior sobriety (long) willingness to work maintain intimacy | response if domestic violence response if relapse |
| Psychodynamic Therapy | none initially | time limited therapy follow-up sessions | understand underpinnings interaction between behavior and psychological states |
| Behavioral Systems | family maintain drug diary biweekly reports from community homework: regular diary keeping | relapse prevention— generalize skills positive contingencies control external factors | master skills for temptation replace bad with good behavior response covariation, e.g., self-relaxing |
| Cognitive Therapy | involving wife and father is desirable but dangerous homework essential: self-monitoring, scheduling, breathing, etc. | slow process follow-up sessions | increase sense of hope learn treatment process understand beliefs increase self-efficacy periods of abstinence stronger social support use time effectively reduce cravings explore family issues |
| Rational Emotive Behavior Therapy | careful involvement of family homework: bibliotherapy, REBT self help forms, imagery, be alone without drinking, listen to criticism | follow up sessions relapse prevention skills fade session frequency anticipate problems review progress | internalize rational beliefs |
| Client-Centered Holistic | spousal support relapse prevention homework depends on content | not applicable since therapy indefinite external supports | develop life plan strategies to cope with anger and impulsivity positive reasons for change |

*(continued)*

| | 13. Family/Homework | 14. Termination | 15. Mechanism of change |
|---|---|---|---|
| Client-Driven, Research-Guided Treatment | Community Reinforcement Model homework is question—past non-compliance | determined by client continued support group follow-up sessions | behavior change environmental change |
| Relapse Prevention | involve spouse homework: self and couple monitoring, identify risk situations anger management, attend AA | continued support group identify indicators for follow-up sessions | identify causal mechanisms reduce harmful effects of use increase motivation for change medication, family therapy balanced lifestyle |
| Family Therapy | involvement of ex-wife, father, mother, siblings, children AA attendance homework: daily records, review sessions, problem solving | relapse prevention continued support group follow-up sessions | assessment of alcohol use feedback of family knowledge of effects more positive reinforcers new coping skill |
| Community Reinforcement Approach | eventual couples therapy homework: nondrinking pleasures problem solving | relapse prevention positive expectations continued support group follow-up sessions | effects of positive behavior nonconfrontational format learn what he values |
| Erickson Utilization | consult with family homework: skills with wife/children | | positive interaction between belief, attitude, behavior |

# Index